PRAISE FOR *SEVEN SEASONS OF BUFFY*

"A fun, sassy, intelligent and sarcastic book by and for those who understand the fascination with The Slayer, her friends and her foes. I loved it!"

—Nora Roberts

———

"This collection of smart, sassy, mind-bending essays is a fitting tribute to Joss Whedon's beloved series. Read them and weep—for the loss of a great show that clearly encouraged its fans to think great thoughts."

—Michael Logan, *TV Guide*

———

"Rejoice, O Buffyphiles! It's a delight to learn that the most famous writers in the business are also the biggest fans of our favorite show, and they live up to their promise! This captivating collection will make you cheer, laugh, growl (with glee!), and think—the same as the series! From sublimely thought-provoking to slapstick hilarious, this book is just as relentlessly entertaining, capturing the essence of what we love about the Buffy the Vampire Slayer!"

—P.N. Elrod, author of *The Vampire Files*

———

SEVEN SEASONS OF
BUFFY

ALSO EDITED BY GLENN YEFFETH

Taking the Red Pill:
Science, Philosophy and Religion in The Matrix

Edited by Glenn Yeffeth

SEVEN SEASONS OF
BUFFY

Science Fiction
and Fantasy Authors
Discuss Their Favorite
Television Show

BENBELLA BOOKS • Dallas, Texas

First BenBella Books Edition April 2003

BenBella Books
6440 N Central Expressway, Suite 508
Dallas, TX 75206
(214) 750-3600
www.benbellabooks.com

Printed in the United States of America

10 9 8 7 6 5 4 3 2 1

Seven seasons of Buffy : science fiction and fantasy authors discuss their favorite television show / edited by Glenn Yeffeth. — 1st BenBella Books ed.
    p. cm.
  ISBN 1-932100-08-3 (alk. paper)
  1. Buffy, the vampire slayer (Television program) I. Yeffeth, Glenn, 1961–
PN1992.77.B84s48 2003
  791.45'72—dc22

Cover design by Melody Cadungog
Interior designed and composed by John Reinhardt Book Design

Distributed by Independent Publishers Group. To order call (800) 888-4741
www.ipgbook.com

Dedicated to Joss Whedon,
for your kindness, support and,
most of all, for seven seasons of Buffy

Contents

Foreword

TASTE OUR STEEL

Why do we care?

I don't so much pose the question in the general sense (though we can discuss that if you wish, I think it has something to do with electrolytes) but rather as it relates to a certain vampire slayer from Sunnydale.

Why do we care about Buffy? Why do we care *so much* about Buffy?

Why are we watching her and reading about her and dressing up like her and writing the occasional Buffy/Chaos Demon/Staff Writer fanfic about her?

I'd like to suggest that it either a.) has something to do with leather pants or b.) comes down to the integrity of intent behind the show itself.

"Integrity of intent." What does that even mean? To be honest, I'm not quite sure. But I do know that if you find yourself wearing leather pants, a halter top, and claddagh ring in a bar in Santa Monica and your friends and/or a German person start telling you that *Buffy the Vampire Slayer* is nothing more than a silly little show about vampires, you can whip out a phrase like "integrity of intent" and they will be so amazed by your keen intellect they will bow down before your giant brain or, in the case of the German person, try to fight you.

German people love to fight. That's my point.

If you look at the way Joss Whedon constructed his little show, you'll see that every episode has something important to say about the human condition. (Sounds simple enough, right? You'd be amazed at how the notion of plot-for-the-sake-of-plot-alone has overtaken the corporate entertainment mentality. Actually, you probably wouldn't be amazed. You seem pretty smart. You don't need me telling you these things. Also, your hair looks great today. Also, I agree with you when you say $120 is far too much to pay for a pair of blue jeans.) Every episode emanates from a relatable emotional place; we care because the intent behind the show is pure.

"Wait. Are you saying the show *means well*? That's your point? Isn't that what they say about autistic children and old people?"

No. I mean, yes. I mean, I don't know. (And who says that about autistic children? That's terrible.)

I'm saying those of us who care see ourselves in Buffy. She represents our voice. And so we celebrate this silly little show and we occasionally punch out German people in bars because we've somehow come to understand what it feels like to be a teenage girl whose duty it is to rid the world of vampires.

And so what you've got in your hot little hands here, dear reader, is a collection of the best and brightest science fiction and fantasy authors around doing just that (and by "that" I mean "celebrating this silly little show," not "punching out Germans." That's a different book entirely.) And as you read through these essays, you'll see the passion these heavyweights have for *Buffy*, and hopefully you'll come to understand there's a large, diverse group of people out there who, deep down, are simply young teenage girls jumpkicking vampires and yelling, "Close your eyes Angel . . . and taste my steel!"

What I'm saying is, you are not alone.

Drew Goddard used to argue that Buffy the Vampire Slayer *was the greatest television show of all time. Then he got a job working for the show. Now he has to say things like "It's impossible to judge one work of art against another," and "It's an honor to be included in the same sentence as* Dr. Quinn, Medicine Woman," *and "As long as we've helped one impoverished, inner-city child, well, we've done our job."*

David Brin

BUFFY VS. THE OLD-FASHIONED "HERO"

In a now-infamous Salon article, David Brin takes on the virtually sacred Lord of the Rings trilogy, pointing out that the works celebrate the attempts of the hierarchy of a feudal order to squash the revolt of a more egalitarian society. As Brin points out, in the Lord of the Rings "the good guys strive to preserve and restore as much as they can of an older, graceful and 'natural' hierarchy, against the disturbing, quasi-industrial and vaguely technological ambience of Mordor, with its smokestack imagery and manufactured power rings that can be used by anybody, not just an elite few . . ." Brin goes on to note Hollywood's inherent bias toward feudal systems and dynastic elites, citing Star Wars as another prominent example. But Brin does credit one Hollywood creation with deliberately subverting hierarchy and embracing the common folk. And that creation is . . .

WHAT DOES IT TAKE to be a shining new star in Hollywood these days?

Well, if you're female, it helps to be beautiful. An ability to act? Kind of useful. Success may also come with knowing the right people. That much has always been true.

1

But nowadays another essential trait has been added to the list of starlet requirements. *You gotta be able to kick ass.*

Think about it. Can you name any hot new Hollywood sensations who can't do a leaping decapitation kick? From *La Femme Nikita* and *Charlie's Angels* to *Witchblade* and *Xena*, the trend has been amazingly consistent. And leading the charge has been the winsome but mighty *Buffy the Vampire Slayer.*

Oh we still like our heroines to be gorgeous. We're still terribly sexist. But you have to admit, it's a more *respectful* sexism. That's how progress comes, in stages.

Nowhere is this progress better typified than in *Buffy*, with its wonderfully charming mix of the silly and the serious, the assertive and the sweet. Old-fashioned values of love and romance are retained while making it clear that women are no longer willing to be pushed around.

And it goes much deeper than that. For *Buffy* hearkens to the greatest modern movement, though one we hardly ever comment on—the momentous movement to change the way people view authority. A movement that pervades our culture, calling into question the whole issue of conformity and obedience. Unlike any other culture, ours has taken to saying—prove it!

In *Buffy*, an expert or authority figure is judged good or evil by a simple set of standards that have nothing to do with their status or class or birth. Even a vampire can be a good guy. The sole criterion that matters is whether you treat others decently.

Nor is Buffy alone pushing this message. Take *Xena* and *Hercules*, two fairly lowbrow popular television series in which authority figures were portrayed as evil in direct proportion to their rudeness or callousness toward commonfolk. Xena might rescue an exiled king from invaders and restore his throne, but only if he treats people nicely and promises to set up a democratically elected city council. Any time someone is abused by an Olympian, that 'god' is sure to face dire punishment from our heroine!

Yes indeed, Buffy ain't alone. She's leading an important movement. Our myths are the way we prepare our minds to think and our wills to act. And her stories are right up there, promoting individualism, tolerance, eccentricity, openness, and suspicion of anything that reeks of snooty superiority.

Ah, but she has her work cut out for her. The will toward worshipping Olympians and demigods still roils within us. After all, we spent thousands of years in feudal settings that were totally undemocratic.

Social structures were pyramid-shaped, with a narrow elite dominating ignorant masses. Starting with Homer's *Iliad* and *Gilgamesh*, nearly all of the bards and storytellers worked for the chiefs, aristocrats, and kings who owned all the marbles.

In his famous book about *The Hero's Journey*, Joseph Campbell spoke lovingly about the positive aesthetic elements of these old myths . . . without even once mentioning their dark side, like the deep assumption that humans come in neatly packaged social castes. That secrecy and mystery are more important than cooperation and skill. The surrounding society doesn't matter. Neither does daily life.

None of this is true of Buffy, who values daily life and the vibrant society around her. What does she need after a stint of saving the world? A bath and then a trip to the mall! She's normal and likes it. Well . . . all right, maybe above average. All right, she's *way* above average! But she also likes being one of us. That matters.

Older stories played a different tune—that lords and "better" folk had a right to exercise capricious power at whim. You could choose which demigod to root for—say, Achilles or Hector. But there was no disputing the super hero's ultimate right to deal with mortals however he wished. Small wonder this pattern crossed nearly all cultures and eras. After all, the chiefs and kings were the ones who had all the cash and beer. Storytellers needed patrons. They cozied up to the mighty whenever they could.

You don't think people preach that message anymore? Look closer! Today you see it exemplified in highly popular epics like the *Star Wars* saga and *Lord of the Rings*. Oh, sure, in those tales the "good guys" are prettier than the villains. The towering lords and secret cultmasters on one side utter nicer phrases than the "evil" secret masters do on the other side. What the secret masters on both sides have in common is that they are snooty, bossy, mysterious, and oh so superior.

Look at them with open eyes. With *Buffy*'s eyes. Nearly all the pivotal characters in old-fashioned stories are born profoundly superior to those around them . . . not just a little smarter, but indisputably and qualitatively greater than mere mortals. Moreover, the distinction is not earned by hard work or skill or give-and-take. The justification for power is inherited genetic supremacy. Whole classes of people (or aliens or orcs) can be annihilated because they are members of a group.

It seems a pity that all fantasy stories get jumbled together, often sharing the same eager fans. They shouldn't be. Because the deep moral lesson of *Buffy* is the opposite of *Star Wars*. It has nothing at all to do with feudal legends or *Lord of the Rings* . . . or even *Dracula*, with its gloomy maunderings about futility and the past. Go ahead, picture Buffy in those tales. She'd knock those epics off their carefully laid rails with the very first irreverent, questioning words out of her mouth.

Kings and wizards may seem romantic, but they had 6,000 years to deliver human happiness, and all they ever did was push us around like vampires. And Buffy doesn't take it! Notice the episodes set in the past. The Slayer is never one to accept a brat's authority, just because his dad wore a crown.

If this were 1776, she'd hack off her hair and join the Continental Army. If it were 1850, she'd be liberating slaves via the Underground Railroad. I can picture Buffy as a suffragette, or helping the French Resistance, tossing Nazis like kindling in order to free their prisoners.

Those jobs were already done by her aunts (and some uncles). So? This is a new millennium. Time for the next task. Go girl!

Buffy is our future. Brash, open-minded, open-hearted. Always willing to give someone a chance, even if they're low-born, or even (ew!) ugly. Always questioning authority while willing to cooperate and learn something new. To Buffy, old isn't always better (as it is in *Star Wars* and Tolkien). She's stylish, hip, caring, sweet, and nowhere near as dumb as outsiders might think.

Oh, she knows what she's doing, all right. We oughta listen.

Anyway, she sure can kick butt.

David Brin's best-selling SF novels have won Hugo, Nebula, and other awards and have been translated into twenty languages. His 1989 thriller, Earth, *foreshadowed global warming, cyberwarfare, and the Web. A 1998 movie was loosely adapted from his Campbell Award winner* The Postman, *while* Foundation's Triumph *brought a grand finale to Isaac Asimov's famed Foundation universe.* Kiln People *portrays people using "home copiers" to be in two places at once. David's nonfiction book* The Transparent Society *deals with openness, security, and liberty in the future; it won the Freedom of Speech Award of the American Library Association.*

Roxanne Longstreet Conrad

IS THAT YOUR FINAL ANSWER...?

Seven seasons of Buffy *made it increasingly clear that the forces of evil are not composed merely of random vampires, bug-ladies, and mummy-girls. The forces of evil are organized and systematic. They have long-range plans, hierarchies, schools and training facilities. Obviously these schools are located in a far-off hell dimension, virtually inaccessible to humankind. But virtually inaccessible is not the same as completely inaccessible, as proven by our intrepid researcher, Roxanne Conrad, who, best we can figure, managed to infiltrate a demon school and escape to tell the tale...with proof!*

SPATIAL INTERDIMENSIONAL METAPHYSICS
Final Exam, Semester 2

INSTRUCTOR: Vardath of the Outer Cold Darkness, Ruler of Visanganeth, Shatterer of Hearts, Most Dread of Dark Sovereigns, Ph.D., M.D., D.M.oD., S.J.

T.A.: Bob Jones, B.B.A.

STUDENT NAME: *Korelva Norn*
STUDENT LEVEL: *Quell-nar Demon* (trainee)

INSTRUCTIONS: The following question should be answered in a mathematical/mystical equation, with supporting proof provided in the detail section below. This question counts for 100% of your final grade. Any answer judged incorrect will result in the permanent forfeiture of your immortal soul to the fiery reaches of torment (or other hell-dimension, as availability allows).

We know we've previously told you that six pop quizzes administered by the Demon Prince Alkeerzath counted toward your final grade. We lied. Sue us. We're evil. So are you.

QUESTION 1: IDENTIFY AND PROVE (WITH EXAMPLES) THE IDENTITY OF THE MOST POWERFUL INDIVIDUAL FORCE FOR GOOD IN THE REALM OF SUNNYDALE, CALIFORNIA (aka, the Hellmouth). You may consult your notes during this exam. Creation of interdimensional portals or spells to make the instructor (or teaching assistant) forget your existence will be punishable with eternal torment (see above).

Good luck. (Well, not really. We're evil. We hope you fail and suffer mindless agony forever.)

INSCRIBE YOUR CHOICE FOR THE PULING, MISERABLE WORM OF A CREATURE THAT WE WILL EVENTUALLY GRIND BETWEEN OUR SHARP POINTY TEETH (the Most Powerful Individual Force for Good in Sunnydale):

ALEXANDER (XANDER) LAVELLE HARRIS

INSCRIBE YOUR MYSTICAL/MAGICAL EQUATION IN SUPPORT OF THIS IDENTIFICATION:

$M = (S^x \times S^{ax} \times S^s \times S^i)^6 - (E^6)$

Where:
  M = Most Powerful Individual Force for Good
  S^x = Saving of the Slayer (unassisted)
  S^{ax} = Saving of the Slayer (assisted)
  S^s = Saving of Scoobies
  S^i = Saving of Innocents
  E = Reduction for Evil Acts

INSCRIBE YOUR SUPPORTING PROOF (preferably in the blood of others, but your own may be used if you cannot overcome your fellow students):

Hail to Your August and Awful Majesty, Professor Vardath[1].

Obviously, you seek to trick your lowly, humble, crawling students into incorrectly identifying the Slayer BUFFY ANNE SUMMERS[2] as the most powerful force for Good[3] in Sunnydale.

However, it is clear that had the Slayer[4] been equipped only with the traditional weapons of these champions of Good (i.e., a Slayer's Manual, some rather inadequate training, and a bumbling, well-intentioned Watcher) she would swiftly have been dispatched, probably well before she needed to be included in the syllabus.

However, the current Slayer[5] has been untraditional in her approach to fighting our courageous and much-maligned Forces of Evil. This is illustrated quite clearly by her choice of allies.

Clearly, upon examining the group of somewhat-human beings she has gathered around her, there are some outstanding candidates for Most Powerful Individual Force For Good (M.P.I.F.F.G.) on the Hellmouth.

(I discount the Slayer[6] as the M.P.I.F.F.G. simply because without the nontraditional—and clearly impressive—supporters she has assembled, she would even now be a molding corpse in a forgotten grave. Actually, she HAS been a molding corpse in a forgotten grave, but that didn't work out so well for us. Bad luck, incidentally, sir.)

I bring your august and spine-cracking attention to the least likely suspect: ALEXANDER (XANDER) LAVELLE HARRIS. He has a traditionally heroic profile: outsider, handsome (according to ridiculous human female standards), witty, handy with power tools. He even has a dark, tragic childhood to add pathos and mystery.

It cannot possibly be an accident that this human is the ONLY member

---

[1] I crawl before you, o enormous godlike manifestation of evil. May you reign forever and crush the forces of good like tiny little crushable things. Etc.

[2] Cursed be her name, in every dimension! Hail Vardath!

[3] Good being a somewhat fluid term, even in the Realm of Sunnydale. See, for instance, our fallen brother Angelus, the once-formidable Spike, or the occasionally (and deliciously) evil Willow Rosenberg.

[4] Ibid (2).

[5] Ibid (2).

[6] Ibid (2). Oh, whatever! Just assume an Ibid, already.

of the Slayer's "Scooby Gang" without superpowers.[7] He is not possessed of great Magicks, not superbly toned and flexible, not a mystical Great Key, not a former Vengeance Demon, and not either of the two currently ensouled Vampires. (He is not even, to our knowledge, gay.) He has never meddled with Dark Powers in search of thrills. He is, in fact, startlingly mundane, and would be considered mundane even in Akron, Ohio, much less at a mystical convergence of the outré such as the Hellmouth[8].

IN THE BEGINNING

"Oh, huh, I laugh in the face of danger. Then I hide until it goes away."

Xander was, in fact, the very first person in Sunnydale to recognize the Slayer's unusual nature. As her first friend upon her moving to the Hellmouth, he immediately brought a number of vital skills to the battle: witty repartee, an unexplained knowledge of the extensive tunnel system below Sunnydale, and a willingness to face emerging evil, unusual in any Sunnydale resident, where repression is a much-prized survival skill.

On the down side (or up side, for Team Evil) Xander was also cursed (blessed) with a fashion sense that could only be described as horrifyingly sadistic.[9] He also displayed an encouraging streak of stupidity in those early days, not to mention preoccupation with several of the 7 Deadly Sins™.

However, in addition to saving the Slayer's life during the Harvest,[10] he also was the first of her companions to stake a vampire. He continued this irritating and heroic trend by saving the also much-loathed Rupert "Ripper" Giles during a school talent show, and decapitating a poor, defenseless demon. (School functions on the Hellmouth: always exciting.)

Oh, yes, he—and only he—revived the Slayer from her first death at the hands of the Master[11], which was obviously an enormous setback for the Forces of Evil (please refer to my extra-credit assignment, "Fourteen Better Ways to Kill the Slayer," for some thoughts on how we might avoid this embarrassing problem next time).

---

[7] In his own words: "Ah, no. You're not the only one with powers, you know. You may be a hopped-up uber-witch, but . . . this carpenter can dry-wall you into the next century." ("Grave," 6-22)

[8] Through which we will erupt and consume all life on Earth. Real soon.

[9] As we all know, even in a hell dimension, plaids with stripes is Not Done.

[10] I speak for us all when I say that as Harvests went, that one was a crashing disappointment. There was almost no munching of innocents at all.

[11] Frankly, I was disappointed in the Master. I expected him to show a little more initiative when faced with a bunch of teenagers who couldn't even be troubled to show up for class more than twice a day. I think I speak for us all when I say I was glad his bones were ground to dust. Yay.

FIRST YEAR SCORE:
Unassisted saveage of the Slayer: 1
Assisted saveage of the Slayer: 4
Saveage of other "Scoobies": 3

THE SECOND YEAR

"Well, at least I'm the lameness who cares, which is more than I can say about you."

None of Xander's accomplishments would have been overly upsetting to our glorious and brilliant plans for sowing bloody discord, vengeance, and evil, but unfortunately he showed no signs of veering from his right-minded course. In fact, during the Slayer's absence, her Scooby Gang[12] apparently not only survived the summer's supernatural visitations, but thrived and—indeed—managed to save some innocent lives. Well, one. And mostly by accident. But still. (Curse upon them.)

By saving the increasingly good and ever-annoying CORDELIA CHASE from her proper doom at the hands of fellow evil high-school students—more than once—Xander paved the way for the current troubles with our Los Angeles branch office of Wolfram & Hart.

During Spike's invasion of Sunnydale High, the Slayer would have been caught without a stake—and subsequently, extremely dead (possibly even permanently!)—but unfortunately Xander was able to toss her the weapon in the nick of time. Worse, he continued his unpleasant habit of saving others. "If you're gonna kiss anybody, it should be me," he is reported to have said to an Incan Mummy, which is nauseatingly heroic (in that the Incan Mummy was pretty well wrinkled at the time). He summoned Angel[13] to save the Slayer on at least three occasions during his second year as a Scooby.

His infiltration of the Delta Zeta Kappa fraternity—and subsequent hazing—was instrumental in allowing the White Hats to destroy our most excellent and phallic brother Machita. (On the Evil side, however, the destruction of Machita did cause an economic downturn from which the country is, even now, still reeling. Yay.)

---

[12] We believe this refers to a top-secret holy society, but so far, we have only been able to determine that it apparently involves worship of a large canine. Possibly this could refer to the werewolf. He is very laconic.

[13] Aka Angelus. He is a lot more amusing when he is Angelus. Blood, maiming, torture. Leather pants. I live in hope that he will once again experience eternal bliss. In fact, I respectfully recommend that the most evil and glorious Vardath commission a project to study how best to provide Angelus with this escape. It could prove most useful in upcoming years. My sister is particularly eager to participate.

The most credible evidence of Xander's pivotal role as the M.P.I.F.F.G. is his transformation from nerdy high-school student to lethal soldier during Halloween of that year.[14] In fact, during his second year as a Scooby, he saved, saved, and saved again. Irritatingly often, in fact. Willow . . . Cordelia . . . Buffy . . . Willow . . . Buffy . . . all of Sunnydale . . . Buffy . . . Buffy . . . the Sunnydale Swim Team (what's left of it) . . . Buffy . . . and, most irritatingly, Rupert Giles. Again.

Most horribly, by procuring the rocket launcher that served as a technical end-run around our No Weapon Forged ironclad guarantee with The Judge,[15] he ruined our apocalypse. Again.

Respectfully, Professor, I wonder if there was not someone asleep at the Evil Switch for our side, since this puny un-superpowered human has triumphed so often—and humiliatingly—over our Forces of Darkness. Perhaps an Inquisition might be in order. Something tasteful, with iron spikes.

SECOND YEAR SCORE:

Unassisted saveage of the Slayer: 1

Assisted saveage of the Slayer: 6

Saveage of other "Scoobies": 8

Saveage of innocent civilians: 6*

(with force multiplier for potential destruction of Sunnydale)

*Points deducted for nearly destroying Sunnydale with that whole love spell thing. Which so nearly worked for us. I would've paid good kittens to have seen him torn limb from limb by scorned, panting women.

THE THIRD YEAR

> *"Excuse me? Who, at a crucial moment, distracted the lead demon by allowing her to pummel him about the head?"*

With the Slayer once again abandoning her post in Sunnydale, Team Evil had a prime opportunity to destroy all that was good and pure.

Which we apparently, again, muffed.[16]

The Scooby Gang, minus the Slayer, apparently triumphed over 60% of supernatural perils sent their way. The remaining 40% were, apparently, not

---

[14] "You take the princess and secure the kitchen. Catwoman, you're with me." Give him credit . . . for a White Hat, he knows how to bark orders like a Mal-toth.

[15] Personally, I think he was kind of a cheesy blue putz, and cried no acidic evil tears over his demise. But still.

[16] Not that I am in any way implying, great Vardath, that YOU PERSONALLY muffed it. Ever. Have I mentioned I was thinking of endowing a new pentagram in your honor on the Walk of Evil outside of Hell Hall?

properly instructed to simply KILL THEM. It's easy to understand the confusion; obviously, being evil, we like to toy with and torture the innocent.

However, I believe we might want to consider a retraining program to cut down on the taunting and maiming in favor of the KILLING THEM DEAD.

In any case, this percentage presents an important clue that the Slayer is only 40% effective in fighting evil. Clearly, this eliminates Buffy Summers from any serious consideration as the M.P.I.F.F.G., giving Xander the inside track to the title.

Witness the destruction he achieved to our cause in his third year as a follower of the Slayer:

• His use of the moniker "Nighthawk" either struck terror into the hearts of his evil foes, or possibly confused them into believing that he had gone insane.

• During another ill-fated attempt to open the Hellmouth and achieve our goal of hell on Earth, Xander not only saved one Slayer (Faith[17]), he also ultimately saved the other Slayer, all the Scoobies, and assorted innocents by forcing one of our less-than-brilliant evil minions to defuse a bomb. (Zombies. What can you do?) And how many "normal" guys can say they've done the post-fight horizontal mambo with a Slayer? Few. And fewer still breathing.

• Xander actually prevented the horrible deaths of hundreds of Sunnydale students by discovering one of our Evil Minions planting rat poison in the cafeteria food. Coincidence? I think not. The Slayer was entirely on the wrong track. Obviously, Xander was forced to reveal himself as the godlike force for good that he is in this instance.

• Last—and most importantly—he acted as a general during the pitched battle on Graduation Day, marshalling students against the Forces of Darkness. Ascension Day. Another busted opportunity. What a gyp.

THIRD YEAR SCORE:
Unassisted saveage of the Slayer: 1
Assisted saveage of the Slayer: 3
(down from previous years!)
Saveage of other "Scoobies": 5
Saveage of innocent civilians: hundreds, counting the graduating
seniors of Sunnydale High

---

[17] That babe had real evil potential. She's the kind of Slayer we need more of—willing to kick ass, have sex, get drunk, and ally herself with the Forces of Evil. Granted, she's got some annoyingly good qualities, but I'm willing to work with her.

THE FOURTH YEAR

"Are you kidding? I put the semper *in Semper Fi. I might not be able to assemble an M-16 blindfolded like I used to or pass weapons drill from the mobile infantry . . . Might as well face it. Right now, I don't have the technical skills to join the Swiss Army. And all those guys ask you to do is uncork a couple of sassy Cabernets."*

Without Xander, Buffy Summers[18] would be just another corpse being identified from dental records. Who gave Buffy the pep talk to fight back against her enemies at the start of their fourth year of defending the world against evil? Xander. Who fetched her weapons when she was being creamed by Sunday, certainly my favorite vampire of the '80s?[19] Again. Xander.

Granted, he *did* bring back that pesky Chumash vengeance spirit, which resulted in various disgusting diseases inhabiting his flesh. Good one, Professor. Really liked the syphilis thing; that was a nice touch.

His heroics didn't end with just human beings, oh no. He even stepped in to decoy enemies away from the not-then-ensouled-and-still-sort-of-evil Spike. His military experience constantly benefited the Slayer as she struggled against the Initiative.

Without Xander's untimely intervention, Buffy and her new not-very-normal boyfriend Riley might well have melted Sunnydale into a delightful soup, thanks to a nicely conceived scheme on the part of our succubus demons (props to them, that whole "poltergasm" thing was really inspired). But naturally, when the Slayer's at her most vulnerable, who shows up to spoil everything?

Xander.

Let's not forget that when the Slayer needed extra power to beat the crap out of poor Frankenstein—er, Adam—Xander became the "heart" of the gestalt. Yep, pretty sure it was a gestalt. The only thing that saved us from having our Evil Butts totally kicked? They didn't make him the "brains."

Frankly, the year sucked for us . . . again. However, on the side of up, his preoccupation with sex worked for us. Fess up, Professor: was that Anya thing entirely accidental? Or were you planning to distract the M.P.I.F.F.G. with former-vengeance-demon nookie? If so, I worship at your cloven hooves.[20]

---

[18] Cursed be her name, et al

[19] "No studying? Damn! Next thing they'll tell me is I'll have to eat jelly doughnuts or sleep with a supermodel to get things done around here. I ask you, how much can one man give?" ("The Initiative," 4-7)

[20] Which I would anyway. Of course. Gladly.

FOURTH YEAR SCORE:
Unassisted saveage of the Slayer: 0 (hooray!)
Assisted saveage of the Slayer: 3
Saveage of other "Scoobies": 4
Saveage of innocent civilians: debatable.
(There are no innocent civilians anyway, right?)

THE FIFTH YEAR

"Scary, isn't it? I think I've actually turned into someone you want around after a crazed robot attack."

Luckily, the whole Anya thing continued to work for us with Xander . . . plus, once the Hellgod Glory sashayed into the picture in her Fredrick's of Beverly Hills outfits and really cute shoes, well, his usefulness as an ally was strictly limited by his breakability.[21]

He did manage to throw himself in front of a couple of things that might—or might not—have done damage to the Slayer. He also attempted some crisis counseling work with Buffy on her breakup with the virile and tastily depressed Riley Finn. Didn't work out so well, so it's a wash, evil-wise.

However, most notably, he stood up to the formidable Olaf the Troll on behalf of Willow and Anya. It takes a real set of big brass ones to say to a troll, "You are not touching these women." Well, okay, occasionally a human will say that sort of thing, but generally they run screaming once the bone-breaking begins. Xander, however, stood his ground. Points for that.

His only notable contribution to the fight with Glory was, of course, the smackdown he put on her with the wrecking ball, shortly before her inglorious demise at the hands of the enemy. And I ask you, how embarrassing is it for a Hellgod to be dispatched not even by the Slayer, but by her WATCHER? Her DISGRACED, RELIEVED OF HIS DUTIES WATCHER? Yikes. I might want to let a few millennia go by after her re-incorporation before submitting my resume, let her get that out of her system.

It is ominously significant that the Slayer said to the Watcher's Council, "The boy has clocked more field time than all of you combined. He's part of the unit." Clearly, we should have spent more time offering Xander incentives to commit evil acts (or possibly even pyramid investment opportunities) rather than focusing on the redheaded stepwitch. (Not that

---

[21] Now, THERE was a Force for Evil I'd follow anywhere. Quippy, lithe, stronger than most Hellgods, and with a fashion sense second only to Anna Nicole Smith. I'm thinking of applying to her staff after graduation. Her last Evil Minions were hardly management material.

she didn't look beautiful as a villain. Just . . . well. A sudden emergence of fashion sense doesn't substitute for the grit to maim and slay with abandon, now, does it?)

Just as an aside, sir, have you noticed that as people go bad, they tend to pick up some bitchin' fashion sense? Angel: leather pants. Willow: evil 'do and black eyes (black, as we know, accessorizes with EVERYTHING). Perhaps we should open a makeover clinic in Sunnydale. As everyone becomes more fashion-conscious, we may get a corresponding reduction in heroics. Plus, only the Slayer has demonstrated a supernatural ability to fight in high heels.

FIFTH YEAR SCORE:

Unassisted saveage of the Slayer: 0 (two years in a row! YESSS!)

Assisted saveage of the Slayer: 2

Saveage of other "Scoobies": 4

Saveage of innocent civilians: Force multiplier for participation in saving the world from Glory

THE SIXTH YEAR

"Yeah, but then there'd be the flopping and the . . . gasping, and . . . sure, maybe it'd work out, but chances are I'd up and leave you at the helm in your white dress. Then find you spawning with another fish who turns out to be spawning my very good friend night and day behind my back. Then comes the fighting and again with the flopping and the gasping, 'cause hey, Chicken of the Sea here's not doing too good with the women these days."

And here's where you show your true genius, Lord Vardath. When the going gets tough . . . when vampires, demons, Angelus, military-issue Frankensteins and even Hellgods don't do the trick . . . you bring in the really big guns.

Relationship issues.

I mean, it was a great plan to distract the Most Powerful Force For Good with the whole constantly-having-sex-with-a-former-vengeance-demon thing, but this year you destroyed the moral fiber of every White Hat in Sunnydale.

Sure, Xander patrolled while Buffy's corpse molded quietly in its grave. However, after participating in reviving the Slayer, he saved the redheaded stepwitch[22] . . . an ambiguous act, at best, given said witch's slide to the

---

[22] "You made the decision to stop for a reason. You promised us. And can I just ask, what's with the make-over of the damned? I mean, the hair . . .!" (Villains, 6-20)

Evil Side late in the year. And, seeking to pleasure his lover, he summoned a dancing, singing Showstopper of Evil. (I heard a rumor that guy is teaching a Dance to the Death class next semester. If I survive, I'm definitely enrolling.)

The scars left from the musical numbers will never fade from their memory. Or ours. BWA-HA-HA-HA-HA-HA![23]

And—BIG points for us—he leaves his demon-girlfriend at the altar, forcing her to suit up again in the jersey of Team Evil! Wow! Good one.

However . . . and I mention this only in passing . . . he did participate in some saving of lives. When Buffy went nuts with that whole "Am I in an institution?" thing (again, sir, inspired, really) who fought off the slicey-dicey demon, even with his hands tied? Once again, he proves himself the true hero of the piece, while Buffy cowers in her corner drooling. Blah. Slayers. Overrated, I say.

And—of course—there's the most powerful argument of all for Xander being the Most Important Force For Good in Sunnydale.

He stopped black-eyed, killing-frenzy Willow.

No weapons. No fancy backspin kicks. No magic.

Just simple human love.

I mean, we hate him, and all. But clearly. He's, well . . . formidable.

SIXTH YEAR SCORE:

Oh, why even bother? 100%.

No world without him. Game over.

IN SUMMATION

So long as Xander Harris resides in Sunnydale, we're screwed. Evil will never triumph. Slayers come and go, but this Harris character, he looks likely to tough it out. Marry some good woman. Raise a bunch of kids and train them to be good-hearted, power-tool-wielding, salt-of-the-earth heroes.

I suggest an aggressive, go-for-broke campaign to relocate Xander Harris out of Sunnydale to someplace less damaging to our plans. Hollywood, perhaps. He can do no harm there, and our Evil Minions, especially in the Programming Departments at the major networks, are bound to break his spirit in short order.

Respectfully yours, your groveling unworthy student,

Korelva Norn

---

[23] I would inscribe lyrics here, but I feel that even Evil University shouldn't require that much sacrifice for a lousy Prerequisite to Possession class. Suffice to say, they are evil.

DO NOT WRITE BELOW THIS LINE! INSTRUCTOR NOTES ONLY!

TA: Bugger. The little bastard's figured it out. Xander is, indeed, the Most Powerful Force For Good in Sunnydale. This is very distressing. Aren't we required to fail 100% of the class, or risk losing limbs?

VARDATH: Not to worry. Xander has laid the seeds of his own destruction. After all, he once said, "Well, how about this? We whip out the ouija board, light a few candles, summon some ancient, unstoppable evil. Mayhem, mayhem, mayhem. We show up and kick its ass." And lo and behold, is that the First Evil I hear rumbling and slouching toward Sunnydale? I call that a draw. He's no longer the Most Powerful Force for whatever—in fact, I seriously doubt that there IS a Most Powerful Force For Good anywhere in the Sunnydale city limits, a big win for us.

TA: So, about the test . . .

VARDATH: Fail the little loser. He didn't grovel nearly enough, anyway.

> *From the desk of*
> *the Dean of Demonology*
>
> Mr. Norn—
> Sorry. Appeal denied. Pack some asbestos underwear. Oh, and thank you for your gracious sacrifice of your sister and sixteen captured virgins, but here at Evil University, we pride ourselves on academic unfairness. Have a nice day. <:)

DO NOT WRITE BELOW THIS LINE UNDER ABSOLUTE PAIN OF DISMEMBERMENT AND DISEMBOWELMENT!

FIRST EVILS ONLY!

Well, this blows. I go away to Sunnydale for a little game of kill-the-slayer-and-rule-the-world, and minions with not enough to do stuff my inbox with crap. People and others, I am THE FIRST EVIL, not the Forty-Third Annoyance from Pacoima. You cannot seriously expect me to read every undergraduate essay that comes along, no matter how amusing . . .

Oh. I see. It's very humorous. XANDER HARRIS? The most powerful force for good in . . .

... crap. It occurs to me now that if I'd been a little more on the ball, I'd have worked with Propecia or Prozac or whatever the hell her name is, that fashion-victim she-demon who was giving the red-head an evil makeover last year. I'd have killed that he-brat once and for good, thereby giving Tree (Willow? Whatever.) free rein to ... destroy...

Well. Obviously, that wouldn't have worked. If I'd allowed Xander to be given the fatality he so richly deserves, my game would have been over. The world would have been sucked up into a dark evil death-spell thing, which while indisputably evil is not the crazy fun it sounds (been there, so despised that). And while there are lots of brand-name evils out there, do you really want to have Proserpexa at the top of the food chain? Ugh. Can't pronounce her, can't spell her, and she dresses like Cher, which with those hips is NOT pretty.

I digress. Obviously, I must have meant for Xander Harris to thwart the Big Bad and become Hero Boy, so that I could smack him down with ringing authority during my Great Ascension of 2003.

The next snicker I hear will be punishable by the death of a thousand grandmothers with knitting needles. I swear.

Hey, it was a good plan, and it almost worked, if not for those darn ... kids ... why does that sound so familiar? Must assign a few research victims to the problem, make them watch multiple reruns of that awful movie with the cartoon dog until their eyes bleed and they become Harbingers.

Anyway. So very not my fault that the Red Witch turned into Glenda from Glitter Gulch and saved the day by outnumbering me with Slayers. And yes, Xander Harris was the putz who saved her to pull that off. And without Stick (Tree? Shrub? Whatever.), no spell would have been cast, therefore no Slayer Overload to harsh my good vibe.

An argument could be made that the miserable Xander loafed through the rest of his career with the Slayer—but hell, who wouldn't, after pulling off a coup like that? What's he got to prove? That he's EVEN MORE vital than indispensable? Sheesh. Even I don't have that kind of performance rating system. (But you there, in the blue shirt, don't get too comfortable.)

So I'll concede the Xander-linchpin-of-goodness theory. I meant to Evil Dead him, but I got busy. There was the Slayer to torment, live people to taunt, corpses to impersonate ... he was on the list, but you can't expect me to be everywhere and do everybody. And hey, he lost an eye, which is one hell of a lot better than any of the rest of the Big

Boasty Evils have come up with. (Buffy's mother died of NATURAL CAUSES? You don't think this is going to come up in annual reviews, people? Talk about falling down on the job! I'd like to stress that I was not, in fact, the Big Bad at the time. 'Cause that was just, well, embarrassing.)

And lest you think Xander got off lightly, my evil continues to work its magic in subtle yet effective ways. I mean, his love life is screwed. If you really think the chicks will dig the rakish pirate look, you are pathetically mistaken. Petty revenge is so totally mine.

Enough of that, I'm kicking the Xander problem to the curb. Now, about this student who wrote the essay... Narn? Norn. Clearly, he pegged something none of us fully understood at the time. If Xander Harris WAS the most important force for good in Sunnydale, well, our focus groups were way off the mark. We were blinded by the glamour of Red's magic, the glitter of the Slayer's so-not-naturally blonde beauty. This kind of screw-up cannot happen again, if I want to maintain my position as First Evil, and believe me, I am NOT having these embossed business cards reprinted.

What I need is a marketing campaign, something to convince people that whole Sunnydale debacle was a strategic retreat and that I'm just biding my time before emerging more powerful than ever. I'm thinking web site, with a nice Quicktime video. Fluffy, with lots of golden tones and cute puppies dying horribly. Possibly to a Barry Manilow soundtrack.

Get Mr. Norn back, decapitate him, and park him in a conference room with a bottled water and fruit plate. He's my new head of PR.

Get it? Head? . . . oh, never mind. Sulking now.

— T.F.E.

Roxanne Longstreet Conrad is the author of seven published novels: Stormriders, The Undead, Red Angel, Cold Kiss, *and* Slow Burn *(as Roxanne Longstreet), as well as* Copper Moon *and* Bridge of Shadows *(as Roxanne Conrad). Her hardcover mystery* Exile *will be available in late 2003, and a new fantasy series is currently in the works for 2003 and 2004.*

Nancy Kilpatrick

SEX AND THE SINGLE SLAYER

The Watcher's Council, in their wisdom, saw fit to send Giles to Sunnydale in order to guide Buffy in all matters of slayage. And it's fair to say that Giles makes an important contribution in helping Buffy be all that she can be—slayer-wise. But Buffy gets no help at all in an area in which, frankly, she needs a lot more assistance, namely her love life. Nancy Kilpatrick, award-winning author and Goth Queen, has volunteered to fill this desperately needed role . . . and not a moment too soon.

THE MATING GAME

BUFFY BUFFY BUFFY! Honestly, girlfriend, for a while there, those of us in cableland thought you'd never get laid! Oh, admit it: it took you forever to hit the sheets! Of course, with you being a kind of virgin huntress a la that ancient Roman deity Diana, seasons were bound to come and go before a good-enough guy flew into your sights.

Now, season one everybody felt hopeful. I mean, here's a snapshot: you and Angel lip-locked. Kissing is normal for a teenager, and obviously being normal is *the* driving force in a girl hardwired to slay. But as the entire world is no doubt aware, Angel is, alas, a vampire. The undead. The unclean. You knew it, we knew it, and while vampires surely don't fall into the truly "normal" realm—I mean, fantasies aside, did you ever really believe you two would end up in the 'burbs with 2.5 of anything?— still, there's something about those preternatural guys who live out their

19

dark side that make them simply irresistible. And all things said, a kiss is still a kiss, right? Who knew where this kiss could go? Well, we all did! And hope springs eternal, the perfect time frame for vamping the vamp. A nosferatu returning to a mortal state isn't unheard of, which means anything was possible. Mutual attraction built and I think we all experienced a sense of relief that at least *something* erotic was happening for our modern-day Artemis, she of strong limbs, she who cuts up, queen of transformation, and all that.

In retrospect, the relationship with Angel seemed to be going well. What a perfect boyfriend! Sexy, honest, true blue. Just that little glitchy thing, him being a bloodsucking killer and all. Of course, somewhere in there you had fleeting thoughts about that Billy "Ford" Fordham— yes, your continuous-loop longing to be normal. But he had his own nasty agenda, and certainly became a good example of what-you-see-is-*not*-necessarily-what-you-get. And, of course, Xander has always (more or less) been waiting in the wings, the proverbial nice guy who finishes last. Solid. Dependable. In his case, a little klutzy. In short, boring. Not in the running. Face it, a girl in your line of work needs a guy who can keep up with her, and Xander, endearing as he is, could never compete with Angel, either in the realm of the flesh, or by engaging the imagination. Sad but true, a Slayer wants a little fire in the belly of her demon lovers.

So, it had to happen. All of us sat out here week by week, eating low-fat potato chips, peering intently at the great two-dimensional window of imagination, wondering along with you just what it would be like to have sex with a prince of darkness. Angel so handsome! Not to mention charming. Mysterious . . . You more than get my drift. That night at his apartment, well, it was inevitable, and when the lights faded to black, we voyeurs let our fantasies run rampant. We died (so to speak) and went to heaven!

WHEN GOOD BOYFRIENDS GO BAD

Now, as almost every female knows only too well, a night of bliss doesn't always lead to happily-ever-after. And girl, sad to say, I have to tell you that what happened to you next isn't all that uncommon, metaphorically speaking. Many of us have had a loving partner by night who, by the next night, has turned into something "other." It's bloody scary! Not every XY can tolerate humanization! History is full of stories about guys who abstained in order to retain lofty philosophical or spiritual ideals that precluded earthly desires to the point of violence, and others who refused to consummate with the ladies so that they had testosterone in abundance for warlike or sportslike destruction of their fellow man. It's a fact, girlfriend—males have a hard time with intimacy. Like I'm telling you anything you haven't thought about! It puts them in touch with themselves, and that might not be a person whose hand they want to be shaking. That they so often negate the good things that happened and reduce what was a powerful emotional experience to "It didn't mean anything at all," well, there's the rub! All of us out here were shocked on your behalf, but not surprised.

MOURNING RITUALS

What followed was the inevitable déjà vu: tears, guilt, anger, sadness. Oh girlfriend! Been there! Done that. Burned the Kubler-Ross T-shirt! Nothing heals a wound but time, which surely must have seemed eternal as you danced your way to the end of love.

Angel was running amok. What could you do but let yourself flow down the only waterway that made any sense, the River Styx. The guy became history in the making. Everything you loved about him seemed to have vanished like a mist burned away by the sun, leaving a killing machine, hell-bent on revenge, and determined to cause you grief at every turn. The worst for you was the emotional coldness, as though the love never happened. What's left but out-with-the-old, in-with-the-new? You had to try to erase him from your psyche. Never shunning the tough decisions, that's what you did, Slayer girl, and yes, it was heartbreaking to watch your internal struggle.

Sometimes people understand, sometimes they don't. It's hard if they don't, especially when it's those we're close to. Sometimes the only way to cope with all this is to just leave town. Get away for a while. Find a new place. Make a fresh start. Even a temporary change is as good as a rest. Sow the seeds in a virgin field, and see if the love flower can blossom again. And hey! Maybe in your time of grief you could even meet somebody who offers a bit of comfort, if you know what I mean.

DESTINED TO DIE

Let's see . . . season three brought the possibility of change in the boyfriend arena. Scott, but that didn't go anywhere. None of us thought it would; he was a wimp. How could he compete with Angelus?

But old loves never really die, they just alter form. Angel's resurrection left you between a rock and a hard place. It's tough being friends after shared intimacy; all the old pulls are there, and it's so easy to end up melding. But embedded deep in your awareness was the vibrating pain of knowing just how ugly it could, would, turn out. We're all two-legged Pavlovian dogs when it comes to associating pain and pleasure from the past with the present. Anything more than a kiss with Angel would bring out his Demon Within. You settled for a working relationship. Or so you tried to tell yourself. But love never dies, apparently, even when we know it is in the terminal ward, and picking at old wounds keeps those protective scars from forming. The dead-end relationship just keeps going, and going, and going... Nowhere. You're his girl. Always. But gee, isn't that impossible? One of you had to make the break. And between you and me, honey, there's nobody out here who does not hold to the belief that Angel truly loves you, enough to leave you, or something like that. It's confusing. One of those paradoxes no woman ever really is completely sure of.

REBOUND "R" US!

So, onward. And you did battle on, romance-wise. But face it, Buffster, Parker was only a distraction. He was not the guy for you. Oh sure, you bumped into him at the right place, and the perfect time, and indeed he helped you, if not to forget at least to gain a bit of perspective on Angel, and maybe a touch of your slinkster confidence back. But Parker was high maintenance. Basically, another wimp.

Riley. Well, I think we were all amazed when you got involved with soldier boy. Especially with Angel still lurking. Still, Riley was no normal guy. And frankly, despite your love affair with the conventional, it's obvious to most of us who know you better than you know yourself that you'll never be able to maintain a relationship with someone who isn't strange. At least the guy could keep up with you!

Somehow, though, Riley never seemed like "Mr. Right." Okay, he had that long-term potential, even though he was way reluctant at first, and not really accepting of your career choice. But ultimately, you worked well together. Here at last was a guy you could actually talk with, who understood you, and vice versa. Your own species, even. Yet underneath it all was this sense of something missing. He just did not inspire the great passion in you that Angel did, that was obvious. So nobody was truly surprised when you let comfort zone get away. Think of him as a good starter marriage, although it sure must have grated when he committed conceptual bigamy by showing up with a wife!

And then there was Ben. Enough said.

Then finally, Spike, and what was with that? Aren't you a bit young for Alzheimer's? You made it with one vampire, and look what happened! Spike appeared to be a reform waiting to happen but to my mind he was always more of a full-blown catastrophe. No matter how much he might have wanted you, and vice versa, this would never have worked. He didn't have the integrity, the substance, even if he did possess a soul he could feel in the end, or so they say.

Spike gave his life for you, for all of us, and for that we thank him. But a hero does not a good husband make, and fate, it seems, saved you from what would have been a huge mistake. Do not be fooled by a guy addicted to peroxide again!

No, girl, I'm afraid to tell you that it seems you are destined to be alone. A Boadicea of your time, warrior queen, too strong for any potential mate. The only one who can meet you is Angel. He's still there. He came to your mom's funeral. He's always been there for you, helping you, listening to you, working things out with you, loving you, rescuing you on occasion. And yet a relationship with him that involves actualized physical love and all that it entails is a treacherous maze with no way out. What's a vampire hunter to do?

SLAYERS JUST WANNA HAVE FUN

Dismal as it seems, you've got to look at the half-full glass. Consider yourself lucky. I mean, at least you didn't end up preggers by some sexy vampire dude. Now *that* would be a conundrum!

Want some advice? Even if you don't, here it is: Get over yourself, girl! Release yourself from that tragic notion of normalcy, do not pass GO, do not collect $200. It's a myth anyway. Who do you know who is normal? Accept the fact that you will always have a hard time finding a guy in his right mind who will pair up with a girl who kills vampires and other assorted supernatural entities every night of the week. I mean, lesser girls than you can't find a decent boyfriend!

You're in that same grim boat as every female throughout history who has been strong of mind, firm of body, and more or less pure of spirit. She Who Knows Herself. Who line dances to her own rockabilly band. And now that you've dispersed your power to any girl who wants it, well, things can only get tougher for all of us. You don't seem to have lesbo tendencies, so for you there's pretty well only one real option: Wait for the guy who can live with you being the way you are. It's the only road to happiness. Admittedly, those guys are few and far between. Rarer than a vampire who doesn't drink blood. But they're out there, just not lingering at every cemetery gate.

In the meantime, don't take any of the dudes sniffing their way across your path too seriously. Just play the proverbial field. And while you do, don't expend one freckle's worth of energy worrying about what people say, because most of them are sheep anyway, hardly worthy of saving, but you seem compelled. Look, girlfriend, we on the bleachers have your best interests at heart. Just because a girl is cheerleader-cute, and WWF sexy doesn't mean she has to shag every pimply nerd who passes her door, with or without blood running through his veins, in the hopes that he is The One. Maintain your standards! Like the virgin goddesses of old, only give yourself to He Who Is Worthy Of You!

Remember, Buffy, you are not alone. You come from a long line of chicks with a mission, whose agenda is first and foremost to rid the world of malevolence. Xena and Wonder Woman are role models. But honey, you've got to ease up a little. And now's the perfect time, what with Hellmouth having been cleaned out, and all your new sister-slayers the world over working overtime on evil, and now that you're not fighting monsters 24/7, give a nod toward partying. Have some fun. Let the universe provide you with a bit of lighthearted meaning. That's the Zen approach, which is part of your training, or do I stand corrected? Don't worry about the future, just live your life, and as you're doing that, that's when the impossible not only becomes possible, but probable. As Angel said, he's not getting any older. And to quote Mr. J. Lennon, "Life is what happens when you're busy making other plans." Party on, Buffy!

Award-winning author Nancy Kilpatrick has published 14 novels, 150-plus short stories, five collections of stories, and has edited seven anthologies.

She has also penned three comic books, co-scripted a bilingual stageplay, and written a slew of nonfiction. Much of her work involves vampires; for example, her popular Power of the Blood series, which will be reprinted this year (Mosaic Press), and her newest title Eternal City *(Five Star Books/Gale Publishing).*

In 2004 she will publish The Goth Bible, *a nonfiction profile of the modern gothic culture (St. Martin's Press), and* Goth Gurrls & Boiz, *an anthology she is co-editing with Nancy Holder (Roc/NAL). Nancy is currently writing the screenplay for one of her books,* Near Death, *being produced by C3 Productions.*

Check her website for the latest news: nancykilpatrick.com

Sherrilyn Kenyon

THE SEARCH FOR SPIKE'S BALLS

Best-selling author Sherrilyn Kenyon is perhaps most famous for her steamy Dark-Hunters series, described as "Buffy the Vampire Slayer meets Sex and the City." It's hard to think of anyone better suited to discuss this critical and long-neglected topic.

I HAVE BEEN A HUGE FAN of Buffy since the moment the first episode aired where she was lying in bed, dreaming of the evil baddies coming to town. I was with her in the car as Joyce Summers drove her to Sunnydale High where Buffy met the people who would one day form the nucleus of the Scoobies. And I knew then that this was going to be one of those shows that went down into television history.

For all the beauty and wonder of *Buffy the Vampire Slayer* though, branding itself into our culture and collective hearts, I have noticed one disturbing trend in the series: the emasculation of the male characters. I have a theory about this. My belief is that Buffy is, in fact, her own special breed of vampire. Whereas traditional vampires suck the blood from their victims, Buffy drains the testosterone from the characters she is involved with—this appears to be the true source of the Slayer's power.

Nowhere is this better illustrated than with the Spike character.

Spike is now a veteran of the series, but he wasn't one of the first to fall victim to Buffy's gonad vampirism. He is simply her most recent victim.

25

The first victim was Angel. Angel is a mysterious character during the early episodes. We know very little about him other than he's debonair and a master of the one-liners; meanwhile, Buffy at this time is a soft ingénue who is just learning her powers and skills. She has yet to discover her own vampirism.

Yet as Angel becomes more involved with Buffy, we see in him a dramatic change where he becomes weaker while she grows stronger. When he finally succumbs to her and they sleep together, I believe it isn't so much his soul leaving him that turns him into Angelus as it is Angel seeing the writing on the wall and knowing that if something doesn't change instantly, he will be as dead from her testosterone-drainage as a vampire victim is from blood loss.

Enter the evil vampire Angelus. Now anyone who knows me knows I have a fondness for truly evil characters. Something about the baddest of the bad makes me rub my hands together in glee and sit up straight to watch them go.

But notice: While Angelus grew in viciousness, Buffy became a kinder, gentler Slayer. She lost a great deal of her humor and lightheartedness during this season and became (I really hate to use this word) whiney.

Ultimately, her backbone isn't returned to her until the end of the season when she kills Angelus and then runs away from home, never to be the same again.

It is at this point that our cycle really begins.

Angel is resurrected by The First, or at least we are led to believe this. The First is that ambiguous evil that has birthed all evil.

Instead of the strong Angel who captivated us during the earlier years, the new Angel incarnation is a shadow of his former self; meanwhile, Buffy is stronger and better than ever. She has commenced her testosterone-feeding.

No one is immune to this. Think about it. Xander, though often nothing more than comic relief, had his moments of heroism early on. Remember Xander the Hyena, or the Lover, or my personal fave, Apocalypse Now Xander who was all testosterone in the one Halloween episode where Buffy reverted to being a helpless Southern belle? Buffy got her Slayerdom back—and poof, Xander was emasculated again.

Sad, but true.

Even Riley Finn succumbed to her gonad-feeding frenzy. In the early Initiative episodes he was Mr. Bad-Ass-Take-Charge-and-Get Out-of-My-Way. He was the epitome of Soldier (note the capital S) until he became involved with Buffy.

Our GI commando was transformed from SEAL potential to amoeba in one short season as Buffy sucked the masculinity right out of him. We watched him slide down to the darkest pits where he paid vampires to suck his blood so that he at least had some form of control over his drainage. Finally he could stand no more of it and had to leave Sunnydale because he knew he could never be a man so long as Buffy was sucking the testosterone out of him.

In fact, as we all know, he rediscovered his manhood down in South America without her. Remember when he came back season before last as a special guest? He was our beloved commando all over again—scarred and everything. He kicked butts and took names; meanwhile, the Buffy character reverted back to being whiney. Once he's gone, she's strong again.

But I think the most tragic example of Buffy's feeding comes from the character of Spike.

Ahhh, Spike. The mere mention of his name makes me smile and at the same time makes me sad. Now here was a truly great villain. From the moment he walked in and toasted the Master's protégé to the episode where he went to blow the Slayer away even while he had a chip in his head, he was BAD.

Before he allowed Buffy to drain him, he was the Dirty Harry of the vampire world. Even with his wings clipped by the Initiative, he was still his nasty barbarous self, pitting Scooby against Scooby and letting fly stinging comebacks and one-liners.

Until the day he discovers his Slayer obsession. He loves Buffy. From there it is a slippery slope that leads him down to the sad shape he's in now.

Here we really see the fact that, much like the Stygian Witch's Eye, there can only be one set of balls per episode and it must be handed back and forth between the characters. Since the show is named *Buffy*, by default the balls will always revert to Buffy.

Whenever Spike is strong, Buffy is weak. Case in point, when Buffy dies, Spike takes care of the Scoobies and Dawn; when Buffy returns, he becomes submissive to her and allows her to run roughshod over him even when she's clearly wrong.

This culminates into Spike deciding that he can't stand handing his balls over to her anymore. Becoming the vampire we remember from the beginning, he journeys to the ends of the earth where he can battle it out to become what he was before. Of course both Spike and the viewers believe he will become his former evil self.

But since he is now involved with Buffy and she has him under control, like Dracula with his Renfield, Spike doesn't revert to his former vampire self. He, just like Angel, gets his soul back and is now nothing more than Buffy's punching bag.

Gone is the Spike of legend, the Spike who once slew two Slayers without hesitation, and in his place is a tragic shell that is often abused by not just Buffy, but all the cast.

It appears that in the Battle of the Balls, Buffy has finally won the ultimate victory. Poor Spike wasn't as lucky as Angel or Riley, who were able to leave before they became Buffy's Renfield. Spike is now on the level of Xander, who once put into words the feelings of every male character on the show: "As of this moment, it is over. I'm finished being everyone's butt monkey." But as we have seen, he didn't leave and he hasn't regained his manhood.

Now that Spike no longer has balls, it begs the question: who will be next? I thought for a minute Willow might have them, but, as we saw, Buffy the Testosterone-Sucking Vampire, with the help of her emasculated Xander, defeated her.

I believe this is why Buffy had such a hard a time defeating The First during the final season. The last time she faced The First, she had Angel to feed from. With Spike, Xander, and Willow completely drained of testosterone, she had no one to turn to for power.

Enter Faith. Why else would we bring Faith back? Not to mention the fact that poor Faith also fell victim to Buffy's gonad suckage. At one point, they even had to knock her unconscious so that Buffy could suck her dry.

I will never forget sitting down to view the final show. I like to call this the Symphony of the Balls. It was truly spectacular to behold. Like some legendary football game, we watched the great ball handoff between the characters.

It's in Faith's hands, no wait, she's injured, handoff to Buffy. No, Buffy can't handle the testosterone charge, quickly pass to Willow. Wait no, give to Xander, oh wait, Anya has them. Ultimately, it came down to Buffy and Spike. Spike, though he was fighting off to the side, was the vampire we knew him to be. The man who defeated the demon to get his soul back. The one who took his punches and then demanded arrogantly, "Is that all you've got?"

This Spike was worried because his medallion wasn't working. I kept waiting for him to proclaim to all, "I don't need no stinking medallion. I'm here to kick them back into oblivion." He never did. It's not until Buffy goes down with a vicious wound that drains her testosterone that it is immediately transferred to Spike.

Finally, in the end, through the medallion, Spike receives his balls again, only to die holding down the fort while Buffy and the rest of testosterone-slayer potentials run for it.

With Spike and Sunnydale gone, I will never forget my curiosity as I sat there looking at all of them. Willow in the final minutes had dispersed the Slayer's strength to the world. All potentials now have their full Slayer's strength without Buffy dying.

Which is good since so many of the cast died. Now Buffy has an open banquet of people she can suck the balls from. The sky's the limit and the Slayer is now guaranteed to be able to carry on for eternity.

USA Today best-selling author Sherrilyn Kenyon has been a devout Buffy fan since the very beginning. She lives outside of Nashville, Tennessee with her husband and three sons. Raised in the middle of eight boys, and currently outnumbered by the Y chromosome in her home, she realizes the most valuable asset a woman has for coping with men is a sense of humor. Not to mention a large trash bag and a pair of tongs.

Versatile and prolific, she has successfully published in virtually every known genre and subgenre. Writing as Kinley MacGregor and Sherrilyn Kenyon, she is the best-selling author of several series, including, The Dark-Hunters, Brotherhood of the Sword, The MacAllisters, Sex Camp Diaries and BAD Boys. Her novel Fantasy Lover was voted as one of the Top Ten Romances of 2002 by Romance Writers of America. For more information, you can visit her online at one of her websites: sherrilynkenyon.com or kinleymacgregor.com.

Scott Westerfeld

A SLAYER COMES TO TOWN

As Scott Westerfeld explains, Buffy falls into a long-standing science fiction and fantasy tradition that includes Dracula, The X-Files and, for that matter, Abbott and Costello Meet the Mummy. Buffy is a so-called Trespass story, except when it's not . . .

CREATIVE WRITING TEACHERS are fond of sweeping generalizations:

"Never use adverbs."

"Never begin a story with the word *the*."

"There's only one plot: the shift from innocence to experience."

A friend of mine in Louisiana had a writing teacher who enjoyed proclaiming, "The king dies and the queen dies. That's not a story. The king dies and the queen dies of grief. Now *that's* a story." I'm not sure what that's supposed to mean, nor what any of these sayings are supposed to do for young writers. Probably make all but the most dedicated break down and get a real job.

But recently I heard a good one: "There are only two plots: a stranger comes to town and someone goes on a journey." This aphorism helped distill an idea I've developed over years of reading and writing science fiction and fantasy, resulting in my own sweeping generalization: "There are only two kinds of fantastic story: the Alternate World and the Trespass."

What do I mean by this? Allow me to define my terms.

In "Alternate World" stories, the reader goes on a journey to another era, another planet, a world that follows different rules. Alternative histories, stories of the far future, and tales of elves and magic fall into this category. In their own way, *Lord of the Rings*, *1984*, and *Star Wars* are all Alternate World stories.

In "Trespass" stories, a stranger comes to town. Something fantastic—whether *The X-Files'* aliens or Anne Rice's vampires—invades our familiar world of credit cards and disposable razors. Reality is shown to have cracks and fissures we haven't seen before.

I must admit, before becoming a Buffyphile I had a deep prejudice against Trespass tales. The techniques that bring Alternate Worlds to life are those that originally drew me to read and write science fiction: the top-to-bottom world building, the ubiquitous and yet subtle exposition, the filtering of a strange reality through a viewpoint character who finds that reality commonplace. This kind of tale was what I considered to be speculative fiction at its most literary, sophisticated, textured, and, most important, subversive. SF allowed me to visit and create worlds that had completely different rules from our own, and that called everything in our "normal" world into question.

On the other hand, Trespass stories felt rather more comfortable, designed for readers who prefer to start with something familiar. And there seemed to be a conservative principle at work in most, a tendency for the alien invader to evaporate at the end of the tale. We've all seen this plot, which I call the Elastic Trespass story:

1) "Monsters! I can't believe this is happening!"

2) "It's true, there are monsters! Let's kill them."

3) "Oh, no! When you burned down the house to kill the monsters all the evidence was destroyed. No one will ever believe us now!"

In the Elastic Trespass, as in a sitcom, everything goes "back to normal" at the end of the episode. A return to an unperturbed, normal, daylight world is always effected. E.T. goes home. It's as if there's some sort of natural law at work, a principle of conservation of normality, that makes all the evidence disappear by the story's denouement. Either all marks of the alien are erased by happenstance, or the characters engage in a frantic cover-up, apparently unwilling to take credit for saving the world.

(A close cousin to the Elastic Trespass is the Elastic Time Travel story, that old chestnut in which time-travelers wind up on the *Titanic* and no matter whom they tell about the iceberg all they get is "But this ship is unsinkable!" and the ship sinks anyway. History *had* to happen that way.)

The elastic form of the Trespass story is inherently conservative, saying as it does that the stranger who comes to town is fundamentally unknowable. We can't incorporate the alien into our normal world, because that would imply that the world can change. So when the Other pops up, our heroes stomp it into the ground, obliterating all evidence of its passage. Like history, middle-class normality is fixed and unalterable, no matter how many fantastic creatures, ancient curses, and mystical portals might exist in the margins.

This principle is especially strong in stories with young protagonists, partly because no one ever believes kids anyway. It's as if the young adult Elastic Trespass tale is a training ground for adult conformity. Children in these stories always hide E.T. in the closet, repress their own memories, and find themselves unable to break the conspiracy of silence that is the adult world. In C.S. Lewis's Narnia books, at least one of the kids, George, grows up to "remember" that his trips to Narnia were all a game. He manages to enter adulthood only by repressing the fantasies of childhood. Only they weren't fantasies; they were alien realities! (Naturally, he's the one who winds up with the best-paying job.)

When I watched the first few episodes of *Buffy* with an uncritical eye, the show seemed destined to be trapped in this mold. The vamps conveniently turned to dust when staked, leaving no evidence. The protagonists were marginalized kids, and their adult mentor a mere high-school librarian (and a bit of a toff), a marginal adult without real-world credibility. Buffy hid her calling from her mother and from the adult world at large. Despite her extraordinary powers, she and her friends (and her viewers) instinctively knew the rules of young adult powerlessness: "They won't believe us anyway," and "We better leave everything as we found it, or we'll be in big trouble." It's okay to save the world, but not to change it.

But something about *Buffy* kept me watching. From the first episode, the show was playing with the conventions of the Elastic Trespass tale, subverting the genre traditions in subtle (and sometimes obvious) ways. In Joss Whedon's hands, the elastic of middle-class reality wound up stretching and twisting into new and unexpected forms.

One of the ironclad rituals of the Trespass is the Passage of Disbelief, the moment where the protagonist says, "This can't be happening!" Now, we've all read and watched a million versions of this scene.

And not only main characters have to come to believe that the Trespass is real, but often they must convince their friends and parents, the police, newspaper reporters, government officials, and whoever else they need help from. But it's a waste of the viewers' time, because we've seen the movie trailers or read the back of the book, and we already know the vampires or aliens or killer tomatoes are real. We just want to skip to the part where everyone's on board, especially to avoid dialog like "There must be a rational explanation for all this!" or that most embarrassing line in any science fiction movie: "This is like something out of a science fiction movie!"

Thankfully, the writers of *Buffy* employ a number of strategies to subvert this little ritual, using humor and understatement to breeze past the usual protestations of disbelief.

Buffy herself, of course, has had a movie prequel to adjust to her place in the fantastic scheme of things. In the pilot ("Welcome to the Hellmouth," 1-1), she takes over Giles's recitation of a Slayer's duties with, "'. . . the strength and skill to hunt the vampires, to stop the spread of their evil' blah, blah, blah. I've heard it, okay? . . . I've both been there, and done that." For the Slayer herself, at least, no time is wasted in disbelief.[1]

At the end of this scene, Xander emerges from the library stacks, having overheard Giles's exposition, and condenses his initial Passage of Disbelief to a simple "What?"

After Willow and Xander are saved from the Master's henchmen in the pilot's conclusion ("The Harvest," 1-2), they receive a full briefing from Giles. But it is Buffy who mockingly provides the ritual litany of "rational" explanations.

> XANDER: "Okay, this is where I have a problem. See, because we're talking about vampires. We're having a talk with vampires in it."
>
> WILLOW: "Isn't that what we saw last night?"
>
> BUFFY: "No, no, those weren't vampires. They were just guys in thunder need of a facial. Or maybe they had rabies. It could have been rabies. And that guy turning to dust? Just a trick of light . . ."
>
> WILLOW: "Oh, I—I need to sit down."

---

[1] At this point I'd like to thank Justine Larbalestier for her help with this essay. Her ability to identify *Buffy* episodes based on half-remembered fragments of dialog is uncanny (in the sense of disturbing). And also thanks to William Smith, editor of *Trunk Stories*, who has kept me supplied with *Buffy* videotapes during my time in Australia.

BUFFY: "You are sitting down."
WILLOW: "Oh. Good for me."

And thus the original Scoobies' Passages of Disbelief are dealt with, once and for all. Five minutes of screen time later, Xander is ready for action, uttering a line that could be from any *Buffy* episode of any season: "So what's the plan? We saddle up, right?"

Done and done.

In most Trespass stories, the demarcation between those who know the secret and those who are blissfully unaware is carefully maintained. Initiation is an important ritual. But in *Buffy*, that border is shown to be delightfully fuzzy. When Jenny Calendar is recruited into the Scooby Gang ("I Robot, You Jane," 1-8), Giles attempts to break the existence of demonic forces to her gently.

GILES: "I need your help, but before that I need you to believe something that you may not want to. Uh, there's, um . . . Something's got into the um, inside, um . . . There's a demon in the Internet."
JENNY: "I know."

End of scene.

In the standard Elastic Trespass tale, Jenny would have sputtered in disbelief, requiring hard proof of Giles's extraordinary claim. But instead it is Giles who winds up sputtering. When in the next scene he asks if Jenny is a witch, she answers, "Technopagan is the term. There are more of us than you think."

That last line could be the motto for Sunnydale's Trespass-aware citizens. While guarding supposed non-initiates from the dark truths of the Hellmouth, the Scoobies are repeatedly shocked to discover how pervasive secret knowledge is in Sunnydale. In "Lie to Me" (2-7), Buffy attempts to explain away a vampire attack glimpsed by her old school friend, Ford.

FORD: "What's going on?"
BUFFY: "Um . . . uh, there was a, a cat. A cat here, and, um, then there was another cat . . . and they fought. The cats. And . . . then they left."
FORD: "Oh, I thought you were just slaying a vampire."
BUFFY: "What? Whatting a what?"

Again, Ford doesn't sputter, Buffy does. Ford went to Buffy's previous high school, and already knows that she's the Slayer. The mystical forces at work in the Buffyverse are a matter of teenage rumor, dark and knowing humor, an open secret, so even bit players don't waste time with the usual Passages of Disbelief. Any number of Sunnydale residents, students and adults, turn out to be more or less aware of that ultimate Trespass, the Hellmouth, and all it implies about the reality of their world. Time after time, Buffy's grateful rescuees blurt out some sort of reversal similar to Ford's. Perhaps the most underplayed of these inverted Passages of Disbelief comes from the laconic Oz ("Surprise," 2-25).

> WILLOW: "Are you okay?"
> OZ: "Yeah. Hey, did everybody see that guy just turn to dust?"
> WILLOW: "Uh, well, uh, sort of?"
> XANDER: "Yep. Vampires are real. A lot of them live in Sunnydale. Willow will fill you in."
> WILLOW: "I know it's hard to accept at first."
> OZ (nodding): "Actually it explains a *lot.*"

Like the dark secrets at work in any small town, only the most willful Pollyanna is completely unaware of Sunnydale's special dangers. Even the optimistic Larry, in the long traveling shot that opens Sunnydale High School for season three, isn't entirely clueless: "This is our year. I'm telling you, best football season *ever.* . . . If we can focus, keep discipline, and not have as many mysterious deaths, Sunnydale is gonna *rule.*" ("Anne," 3-1)

The pervasiveness of this open secret is most touchingly demonstrated in "Prom" (3-19), when the students of Sunnydale High elect Buffy as Class Protector, recognizing her years of service as Slayer. As Jonathan explains in his presentation speech, this award is ad hoc ("This was actually a new category. First time ever. I guess there were a lot of write-in ballots.") and represents a shared knowledge rarely given voice: "We don't talk about it much, but it's no secret that Sunnydale High isn't like other high schools." But it is precisely on this unofficial level that understanding of the Trespass operates in Sunnydale. The official line may be that monsters don't exist and that the fantastic and mystical must be repressed. But in the Buffyverse there is a significant space set aside for improvised and heartfelt recognition of realities outside the official narrative, and write-in votes for the people's hero do not go uncounted.

Of course, the Passage of Disbelief is only half of the Elastic Trespass. With every monster that emerges from the Hellmouth, the elastic of reality is stretched out of shape, and according to the rules it must snap back to normalcy. After each resolved crisis—the monster slain, the spell reversed—comes the inevitable Cover-Up. All evidence must be erased. (Famously, the original Scooby Gang of *Scooby-Doo* never needed a Cover-Up, invariably discovering that there were no real mystical forces at work. It was always just "old Mr. Withers the caretaker, trying to scare folks away."[2])

Buffy knowingly underplays its Cover-Ups, trotting out genre clichés without much time wasted on believability. At the end of "Harvest" (1-2), Cordelia recounts the rumors meant to explain the mass vampire attack at the Bronze. "Well, I heard it was rival gangs, you know, fighting for turf. But all I can tell you is they were in an ugly way of looking . . . I mean, I don't even remember that much, but I tell you it was a freak show." Moments later, Giles provides, "People have a tendency to rationalize what they can, and forget what they can't."

Memory repression is a frequent device, but even such tenuous Cover-Ups aren't always in earnest. In "The Pack" (1-6), Xander claims to be unable to remember his experiences when possessed by a hyena spirit (particularly his attempted seduction/rape of Buffy, one suspects). But Giles comes to doubt his story.

> GILES: "I've been reading up on my animal possession, and I cannot find anything anywhere about memory loss afterwards."
> XANDER: "Did you tell them [Buffy and Willow] that?"
> GILES: "Your secret dies with me."

In the climax of "Bewitched, Bothered, and Bewildered" (3-16), after Xander is saved from an adoring but violent horde of love-spell-bedazzled women at the last minute, Cordelia offers the gathered crowd this stunningly lame Cover-Up line: "Boy, that was the best scavenger hunt ever." In the next scene, Buffy rolls her eyes at this one.

> BUFFY: "Scavenger hunt?"
> XANDER: "Your mom seemed to buy it."
> BUFFY: "So she says. I think that she's just so wigged at hitting on one of my friends that she's repressing. She's getting pretty good at that. I should probably start worrying . . ."

---

[2] And he would have gotten away with it, too, if it weren't for those gosh-darned kids!

More often, the Cover-Up is left to entities other than the Scooby Gang. As early as "Out of Sight, Out of Mind" (1-11), government agents show up to take the invisible girl away for covert ops training. And in "School Hard" (2-3), maintaining the secrets of the Hellmouth becomes a matter for local Sunnydale officials. Parent-teacher night is invaded by Spike and his gang, and Principal Snyder barely survives, coming into close contact with the vampires. It seems as if there will be some hefty Covering-Up to do. But instead of Buffy making explanations and excuses, we overhear this exchange between the police chief and Snyder:

> CHIEF: "I need to say something to the media people."
> SNYDER: "So?"
> CHIEF: "So? You want the usual story? Gang-related? PCP?"
> SNYDER: "What did you have in mind? The truth?"
> CHIEF: "Right. Gang-related. PCP."

This conversation not only neatly provides a Cover-Up, but again shows the fuzzy border between knowing and not-knowing in *Buffy*. If the chief of police recognizes a vampire attack when he sees one, then knowledge of the mystical must extend beyond the unspoken secrets of high school. After this scene viewers must ask themselves, How far up does this Cover-Up go?

As we learn in the third season, adult awareness and even complicity goes all the way to City Hall. And, of course, in season four the federal government itself is implicated. (Presaged by government involvement in "Out of Sight, Out of Mind," 1-11). As the wider world beyond Sunnydale becomes embroiled in the crises of the Hellmouth, we are forced to reconsider to what extent *Buffy* is set in "our" world. Despite the credit cards and SUVs on screen, the show begins to leave the strict confines of the Elastic Trespass tale, until the Buffyverse seems almost transformed into an Alternate World.

Of course, every fictional TV show takes place in a fictional reality. Although there is a Tom's Diner in New York, we don't expect to find Jerry and Elaine there. But such shows work to minimize their departures from the familiar. In *Seinfeld*'s New York, the Bronx is still up and the Battery's down.

A show like *West Wing*, however, has a far more problematic relationship to reality, given the high profile of the US president. This discomfort is especially apparent when events like the September 11 attacks must be portrayed on the show, but only by analogy. *West Wing* worked best in the relatively sedate 1990s. Presumably, as our current unsettled era goes on, that show's reality and ours will unavoidably drift further apart. (Eighteenth- and nineteenth-century novels frequently used blanks in proper names to prevent this sort of discomfort, referring to the town of "————shire" or "certain officers of the ————rd Regiment.")

But of course my privileged term "Alternate Worlds" refers to fictions like *Dune* and *Brave New World*, in which new realities are created wholesale. The Buffyverse may become less and less like our reality, as its bestiary of government agencies, demons, and alternate dimensions expands, but when those demons rampage in Sunnydale's pedestrian malls, they still encounter coffee shops and sushi bars. In my book, that's a Trespass.

Except when it isn't. Because there's that *other* kind of *Buffy* episode. That one in which reality changes around the characters, altered for one screen hour into a different universe. The Scoobies are the same, but the rules have changed.

Nightmares come true, Halloween costumes possess their wearers, a high-school loser is the super-competent center of a cult of personality, the conventions of the Hollywood musical replace the familiar structures of social discourse ("Nightmares" 1-10, "Halloween" 2-6, "Superstar" 4-17, "Once More, with Feeling" 6-7, respectively). In these episodes, the new rules of reality must be decoded and understood, the cause unmasked, the change reversed. The Trespass is *the world itself.*

But "The Wish" (3-9), in which Cordelia inadvertently asks Anyanka to change the history of Sunnydale, creates not so much a Trespass as a fully-fledged Alternate World. In this reality, Buffy never came to town, the Master completed the Harvest, and the elastic of normality has snapped. The worlds of light and dark have become intermixed: the Bronze a vampires-only club, the abandoned factory back in business as a human abattoir. Vampires are no longer hidden; the open secret is no longer a secret at all. And as goes Sunnydale, so goes the world. Even Cleveland is experiencing "a great deal of demonic activity." The result of Buffy's absence is apparently nothing less than the beginning of the end of the human era. This is *It's a Wonderful Life* on a grand scale, or perhaps a quicker version of Ray Bradbury's cautionary time-travel story "The Sound of Thunder," in which the accidental trampling of a butterfly millions of years ago turns the present into something barely recognizable.

Like any Altered World, "Vampworld" (as *Buffy* fans have dubbed it) has its own internal logic, its own rules: humans no longer wear bright colors and always get home by dark. It's not a fevered dream, but a meticulously worked out reality. Curfew signs and strands of garlic replace the HIV/AIDS awareness posters on the high school's walls, and classes are suspended for the "monthly memorial." As Anyanka explains to Giles: "This is the real world now. This is the world we made."

Interesting choice of words. In the Buffyverse, "we" are responsible even for a reality created by a wish. Vampworld is the world as it very well might have been, had Buffy been a little weaker, a little less lucky, or picked the wrong time to move to Cleveland.

Of course, this contingent nature of reality is to be expected; the Buffyverse is a place in which the world is contested real estate. In "Prophecy Girl" (1-12) (the episode to which "The Wish" is, in effect, an alternate outcome), Willow describes the horrific aftermath of a pre-apocalyptic vampire attack. "And when I walked in there, it wasn't our world anymore. They made it theirs. And they had fun."

This Trespass means business. It doesn't just cross the borders of normality, it invades with intent to remake normality in its own image. It is a potentially world-altering Trespass.

But only potentially. Unlike the wounded future of Bradbury's "Sound of Thunder," the Buffyverse snaps back to its "normal" state at the climax of "The Wish." Giles smashes Anyanka's necklace and history is repaired, with none of the characters even remembering what happened. (Because it *didn't* happen.) *Buffy*'s Altered Worlds are Elastic. Nightmares lose their grip on reality; Halloween archetypes turn back into cheap costumes; Jonathan turns back into a loser; the last song ends.

So how do these Elastic Altered Worlds fit into my schema? Are they like that tedious Elastic Time Travel story, the one in which the *Titanic* sinks no matter what the travelers do, proving that history is immutable? Not quite. In "The Wish" (3-9), history is not itself elastic, naturally springing back into its "rightful" state. Setting it aright takes hard work. Not only the work of Giles overpowering Anyanka and smashing her necklace, but, by implication, all the work that Buffy has done since coming to Sunnydale. The possibility of Vampworld, and its disappearance, prove that Buffy and the Scoobies are not powerless observers of history. They are nothing less than makers of history.

As the climax of "Prophecy Girl" approaches, the Master watches the Hellmouth creature emerge, saying, "Yes, come forth, my child. Come into my world."

Buffy reveals herself, and retorts, "I don't think it's yours just yet."

Across a certain number of story arcs, any fantastic fictional world begins to change and to reflect the alien forces at its narrative center. Like the Bush-era, post–September 11 *West Wing*, the Buffyverse resembles the nonfictional world less and less as time goes on. But one of the great strengths of *Buffy* is that the show doesn't shy away from plot points that have no escape back into normality. No Trespass—an army of zombies, a town unable to speak, a mayor transforming in public into a giant demon—is too extreme for a half-baked Cover-Up line. Or none at all.

Buffy does not repress her memories, no matter how strange or painful. She doesn't sputter with the arrival of every new monster; just saddles up. Her friends and family die, some never to be reanimated. The strangers who come to town—werewolf, demon, or witch—turn out to be something knowable, even worth loving. The elastic gradually frays until it's beyond fixing. The fantastic leaves its mark on the world.

The Buffyverse is not simply a Trespassed world, one that snaps back to middle-class normality as a function of natural law. It's not quite an Altered World either; there are those credit cards and cell phones. But it is a world that, like ours, can be and is changed, for better or worse, by the actions of the people who live in it.

Scott Westerfeld's fourth and latest novel is The Risen Empire. *A sequel,* The Killing of Worlds, *will be released in late 2003. He lives in Sydney, Australia, but escapes its cruel winters by fleeing to New York City.*

Peg Aloi

SKIN PALE AS
APPLE BLOSSOM

I miss Tara...

*B*UFFY THE VAMPIRE SLAYER is thinking man's eye candy. Thinking woman's dramedy. Prime-time soap opera for Trekkies.
Strokevision for loner Lovecraft buffs. Textually rich, emotionally dense, psychologically juicy, it's as layered and complex as *Twin
Peaks* without the po-mo pretension. Douglas firs, doughnuts, and log
ladies? Huh-uh: palm trees, herby potions, and vampires, oh yeah.
Even academics like me can get away with penning essays and presenting them at conferences, and in between the sandwiches and min-
eral water and panel discussions and comparing of CVs we all feel a
delicious glee: watching and analyzing this sexy show is legit, somehow. But none of us need fool ourselves: if we still have pulses, we
watch in part because the young nubile characters are so damn fine.

Hetero-confession time: I have a thing for Giles. He's urbane, handsome, brilliant, compassionate (yet capable of cold-blooded calcula-
tion when it's called for), and he sings like a dream. But I feel a need to
explore my love for one of the show's female characters who I find to
be a perfect foil to Buffy's California cheerleaderliness, Anya's sexpot-
alien-bombshell, Willow's bad-grrrl-geekitude, Drusilla's nasty little-
girl strangeness, or any of the assorted other femme fatales, nocturnal
emissaries, or lambs-for-the-slaughter who appear from time to time,

41

sometimes only for the duration of your average Clairol Herbal Essence commercial. One woman walks alone, in quiet strength, with languid gait, street-urchin eyes, shepherdess hair, New Romantic fashion sense, and a penchant for logic of the acid-flashback variety. Tara is to *Buffy* what brainy rebel Lindsay was to *Freaks and Geeks*, or raven-tressed Sam was to *Popular* (both those excellent shows were, sadly, cancelled prematurely), or Audrey Horne to the aforementioned *Twin Peaks*: undeniably sexy but set slightly apart from the cast's more glamorous females, too smart or political or strange, more "striking" than "beautiful." In the spirit of praising the offbeat and the undersung, I offer a paean to Tara Maclay and to Amber Benson's unforgettable portrayal.

Okay, she's blond; this differentiates her from the brunette goddesses just mentioned. And, truth be told, at first glance she's your classic corn-fed all-American bland, flaxen beauty. She has nice cheekbones. She's taller than average. There may be a Nordic origin to that peaches-and-cream coloring. But there is something about Amber Benson's beauty, her earthy authenticity, her solidity, that is refreshing and decidedly not in the typical angular Anglo-Saxon Hollywood mold. Mostly it's her body. This is not to suggest that Buffy's bevy of other babes— Miss Gellar, or Miss Hannigan, or Miss Caulfield, or indeed Miss Trachtenberg (I can call them all "Miss" without seeming condescending and arcane, 'cuz I'm a girl, okay?)—are in any way lacking in toothsomeness or serviceability. But, let's face it, they're twigs. Like most actresses in most TV shows, these young women, lovely though they are, probably do not weigh more than 105 pounds soaking wet (or clad in leather pants).

Amber has heft. Hips. Thighs. Breasts. A slightly rounded belly. In short, she looks a bit more like the rest of us. Goddess help us, she may even be a size 7.

And it is perhaps the ever-so-slight tendency toward the Rubenesque (this is not to imply she is overweight! Just that she is luscious! Like the actress in *Dark Angel* in the first season, or Christina Ricci a couple years ago, before they turned into twigs, too. Like Kate Winslet, the curvy English rose, long may she bloom) that suggests a painterly quality to Miss Benson's looks. Lovely she is, but she is not perfection (her eyes a bit too large, heavy-lidded and far apart, her lips overfull and perhaps not as precisely-shaped as one might like) but her idiosyncratic appeal is unforgettable, haunting, much like the models used again and again and obsessed over by artists like William Waterhouse (the mermaid is the flower-seller is the nymph who finds Orpheus's head), or Dante Gabriel-Rosetti (willowy redheads clutching, variously, pomegranates, lilies, or serpents), or Degas's shadowy dancers, or Renoir's ubiquitous gold-and-pink bather. In Andrew Wyeth's paintings of longtime model and sometime-lover Helga, we see a glimpse of Tara, too: the soft green tones in her skin and hair, the hint of a secret smile on that closed mouth, the nature-spirit trappings of tree-lined country roads, sere meadows, and frosted windows. Helga's loden-green coat becomes Tara's pale-brown suede jacket; one a forest, the other a fawn.

Color and texture touch our senses as surely as pheromones scream "sex" to the neocortex; and the show's costume design plays upon subtle character traits ranging from the culturally literate to the mythic. Willow's togs toggle between numerologically pertinent sports jerseys and gypsy thriftshop tops. Buffy slinks, capitulates, and kicks butt in badass leathers, near-nude colors, and soft ruffles. And Anya just plain owns it, baby, whether in tight denim or creamy bridal satin. But in Tara's clothes (and the sometimes-slouchy, always comfortable way she wears them) we are not swept into flights of fancy, but grounded; not aroused, but soothed. Watch those reruns for the greens and browns that dominate; earthy, yes, but also, according to the color theory of costume design, a sign of a character who is alien, other, or somehow separate from the crowd. Green and brown, the hues of the tree-hugging neopagan, the teenage witch who is too self-conscious to go garbed in goth black.

Not for Tara the nylon sweats and baggy sweatshirts emblazoned with Nike and Tommy Hilfiger insignia—nor the artificially-distressed dark blue dungarees, or the overalls, or the cargo pants and wispy tank tops of the Abercrombie & Fitch clones. We get a frequent suggestion of the pastoral, as channeled through her Southern California retro-hippie garb. Flowing skirts, clingy shirts, color palettes Derek Jarman might have approved of, hip pagan logos, ultra-feminine stylings often trimmed with beads, feathers, shells (more of the pagan, elemental connection) or other ornaments—often, as with the other cast members, her sartorial details are highly suggestive of the emotional tone of the moment, a wry comment upon a plot movement, or a connection to other characters. Remember the green shirt with the hemp leaf outlined in green rhinestones? Cleverly masked by a pendant crafted from a single peacock feather? What about the medieval corset get-up from the musical episode? That scene by the pond looked lifted straight from a Renaissance faire, complete with dancing wenches. There's a Celtic myth flavor to it, the spreading trees by the water; is this Avalon? Are these two beguiling priestesses of Arthurian times, Nimue and Morgan Le Fay; straight out of a pre-Raphaelite painting by Burne-Jones? Close your eyes and smell the orchard. Listen to the birds.

Ah, the musical episode. How can one fail to wax rhapsodic about Amber Benson's singing voice? A pure, shimmering soprano, but with a power and warmth behind it that belies Tara's tendency to stammer and pause before speaking softly. We saw her improvement with this, her growth in confidence as her relationship with Willow progressed and she felt loved and validated. The song "I'm Under Your Spell" celebrates this flowering forth of self (even as it is an ode to sex and a thinly veiled reference to the manipulative magic Willow has recently used on her), and what better way to do this than to allow Tara one of the episode's show-stopping numbers in a score of mostly fantastic songs? Of course it doesn't hurt that she shares a duet with the show's other finest singer, Giles and his smoky, tremulous folk-tenor. I had found myself anticipating this pairing even before I watched it happen . . . when I heard Tara's sweet siren sound I immediately wondered if she and Giles would sing together. And even though Buffy belted nicely and Anya's triple-threat moves and chops were staggeringly good (that retro-number with the Golden Era of Hollywood 1940s lounging robes was a stroke of genius), Tara would be equally comfortable with a pure acoustic folk-club sound, a neo-Celtic pop confection, or a legit Richard Rodgers ballad. She not only sings rings around everyone else in the cast, she can do it in multiple styles. And while she's not the hoofer Anya is, and not the catlike mover Buffy is (even without her stunt double), Tara's dancing in the musical numbers was just, well, so Tara. Quietly competent, not studied or athletic, a wobbly fawn among whippets. As she enchants with her Guinevere gown and silvery voice, we see a woman come into her power, emboldened by love and ecstasy and total acceptance. A shame it's a sham; but as that song climaxes (with Tara realizing Willow's betrayal, and Giles knowing he must leave Buffy), we also hear the passion that remains behind the anger and grief, the passion that will get them through the rough days ahead as Willow must battle her addiction alone and Tara must work her own solitary magics.

Tara's animal grace is also part and parcel of her witchiness. She and Willow merged so well magically because they complement each other: Willow is enamored of books and spells and power and rare magic items, but Tara is of a more earthy stamp: buying tea-lights at the drugstore and herbs from the farmer's market, perhaps, and sitting quietly beneath a full moon after soaking in a rosewater bath. A natural witch, she believed for years she had demon blood, lied to by her family who seemed, after all, to merely want to keep their women down. When the Scoobies stood up for her and refused to let Mr. Maclay take his daughter away, we know they also showed their approval of her relationship with Willow, and after a rough start (no one understood her jokes, for one), they accepted Tara into the Sunnydale family. It always seemed clear that it was Tara who made magic really blossom in Willow, that without a partner in love and witchcraft she would wallow further in greedy spell acquisition and geeky Internet research. In "Tabula Rasa," when the two forget but then remember each other, they have telling reactions while in The Magic Box. Everyone is wondering why they're in such a place and with these people. Looking at the occult detritus everywhere, Willow comments on all the "weird stuff" and implies it's unwholesome (though she lets out a small excited "Ooh!" when she notices a book called *Magic for Beginners*). But Tara's face is knowing when she proclaims "This is a magic shop," as if even total amnesia could not erase her intuitive grasp of her own talents, nature, and karmic destiny.

To paraphrase Bart Simpson (though he was quoting George Burns and speaking of show business), karma *is* a hideous bitch goddess. *Why?* we asked ourselves when the blood droplets flew and landed. Why her? "Your shirt" were her last words: an eerie reference to Willow's near-breakdown when trying to find something suitable to wear for Joyce's funeral, tossing aside her hated, childish togs like Daisy shuffling through Gatsby's shirts. And then, unfathomable, final, sad silence. The golden girl, the gentle woodland fawn, the earthy witch, gone from us. When it happened, I thought of Willow's earlier act of blood sacrifice: luring the hapless fawn so she could procure its blood for Buffy's resurrection rite. On some level that act (irresponsible and wrong-headed to the extreme, and yet also necessary, and unavoidable) set things in motion that culminated in the murder, violence, mayhem and brutality of the rest of the season's narrative arc. One fawn slaughtered, another offered up, the Slayer brought back, the universe in balance again, blessed be.

I know it's fashionable just now to be annoyed at Joss Whedon for killing her off. The level of hurt and indignation among fans has been nothing short of staggering. Of course, much of this rage (often inarticulate in its unfocused emotion) is aimed at Whedon's unthinkable act of betrayal to those viewers who saw Willow and Tara as lesbian role models. I'm one of those lily-livered romantics for whom politics goes right out the window as soon as my heart is ignited. That we were privy to the sweet musings, hot sex, heart-stopping epiphanies and tissue-shredding rifts of these lovers, to me, meant never considering the sociological implications of this couple's representation as the only loving lesbian relationship on serialized television. These two simply *were*, from moment one in "Hush" (4-10) by the soda machine. No sooner met but they looked, no sooner looked but they loved, as tall, trousered Rosalind/Ganymede would say. Their own paths of self-actualization converged like overflowing tinderboxes suddenly upended and neatly arranged into cordwood. Willow's need for approval and Tara's need for unconditional love allowed their supernova trajectory its singular, incendiary thrust toward its triumphant but tragic end; like all witches who burn, martyred by flames, they move on to a place where their gods are the right ones.

Of course, this is not over. I don't necessarily mean Whedon will decide to reunite them, or resurrect Tara or have her serve as some sort of shamanic, psychopompic, or otherworldly mentor, or have Willow find some magical means of contacting her or entering the realm of the dead (although none of these narrative trails would be unreasonable or untenable).

In season seven, the closest thing we have to a reappearance of Tara occurs when Willow becomes romantically involved with one of the new "slayers-in-training" named Kennedy. (For the record, I find Kennedy to be bossy, bitchy, and nowhere near as beautiful and dreamily sublime as Tara. It's like comparing apples and ugli fruit.) When Willow feels her attraction to Kennedy growing, she experiences an unusual transformation; she becomes, to all outward appearances, Warren. In other words, she takes on the mantle of Tara's killer, because her unexpressed rage, guilt, and most of all, her sense of betrayal, take over her Willow persona. Other characters, in discussing the source of the "big bad" that is destroying Sunnydale and, by implication, the world, agree that it was Buffy's coming back from the dead "not right" that engendered this new evil. Anya matter-of-factly states it was Willow's insistence on resurrecting Buffy that has brought them all to where they are now; and this, to Willow, means a burden of unbearable guilt. Heavy stuff for a witch who nearly destroyed the world and everyone in it; far more terrifying for her is the prospect that she was even indirectly responsible for Tara's murder.

In "Conversations with Dead People" (7-7), Willow is contacted by Tara through Cassie, a dead girl who claims to know Tara, who says Willow is not allowed to speak to her because of what she did. But there is deception and cruel manipulation here, as several characters are made to confront their worst insecurities and fears: From Beneath You, It Devours. This suggests karmic turmoil to the extreme, and the California Crew of Light is adept at nothing if they aren't good at speeding up their own karma. But for two lovers to have had the recognition these two did at the beginning, such instantaneous comfort and tension and heat, bespeaks a timeless and enduring connection, a love that spans ages and incarnations, steeped in karmic debt, a ritual bound to circle round and repeat itself until they get it right.

And so we wait for the fawn to be reborn in spring, dappled in green light beneath the weeping willow. Then winter comes and the scattered does provide cover for the king stag. Starvation threatens and acorns vanish. The riverbed creaks and melts. The elf queen metes out death and punishment and is lonely. The forest floor is fragrant and damp with decay. The bluebells push through again. It always happens, it will never not happen.

Peg Aloi teaches creative writing and film studies, and writes film criticism for The Boston Phoenix, *as well as a regular media column for* witchvox.com. *Her poetry has been published in* Obsidian *magazine and on* gothic.net, *and her first published short story somehow became a chapter in some stranger's doctoral dissertation somewhere in New Jersey. Last summer she won the Gorseth Kernow's Morris Cup for a poem about an ancient Cornish landmark she's never actually visited. In October 2002 she attended the first-ever academic conference devoted to* Buffy the Vampire Slayer *in Norwich, England.*

Chelsea Quinn Yarbro

LIONS, GAZELLES, AND BUFFY

Chelsea Quinn Yarbro, who knows as much about vampires as anybody, has come up with a surprising and remarkable theory about the ecology of vampires in the Buffyverse. I resisted Quinn's theory at first, but the more I thought about it, the more I realized that, as Oz would say, "actually it explains a lot!"

N O MATTER WHAT THE GAZELLES may think, lions are good for gazelles, as naturalists have long observed: lions cull the herd by eliminating the weak, the slow, the stupid. Without lions, the genetic quality of gazelles would diminish and the increasing numbers would over-graze the veldt; resulting in starvation and a far more radical culling of the herd than lions achieve. Of course, the lions have a big advantage: gazelles aren't carnivorous. If they were, their battles would be a lot more hazardous for the lions. In other words, the lions would be in the same situation Buffy is, a predator after a prey that can fight back on more than equal terms. Nevertheless, Buffy is good for vampires for precisely the same reason that lions are good for gazelles. The stupid, the crazy, the ravenous all fall to her stakes, and their numbers are kept in check, preserving the intelligent, the capable, the formidable. Just as among lions the lioness is the principal hunter, the female human is the most effective vampire slayer.

And just as the relationship of predator and prey is a very close one, so is Buffy's with those vampires who are clever enough, sensitive

48

enough, *human* enough to know that she is an opponent worthy of their steel, and appreciate her as such, because of their esoteric ecological ties. She also knows that they are opponents worthy of her steel, and that, like it or not, they are deeply dependent on one another. The few who comprehend her necessary role in vampire existence fall under her spell, and only they have the capacity to command her attention and respect. Whether it is the Byronic Angel, the sardonic Spike, or the arrogant Dracula, those vampires who manage, through understanding and skill, to avoid her attack end up in a complex relationship with her, a recognition of the bond they share, and which both vampires and Slayers accept, sometimes with relief, sometimes with attraction, sometimes with repugnance, but always with mesmeric intensity. Theirs is a mutual understanding that goes to the heart of Slayer and vampire alike. It is more than sexual attraction— although that always plays a part in vampiric folklore—that binds them together, it is their shared role in the metaphysical ecosystem of Joss Whedon's *Buffy* universe.

From the beginning, Whedon has maintained the premise that the Slayer's role is to keep vampires in check, and it is stated directly in the voice-over of the opening credits of the first season: *She alone will stand against the vampires.* Simple math shows that she would be unable to rid the world of vampires, but, if she keeps on the job of necessary destruction, the vampires will not overwhelm humanity, and the worst of the vampires will be stopped before they can do anything too damaging to Sunnydale—and, by extension, the world. This view has remained consistent from the start and continues to shape the direction of the series, twisting and turning around this central point. Through that consistency of vision Whedon keeps the escalating highjinx from flying off into incoherence, which has happened to many other series with a paranormal element in its structure. When Whedon wants to show the delicacy of this metaphysical ecological balance, he steps outside his vision via an alternate universe, such as the universe where Willow is a black-corseted vampire with an inclination to boredom. In the Buffy-less Sunnydale, the vampires have run amok, and they are using up humans at such a profligate rate that starvation will be upon vampires in less than a generation, for their human nourishment will be exhausted. By the same token, in a vampire-less universe, Buffy would be a young woman facing those problems that confront almost all young women, a capable person with a lot of determination, but not unique as she is as the Slayer. Or perhaps she would be in a mental hospital, as Whedon has posited. For Buffy to be Buffy, she needs vampires. For vampires as a species to survive, they need Buffy.

Buffy lives at the Hellmouth for just the same reason as lions wait at the waterhole—that's where the prey is. If vampires are going to congregate anywhere, it will be at the Hellmouth, and she'll be there to waylay them. She must be close to the trouble in order to keep the situation in hand. By the same token, vampires—and all other manner of unpleasant supernatural creatures—are drawn to the Hellmouth because it seems to nourish them and give them increased energy. The nightly patrol that Buffy undertakes is like a lion on the prowl, and is done in the preferred leonine-predator way—one or two deputies to drive the prey to the Slayer. The Scoobies are essential to the predator routine that Buffy has developed to deal with her slayage, and their presence reinforces her hunting and the obligations of predation.

Which is why Riley could never sustain a relationship with Buffy—he was one of a band of competitive predators, working on her territory and after the same prey. Unlike Buffy, he was part of a pack-like, secret, large group of young males trying to horn in on Buffy's job, and turning themselves into targets in the process. To make matters worse, the commander of the all-male group was Professor Maggie Walsh, who was on a campaign to eliminate all Buffy's myriad prey, which would disrupt the universal balance of Slayer and vampire. For Buffy to join the Walsh Crusade, she would have had to accept Walsh's authority and agenda, which she could not do, for it would upset the balance of prey and predator. She made her own perverse superman in the hope of perfecting the non- or hyper- human—Adam, her manufactured son and murderer. All this reflected Maggie Walsh's hubris and her zeal, by which she was able to excuse all her excesses and justify the enormity of what she had undertaken. The result was Walsh's attempt on Buffy's life; she could not continue her extermination project without upsetting the balance of the Buffy universe.

That intrinsic conflict was the underlying reason Riley felt that Buffy didn't love him—he didn't have the intense bond that Buffy had with her prey, and in time came to resent the lack of it, to be jealous of the profoundly intimate predator/prey relationship he would never be able to share. Even though he rejected his primary pack, he could not break away from such institutions entirely, and when his loyalty was put to the test, he remained with his pack rather than with Buffy, to help her on her hunt. Strong as his devotion was, he could not cope with the equivocality of the Buffy/vampire nexus. His own experimentation with vampires revealed his desire to know that predator/prey bond, although he couldn't sustain the relationship in the manner that Buffy and vampires enjoy. Making himself a victim could not come close to Buffy's reciprocity with vampires, no matter how many demons, vampires, and other supernatural critters he and his fellow "soldiers" have neutralized. That Riley chose to remain with his own pack isn't surprising, given his own predatory inclination coupled with his absolutist philosophy, though it was a great disappointment to Buffy.

In most folklore throughout the world, vampires are few in number, hunting sometimes in small clans, but more usually alone or in pairs. Folklorically, the most packlike creatures are the werecreatures, which are often said to pursue isolated humans or communities in formidable groups, while vampires tend to cut out one or two humans from the community, wooing them rather than terrorizing them in order to establish a mutual dependence, hence the heavy erotic punch that vampire myths tend to possess, helping to create the fascination with which the vampire is imbued. And the vampire hunters in folklore often have some tie to the vampire, such as blood relation, abandoned lover, or penitent and/or confessor. Buffy may not have blood relationship to her vampire prey, but she is born to this task, assigned by fate to preserve humanity from vampires—she is destined to spend her life in pursuit of her prey in the best predator tradition. It is appropriate that her recognition of the First Slayer validated the predator image—that Neolithic hunter with the spears and shamanistic body-painting—and the task of devoting her life to this calling. From the inception of Slayerdom, the Slayer has been a hunter: in other words, a predator. Buffy may be uncomfortable with the primitive First Slayer, but she is aware that they are linked in purpose, and that predation is crucial to the mission.

Giles's neutrality as Watcher makes it clear that he is not a competing predator—he is there to provide instruction and support, to train and assist the Slayer in her fated work—in other words, he was cast in the role of a metaphysical scout, providing the information Buffy needs to do her work, but unwilling/unable to participate in the actual slaying. As Giles became increasingly active in Buffy's work over the seasons, he became less and less a Watcher, his neutrality diminishing steadily, until he was effectively excommunicated for his participation in Buffy's activities. The more Giles was moved to engage in active evil-hunting, the farther he got from Watching. It also provided the opportunity for him to leave Sunnydale and all that it contained, since he had never aspired to being a predator himself yet he had reached the point of having to become one in spite of himself. It also allowed him to return to save the day with his knowledge, making it possible for Buffy to fulfill her work as Slayer while restoring Giles's task of information provider.

Multiple predators is a tricky proposition in this universe, and Joss Whedon has been at pains to show that secondary Slayers are intrinsically flawed. Kendra was overly rigid in her predation, and her failure to adapt was her undoing. But the more perplexing case of flawed Slayer was the vampire-like Faith. It is necessary for any reputable predator to respect its prey, to understand the importance of their relationship and to honor it. Faith was not a successful predator in any sense of the word, for she lacked respect for her prey, and indeed, for humanity as well; she didn't acknowledge the irrevocable tie between predator and prey, nor did she comprehend her role as protector. Faith was an exploiter of both people—particularly Buffy, who put the pressure of conscience on Faith and provided a living counterpoint to Faith's fecklessness—and vampires, using her slaying as an expression of pride. Unable to function as a predator, Faith could only strive to disrupt Buffy's well-balanced predation. She condemned Buffy for her concerns and her integrity, while seeking to use Buffy as a foil to enhance her own circumstances. From her seduction of Xander to her alliance with the mayor, her ambitions over-rode all other considerations; ultimately she suffered for it, which, in terms of folklore, was necessary because of her betrayal of Slayer ethics as well as her contempt for her predestined work.

Crucial to the acceptance of the tradition of predation is the constant contrast of the mordant wit that makes it possible for *Buffy* to discuss matters that would be either too grim or too far-fetched to hold the continuing attention of the audience. Much like the Mulder period of *The X-Files*, *Buffy* uses ironic humor to underscore the ongoing themes of the series without having to lecture or preach on the subjects. The wry humor takes the sting out of the predation, and also gives the series its deft touch; without the humor, the series would be heavy-handed and ponderous. Predation can be a gritty subject, unsympathetic to most audiences, and conceiving the predator as the good guy is a dramatically chancy device. The Slayer's being a young, attractive, petite woman makes for an opportunity to create a heroine who is allowed a degree of ruthlessness that would be much less acceptable in a large, muscular young man. Being female, Buffy has a fine chance for making pointed observations about her circumstances that in a male performing the same function might seem a sign of weakness, or at least a lack of heroism, or an inadequate comprehension of the scope of the task being undertaken.

As the series has evolved, the skills of the Scoobies have continued to adapt to the new circumstances that continue to crop up in Sunnydale. Willow's pursuit of witchcraft was a natural extension of her general intellectual curiosity, and made it possible for her to continue to contribute to the ongoing predation. The newly-human Anya, with her charming mix of venality and naiveté, brings an insight that simplifies some of the more exotic predations the Scoobies have undertaken. Dawn's elaborate transmogrification to human form removes her from simple kid-sister duties, and retains a very particular potential for handling the more apocalyptic prey. Xander provides the human anchor for all these outré conflicts; it is entirely appropriate that Xander stopped the cataclysmically inclined Willow from ending the world as an expression of grief—only he is sufficiently committed to the here-and-now to interrupt the most dreadful manifestation of predation. Remarkably, Spike, the most ambiguous of Buffy's supporters, has changed the most dramatically as his bond with Buffy evolves in his continuing attempt to participate as fully as possible in this essential relationship; hence, he achieves more than redemption in the end through his altruistic apotheosis, going out in a literal blaze of glory.

With the creation of a cadre of slayers, and therefore enlarging the nature of slayer predation, the Buffy cosmology has shifted its emphasis but not its nature. The complex dance of non-carnivorous predator and carnivorous prey continued to the very end of Joss Whedon's compelling vision.

A professional writer for more than thirty years, Yarbro has sold over seventy books and more than sixty works of short fiction. She lives in her hometown—Berkeley, California—with two autocratic cats. When not busy writing, she rides her Norwegian Fjord horse Pikku or attends the symphony or opera.

Laura Resnick

THE GOOD,
THE BAD, AND
THE AMBIVALENT

When I first began planning this anthology, I received an e-mail from Laura Resnick, which said, "If you don't let me play, I will be forced to kill you . . . I hope you'll be interested in asking me to participate. For the sake of your life." After careful but prudently brief consideration, I invited Laura to contribute. I think you'll be glad I did . . .

I WANTED TO KILL YOU TONIGHT," Angel says to Buffy in "Angel" (1-7), as he's explaining not only his life story to her, but also the truth about his nature.

As Angel's dialogue indicates in that same scene, the *Buffy* ethos equates a soul with humanity, with a conscience, with the ability to experience remorse and guilt. Prior to regaining his soul via the infamous gypsy curse, Angel was (as Giles describes him when first researching Angel's past) "a vicious, violent killer." Two seasons later, when Angel tries to twelve-step the rogue Slayer Faith while she's chained to his wall in "Enemies" (3-17), he recalls the pre-soul clarity and exhilaration of killing without remorse, which he remembers as an addictive pleasure. And when Angel loses his soul in season two's "Innocence" (2-14) and spends the rest of the year tormenting Buffy, killing innocent people, and wreaking havoc in Sunnydale, we see for ourselves just how *evil* Angel is without a soul.

But what's interesting about Angel is not how evil he is when he's bad . . . but rather, how evil he is when he's "good."

"I wanted to kill you tonight," says the *good* version of Angel in that season-one episode, the version of Angel whom Buffy invites into her home, trusts with her life, and grows to love. This is the kind of stark, unmitigated impulse that can (and often does) seize Angel. Many desires and instincts just like this one live inside his skin, and he struggles nightly with them.

When "good" Angel stops his sire, Darla, from killing Buffy's mother in "Angel," his heroic gesture starts crumbling under the onslaught of his blood hunger when Darla shoves Joyce's warm, wounded body into his arms and urges him to drink; his face transforms into the familiar monster-mask of *Buffy* vampires, he licks his lips, and his body is as taut as that of a long-denied lover on the verge of consummation. In season three's "Amends" (3-10), when a tormented, hallucinating Angel comes to Buffy's bedroom to warn her that he has become a danger to her, he stalks her as they talk, his gaze fixed hungrily on her jugular vein. Angel may have stopped feeding on humans years ago, but it's not as if he doesn't still *want* to; and it's not as if we can ever be sure he'll never do it again.

Nor is Angel's struggle with his vampire nature purely gustatory. In numerous instances, Angel's inner demon gains ascendancy in moments of high emotion. When his first-ever embrace with Buffy gets passionate in "Angel," his self-control slips—immediately revealing his demon face. When Angel is near death and refusing Buffy's self-sacrificing cure for him in season three's "Graduation Day" (3-21, 3-22), Buffy deliberately provokes him with physical violence, intentionally inciting visceral anger so that Angel's vampire nature will take control and override his human judgment. When Angel revisits Sunnydale in "The Yoko Factor" (4-20), Riley Finn finds his manner so dark, menacing, and "king of pain" that he mistakenly assumes Angel has gone evil again, and he's stunned when Buffy explains that no, this is how Angel behaves *with* a soul.

Whatever sexual, moral, or spiritual metaphors may be inferred from Angel's storyline in *Buffy*, the key point here is that his characterization is built on the inherent struggle between his evil demon nature and the soul which gives him a "good" human nature; and this perpetual internal conflict is precisely what makes him such a compelling character.

Angel's inner darkness may be supernatural and demonic, but it's a rare person—and therefore a rare *Buffy* fan—who has never once wanted to seize something he has no right to take; never once wanted to give free rein to instinct and desire with no thought for social mores; never once wanted to act out of anger without consideration for the consequences; and never once wanted to break a strict and unsatisfying diet (even in context, cold pig's blood sounds pretty unappetizing). When someone really pisses me off, I don't break out in a monster face and roar like the MGM lion; but sometimes, I'd really like to. In fact, some surveys suggest that more than half of all people in our culture have occasionally fantasized about killing someone. Though we may feel repelled by or wary of the demonic urges living so close to his surface, Angel's struggles are nonetheless *our* struggles—taken to dramatically heightened extremes by the supernatural qualities of the *Buffy*verse.

Of course, this moral ambivalence, this duality of nature, is not unique to Angel; in one way or another, it's at the heart of all of *Buffy*'s most compelling characterizations.

It's a well-known craft premise among writers (and probably a well-recognized one among readers and viewers) that a flawed character is usually more interesting than a perfect one. Stories in the fantasy and horror genres are usually about the struggle between good and evil, in one form or another; and in *Buffy*, good and evil are personalized. Not just in the sense that Buffy regularly comes face to face with evil, learns its name, and then gets to beat it up and kill it; but also in the sense that most major *Buffy* characters manifest both qualities—good and evil, bright and dark, cruelty and compassion. In doing so, they continue to surprise us, as real people do throughout our lives; and they thereby accurately reflect the confusing ambiguity of life in our own world, thus making the supernatural *Buffy*verse compelling and seemingly real because of its visceral truths.

Surely no one, during season one of the show, could look at the shy, obsequious, sweet-natured Willow and predict that she'd one day, due to her own character flaws (as opposed to demonic possession, for example), try to destroy the world. Now, frankly, the season-six twist of Willow becoming "addicted" to magic was just weak writing. Prior to the sudden appearance of this premise in "Smashed" (6-9) and "Wrecked" (6-10), there was no precedent for it in her characterization or in the portrayal of magic, and it was a theme pursued at the expense of the meaningful conflict which had already been well established for Willow—which was the abuse of power: Willow habitually and willfully misused magic for her personal convenience the way some people in our reality misuse wealth or political power, for example.

Starting with season three's "Lover's Walk" (3-8), we see a tendency in Willow to use magic as a shortcut for the ordinary troubles of life; in this particular episode, she tries to cast a spell which will eliminate her mutual attraction with Xander and thereby solve this volatile personal problem. While the incident is fairly minor, it's Willow's first misstep on a long, slippery slope over the next few seasons. She again tries to use magic to solve the emotional problems of her personal life in "Something Blue" (4-9). Although that incident nearly gets her friends killed and wins her accolades from the *capo* of the vengeance demons, Willow nonetheless reverts to such behavior again. In "Tabula Rasa" (6-8), she once again nearly gets all her friends killed by abusing her magical powers in an attempt to make her own emotional life easier (this time with an intrusive spell intended to affect those closest to her). So down that slippery slope this character goes, until this kind of misuse of her power eventually combines with a moment of such terrible emotional rage, upon Tara's death, that Willow becomes the big bad villain whom the Slayer must confront and defeat in the season-six finale.

Sitting through season one, we might have guessed that, say, Cordelia could potentially become a murderous world-destroying bitch wielding enormous power to the detriment of mankind. But who knew that such potential for evil even existed inside of the soft-natured Willow?

It is through this slowly developing good-and-evil struggle within herself that Willow eventually becomes a fascinating character in her own right. Surely Willow's most interesting year is season seven, as she struggles with the evil she has encountered within herself and which, like Angel, she must now learn to understand, incorporate, and utilize with good judgment. Now Willow's magic turns inadvertently against herself, revealing her insecurities as she becomes "invisible" to her loved ones in "Same Time, Same Place" (7-3). Her power also exposes her remorse in "The Killer In Me" (7-13), when she takes on the appearance of the man she murdered, an event which also forces her to recognize how guilty she feels about starting a new relationship while her lover, Tara, lies dead.

All power comes hand in hand with danger as well as with temptations to misuse it, and Willow's struggle with this is real to us, even if her immense magical power is clearly fictional.

Meanwhile, whereas one might have originally assumed *Buffy*'s Cordelia might turn into a major villainess in Sunnydale, she instead becomes, like Xander, a person whom we often don't know whether to love or hate. Cordelia's and Xander's "evil" in *Buffy* is ordinary, familiar, and all too human.

Cordelia is self-centered, snide, arrogant, and malicious. We'd love to hate her; but we can't, because Cordelia mixes too much good with her daily dose of mundane evil. She's brave; she often joins the Scooby gang in battling monsters, and she conquers vampires with mere words in "Homecoming" (3-5). She's honest; note how Cordelia says everything she thinks and never thinks anything she doesn't say in "Earshot" (3-18). She's sincere and capable of love, as we see in her volatile relationship with Xander; and we realize in "Lover's Walk" (3-8) and "The Wish" (3-9), when Xander breaks her heart, that she's as vulnerable as we are. Moreover, rather than whining and feeling sorry for herself thereafter, she relieves her pain by inflicting any number of clever, sharp-edged verbal assaults on Xander in subsequent episodes. Sure, she's a bitch; but who among us doesn't envy how bold and articulate she is when confronting someone who has hurt her?

If Cordelia is the evil bitch whom we can't help liking, then Xander is the good guy whom we can't help despising. Xander is a catalogue of petty weaknesses and minor evils; his characterization is practically a template for a venial sinner. During the gang's high-school years, Xander often speaks and acts out of spite when it comes to Angel. Whether it's something as minor as his many snide little comments or something as major as his urging Faith to kill Angel in "Revelations" (3-7), his jealousy over Buffy's feelings for Angel is always among his motives. Nor is he a guy you'd want your sister to date. Even prior to his nuzzling with Willow behind his girlfriend's back in season three, he demonstrates a roving eye with his obvious sexual interest in Faith ("Faith, Hope, and Trick," 3-3) and his ongoing crush on Buffy while dating Cordelia. He takes Willow for granted, sometimes to a truly insensitive and unconscionable extent . . . right up until she has a boyfriend. It's only when another guy loves her that Willow finally becomes sexually interesting to Xander. In subsequent years, he proposes to Anya, abandons her at the altar, and then attacks her with verbal viciousness when she later sleeps with someone else for solace. And he is harshly judgmental when he learns that Buffy has slept with Spike.

Yet, despite all this, Xander inevitably comes through in the end as a decent, loving, and loyal friend. Moreover, though it's not his "destiny" and he has no supernatural defenses, he nonetheless regularly chooses to be on the frontlines of the battle against dark forces on the Hellmouth. No matter how often we despise Xander for his petty evils, we also always respect him for his virtues.

The seemingly straight-arrow Giles was a rock 'n' rolling rebel who resented and resisted his assigned duty to become a Watcher, and who even dabbled in demonology as a young man. Usually the figure of wise restraint and fatherly wisdom, he betrays Buffy in "Lies My Parents Told Me" (7-17) by colluding in the attempted murder of Spike. The laid-back Oz gets bitten by a werewolf in season two and eventually learns, as did Angel, that there's no ignoring a monster inhabiting your body. By season four, in "Wild at Heart" (4-6), Oz realizes that he can't progress as a person until he learns how to incorporate the wolf.

Faith is a colorful character when first introduced to us, but she becomes far more compelling when she tumbles across the unseen line into the dark side of her nature and then joins Buffy's enemies. Faith's longing to belong is most moving after she's ensured that she can never belong again. Her desire to be a true Slayer only becomes truly apparent in season four, after she has betrayed and abandoned all that being a Slayer means. Prior to her downfall, Faith disregarded the moral principles of Slaying and enjoyed the violence and power. Only much later, as she struggles alone in a mentally unstable state during "This Year's Girl" (4-15) and "Who Are You" (4-16), does Faith start grappling with what it means to be a Slayer, to protect the innocent, to commit murder, and (in the related *Angel* episodes) to atone for evil. Only after her own "demon" has dominated her life can Faith's soul find a place to make its stand, ultimately enabling her to return in season seven as the edgy, wisecracking, self-aware ex-con who's ready to die to save the world. And it is the journey to these extremes which makes Faith so memorable.

Faith's story, of course, is entwined with the schemes of that great *Buffy* villain, Mayor Wilkins. Is there any fan who didn't love finding such immense evil in the form of the squeakily clean-cut, self-righteous, platitude-spouting authority figure whom we have all known at some point in our lives? Yet, as delightful as he initially was, the Mayor continued growing and surprising us until, no matter how evil he was, it was impossible to see him *only* as a villain.

Eschewing the indiscriminately libidinous stereotype of so many boring villains, the Mayor kindly but firmly rejects Faith's sexual overtures when they become allies in season three. Not only does he deliberately choose the role of protective, supportive father figure with her, he also grows to love her in a selfless parental way. He talks with her about her problems, tries to build her self-confidence, and worries about her happiness. His genuine love for Faith is the weakness that Buffy exploits to defeat him in "Graduation Day" (3-21, 3-22). In "This Year's Girl" (4-15) we learn that even as the Mayor was preparing for his Ascension, he made plans to protect Faith from beyond death in case his own schemes turned to ashes (as they did).

Apart from Buffy's mother, the Mayor is the only person candid and clear-sighted enough to confront Angel about the huge sacrifices that his relationship with Buffy will force on her. The Mayor's condemnatory comments about this in season three's "Choices" (3-19), are so articulate and convincing that we realize, as does Angel, that he's right. Though he is Buffy's mortal enemy, the Mayor sees her dilemma with compassionate understanding. Mayor Wilkins is so vivid a character because of the ambivalent responses he continually creates in us with his contradictory nature.

However, probably no *Buffy* character's ambivalence has ever fascinated us as much as that of Spike. His characterization as an exceptional and unpredictable individual began with his very first appearance, in "School Hard" (2-15): A particularly dangerous vampire who has killed two Slayers in his time, he stalks Buffy, despises Angel, kills Sunnydale citizens, and even murders the Anointed One (or, as Spike calls him, the "annoying" one); and yet this epitome of ruthless, bloodthirsty, wisecracking villainy loves Drusilla with a tender and selfless devotion that, frankly, not many human lovers can equal. He humors her strange moods, apologizes sincerely whenever he hurts her feelings, looks after her with the patience of a good nurse, and gives her unconditional, monogamous, and enduring devotion. He goes to great lengths to cure Drusilla's physical weakness. Later, he's emotionally devastated by her abandonment.

Nor is Spike just a devoted (or besotted) lover. Like the Mayor, he's shrewd enough to understand the emotional lives of his enemies. As Buffy notes in "Lover's Walk" (3-8), she can fool her friends about her feelings for Angel, but she can't fool Spike. Though Spike usually uses his understanding of human emotion to torment his victims and inflict pain on his enemies, he can nonetheless demonstrate an unexpected sensitivity. In season four's "Something Blue" (4-9), he snaps at Giles and Buffy for failing to recognize the depth of Willow's emotional pain over losing Oz. In "Fool for Love" (5-7), Spike credibly asserts that he understands Slayers even better than they understand themselves.

After the Initiative has planted the lifestyle-altering chip in Spike's head in season four, Spike's new habits gradually bring him into more frequent and intimate contact with the Scooby gang; and it's ultimately only a matter of time before Spike's empathy and insight combine with his penchant for grand passions and lead to the most interesting development in his story: He falls in love with the Slayer.

Spike's extremes thereafter make him the most challenging characterization *Buffy* has ever explored. His sincere, tormented confession of love is heart-rending in "Crush" (5-14); yet he chains Buffy up in his crypt to make this declaration to her *and* threatens to let Drusilla kill her if she won't admit to having feelings for him! In "Intervention" (5-18), Spike's antics with the Buffybot are wonderfully comedic, but it's nonetheless incredibly creepy that he's had a robotic sex slave made in Buffy's image; yet just as we're thinking that a smart Slayer would definitely stake him for this . . . Spike endures torture at Glory's hands rather than reveal to her that Dawn is the Key she wants, because he'd rather die than let Buffy endure the pain of losing her sister. In equal measures, Spike regularly repels us and wins our admiration.

Eventually, Spike and Buffy enter into a secretive sexual relationship so volatile and unstable that it's frequently unclear to both of them whether he's currently her lover or her *ex*-lover.

So, who is Spike? Is he really the stalker outside Buffy's bedroom windows, the obsessed creep who steals pieces of her clothing to sniff in his crypt? The demon who chains her up and threatens to kill her if she won't say she has feelings for him? Or is he really the strong knight who serves Buffy selflessly in "The Gift" (5-22), faithfully guards her sister in "Bargaining" (6-1), and is Buffy's patient confidante in "Life Serial" (6-5)?

The beauty of Spike's characterization is that he's really *all* of these. He repels us and wins our admiration in equal measure precisely because he *is* equally repellent and admirable. He is both villain and hero; both demon and knight. Any attempt to define him as primarily one thing or the other is bound to fail, because he refuses to remain consistent with either definition. He regularly goes to *both* extremes, and that is precisely why he is such a riveting character.

Spike tells Buffy numerous times that loving her has changed him. Yet in "Smashed" (6-9), when Spike mistakenly thinks his chip has stopped working, the first thing he does is stalk, attack, and try to kill an innocent woman.

Spike has spent more than a century killing hundreds—perhaps thousands—of people, and, prior to having a soul in season seven, he never expresses or demonstrates even a wisp of remorse for any of those murders. As Buffy argues in "Crush" (5-14), the chip in his head isn't moral change, it just makes him like a serial killer in prison. According to the established natural laws of the *Buffy*verse, no matter how exceptional Spike is, no matter how much he loves Buffy, and no matter how much he wants to be worthy of her love, he can never become a compassionate, morally developed, trustworthy being, because he lacks the one absolutely essential ingredient for such a transformation: a soul.

Yet, despite this void, Spike demonstrates over and over that he is capable of love, loyalty, adaptation, even of kindness. Whether because of these qualities, or because of his charm, or simply because he wants it so badly, we *want* to believe he is capable of the changes he keeps trying to claim. And yet, without a soul, he clearly has no moral compass. In "Smashed" (6-9), he tries to kill an innocent woman; in "As You Were" (6-15), he's involved in a scheme to sell deadly demon eggs; in "Dead Things" (6-13), he can't understand Buffy's moral dilemma over having killed an innocent bystander.

However, Spike does have a moral code, and he states it plainly to Buffy: "I don't hurt *you*."

And this is why Spike finally reaches a moral crisis in "Seeing Red" (6-19) after he tries to rape Buffy. Acting upon life without a soul, Spike is ultimately capable of horrifying even himself. At this nadir of his existence, even *he* becomes repelled by his own extremes in one direction.

Being Spike, of course, he then goes to another unforeseen extreme in the opposite direction: He risks his life in pursuit of regaining his human soul, hoping it will make him worthy of Buffy. And, Spike being Spike, his demon nature and his human nature are so incompatibly extreme that trying to incorporate them into one persona makes him mentally unstable at first—and therefore vulnerable to The First in season seven.

Despite the soul, there's enough demon in Spike that The First easily manipulates him into killing many victims; and, in the perpetual paradox which is Spike, despite the demon inside him, he begs Buffy to kill him in "Never Leave Me" (7-9) so that he can't cause any more suffering. In "Lies My Parents Told Me" (7-17), he refuses to feel any remorse for killing Principal Wood's mother, who was a Slayer, because killing each other is what vampires and Slayers do; but he spares Wood's life, despite his anger over Wood's ambush, because he understands—even empathizes with—what his slaughter of the mother meant to the son. So the acquisition of a soul only serves to strengthen the persistent contradictions of this fascinating character.

Finally, the central figure of *Buffy*, the Slayer herself, may not be the show's most ambivalent character, but she, too, endures the same kind of internal struggle. The Slayer has, after all, been in love with not one but *two* vampires. Moreover, she took one of them as a lover even when he didn't have a soul. And we suspect that Faith is not wrong when she suggests in "Consequences" (3-15) that Buffy was attracted to Angel "even when he went psycho," i.e., lost his soul and was evil for half a season. When Spike tells Riley Finn that Buffy likes some monster in her man, he's right; the power of Buffy's feelings for Riley never equals her love for Angel or her obsession with Spike.

It's no coincidence that possibly the most honest conversation of Buffy's adult life occurs with a vampire when she confesses her emotional secrets to one, in season seven's wonderfully twisted "Conversations with Dead People" (7-7). As we see here, there are some things about Buffy that the evil undead are more capable of understanding than her closest human friends are. Indeed, this is precisely Spike's emphatic assertion on numerous occasions, even before they start sleeping together. It's a theme that he explores thoroughly in "Fool For Love" (5-7), and Buffy's riveted attention as he talks in that episode about her inescapable flirtation with death is clear evidence, despite her angry rejection, that he's found a path to the darkest part of her heart. And Buffy exercises these dark impulses in that same scene by intentionally humiliating Spike as punishment for having exposed her this way.

Of course, Spike isn't the first character to probe Buffy's dark side. In "Bad Girls" (3-14), Faith makes a giddy effort to convince Buffy that the Slayer's rightful motto should be "Want, take, have." Under Faith's influence, Buffy clearly starts finding visceral pleasure in the kill, and she winds up gleefully participating in an episode of wanton vandalism and burglary, though she does not follow Faith across the thick dark line into murder and betrayal.

Throughout Buffy's tenure as the Slayer, there is a ruthless, ambivalent side of her character which is, in fact, crucial to her survival. In "Becoming" (3-21, 3-22), as Buffy approaches her showdown with

Angelus, she coldly warns Xander that he'll be solely responsible for saving Giles because "I'll be too busy killing." In "The Wish" (3-9), we see a chilling, dispassionate Buffy, the persona which *our* Buffy would have developed under different circumstances. Much of Buffy's growth as a Slayer has involved her learning to understand, accept, and utilize this dark side, rather than continue denying it. In "Restless" (4-22) and "Intervention" (5-18), the First Slayer makes it clear that a seamless incorporation of dark strength is necessary to a Slayer's success. And by season seven's "Selfless" (7-5), Buffy explains to Xander that an essential part of being the Slayer is being able to do what others find unthinkable—such as killing a friend or loved one.

In her struggle to incorporate character traits that conventional morality tells us we're not supposed to have, let alone accept—and which, nonetheless, many of us either have or fear finding within ourselves—Buffy the Vampire Slayer is not only the bright-and-dark heroine of her own world; she is also *us*. It is precisely because her painful internal ambivalence is all too familiar to us that she inevitably becomes terribly real to us despite her supernatural trappings.

Longtime Buffy *fan Laura Resnick is the author of such fantasy novels as* In Legend Born, The White Dragon: In Fire Forged I, *and* The Destroyer Goddess: In Fire Forged II. *This Campbell Award–winning author of forty SF/F short stories is also the author of over a dozen romance novels published under the pseudonym Laura Leone. She is a regular contributor to the* SFWA Bulletin, *the* Romance Writers Report, *and* Nink. *You can find her on the Web at* www.sff.net/people/laresnick.

Michelle Sagara West

FOR THE LOVE
OF RILEY

Among the great debates in the history of mankind—capitalism vs. commu-
nism, Big Crunch vs. an ever-expanding universe, guns vs. butter, and Kirk vs.
Picard—surely belongs the irresolvable question of who is the better boyfriend
for Buffy: Angel or Spike. Much ink has been spilled on this question (or electrons
splashed, whatever). But this debate, a bit of which goes on in this modest vol-
ume, ignores Riley, hated by many, dismissed by most. Is this right? Michelle
Sagara West makes the case for Riley.

R ILEY.
Just two syllables, but concatenate them in that particular
order, and you'll cause a rash among a surprisingly large
number of the more civil of *Buffy* aficionados. Among the less civil,
you'll be the proud recipient of linguistic eruptions of a particular and
unenviable nature, although if you're into safety, you can cover your
momentary lack of taste by tacking on a *different* last name, and then
turning the subject of conversation to either Angel or Spike.

And why shouldn't people complain? Let me get to that in a moment.
First, let's look at the introduction of Riley Finn.

One, he appeared in the meandering and directionless fourth season.
While many episodes of note—well, one at least ("Hush," 4-10)—made
their debut in season four, possibly the worst of the Buffy episodes to
date also called it home ("Beer Bad," 4-9). His initial introduction—as

65

the target for a large number of falling books—went without a hitch, as did saving Willow's life, and he sealed the "all good" vignettes with a direct punch to the loathsome mouth of Parker, a boy who slept with Buffy and dumped her after his one-sided one-night stand.

How could it have gone wrong from there?

Well, actually, it goes wrong from way, way back.

The Scoobies were misfits. They managed to be cute without projecting *cute* (Alyson Hannigan. Sarah Michelle Gellar. Need I say more?); Alyson Hannigan was the nerd's nerd, Nicholas Brendan's Xander was the witty pop-culture guru who couldn't get a date with something that wasn't trying to eat him or his friends, and Sarah Michelle Gellar's Buffy, although beautiful, was considered too weird for words. The Scoobies were misfits.

People seemed to identify with that.

Hell, I did.

Self-confidence changed the Scoobies slowly but surely—it does that in real life too. Saving the world a few dozen times or more tends to make the little things in life less and less important. But this growing self-confidence is problematic because it conflicts with the major theme of the first three years of the show: that horror is a metaphor for life, especially among outsiders, underdogs, and people who go unheard in the halls of comfortable authority. Buffy, Xander, Willow, Oz, and even Cordelia survived all of this at a point when Joss Whedon's metaphor had just hit the shoals with the benefit of a dim and shaky lighthouse of dubious intent. Sort of like this metaphor just did.

Riley Finn was parachuted into the archetypal Buffy landscape when he very clearly had no such outsider archetype to anchor himself to.

On top of that, he was delivered into the arms of Buffy, a woman who had just lost the Love of Her Life. The end of season two—the death of Angel—marked the coming of age of the Slayer. It's hard to die in the line of duty, and she did that so perfectly in "Prophecy Girl" (1-12) it broke my heart to watch her take that final step.

But as much as that moved me, "Becoming: Part Two" (2-22) was the true heart-stomper, because if Buffy could *kill* in the line of duty, she stood on the precipice of a much, much more difficult act: to kill someone who you are so certain—especially at eighteen—is the love of your life. It's possibly the most dramatic and moving season end I've ever seen.

Nothing that Riley Finn could offer her could come close to that because, for one, he wasn't attempting to destroy the entire world.

Any growth that could come out of the relationship with someone like Riley is a quiet growth.

David Boreanaz should have *stayed* dead, and would have if it weren't for his following in television land. The sacrifice of Buffy's love for him was an act of duty, and the certainty of its necessity, along with the pain of the loss, would have meant so much more in the context of a permanent death. But hell, if Marvel could bring back Jean Grey, writers can do anything.

So, for no reason whatsoever—certainly none that was given an onscreen explanation in anything but a cursory and ill-conceived way—Angel was unceremoniously dumped back in the lap of our heroine, a loose end that was handled with less grace than even television dictated.

And because of this, he lingers like shadow in the myth of Buffy. People even now want them to get back together because they feel that they're fated for each other. I suppose killing a person does that.

I'll confess up front that it was the episode "Angel" (1-7) that first drew me to *Buffy*. I was sick as a dog, and I caught the last twenty minutes of that episode. Being a fan of *Phantom of the Opera*, *Beauty and the Beast*, and a host of other similar tales, it intrigued me. But it was the next episode I watched that sold me on the series: "When She Was Bad" (2-1). This showed that fear and reaction—to death, admittedly something pretty severe—could change the character; that in the Whedon universe, experience *counted*. Angel figured prominently in both. I thought SMG was fabulous; I thought DB was worthy of *Babylon 5*. (I'll get hate mail for that, if it's taken in the proper context, but I digress again.)

SMG carried the weight of their on-screen romance; she projected vulnerability and confused desire in a pitch-perfect way.

I believed in their doomed-from-the-start romance. Isn't that almost the point of it? We almost always believe most intensely in the earliest of our romances, those relationships that are built on air and hope and insecurity and the inability to actually see what we are because we haven't become it yet.

It's the time of life when we confuse love and longing, and believe that they're the same thing. Joss Whedon, fashioning his darkly comedic drama from those early years, brought back this emotional intensity with his gifted cast. Angel was the boyfriend that you sleep with only to discover the morning after that he's really a jerk. And you want desperately to somehow get an explanation that will make him *not* be that jerk.

High-school Love.

But Joss didn't *stay* a high-school student forever.

And neither did I.

What cured me of high-school intensity was experience. I'm not a great believer in pain. I'm not in favor of self-inflicted wounds, although in other ways I'm not terribly militaristic.

Spike is, sadly, another High-school Boyfriend.

All that snide, clever sniping? All that posturing, all that heavy coolness that someone like Spike exudes? Those are high-school things. Attractive, yes, because at that time, and in that place, they speak of power—of those things that aren't our parents or our brothers. Rebellion is always attractive.

But in the end, the little things whittle away at the core of emotional belief, embittering love—which is often fragile in the early stages. Posturing almost by its very nature excludes the type of vulnerability, the type of risk, that honesty requires.

And it's my belief that without it, there is no lasting relationship.

Riley Finn, as introduced, was the antithesis of Angel. Fair, where Angel was dark, directed where Angel was directionless, and focused where Angel was scrambling to redefine himself. Riley was the "nice" boy. The boy next door.

Big crime, that.

Riley Finn was—until the experiments of the Professor came to light—normal. And nice. The type of person who *no doubt* belonged to a Boy Scout troop, possibly even leading it. The type of guy who gets straight As, not because he's a quirky, insecure genius, but because he works at it. The boy who doesn't get wildly drunk, doesn't experiment with drugs, doesn't spend his adolescence experimenting on the fringes of a law he doesn't care for because he doesn't feel like being told what to do.

He is also the type of person who helps old ladies and blind people across the street because they need help and he happens to be standing there. He holds the doors open without drawing enormous attention to himself. He's just . . . nice.

Why is that word such a cultural epithet?

Why does it seem to lurk in collusion with normal to form an equation that says *boring* in the minds of so many people?

What the writers chose to do with Riley in season five was the antithesis of what he was presented to be in season four—and it was perhaps the *only* thing that was done that made him more palatable, barely, to the legion of people who hated him. I understood Riley's

insecurity; I understood the writer's manipulation behind his character change.

But even in this, there was some important truth: Riley grew to
understand that you *cannot* define yourself by love alone. It puts the
weight of the relationship on the shoulders of a single person—and it
takes it outside of the realm of adult interaction. He had no life, after
the initiative was gone; he had—as Graham pointed out—no Mission.
He was dating his mission, and in the end, that wasn't enough.

It took him a while to figure this out. Sometimes that happens.

But I was upset when he left—not for his sake, and not for mine,
but for what it says in general about our tolerance for television drama.
Buffy was no longer a high-school girl. Riley was not a high-school
relationship. In many ways, with his understanding, his lack of ego,
the lack of baggage that he brought to Buffy, he *was* the type of person
that exists in, and for, the long haul.

And Buffy was not allowed to grow into that. The metaphor that
guided the early show failed here. She went from Angel, the HSB, to
Spike, the HSB, and Riley, who treated her with respect up until the
doubts and insecurities overwhelmed him, was given short shrift and
shorter understanding. He deserved so much better.

Was he off whoring with vampires? Yes, maybe; he was trying to
understand what it was in Buffy that was so compelled by the darkness and the need. But compare this to, say, killing everyone in sight
for the sheer fun of it—all arguments of soul or no soul aside—and I
think he still comes out on top. Because in the end, he's still dedicated
to saving the world. He's not lost in the insecurities and the clinging of
the strictly emotional life: he's moved on, found his place, found his
calling. Did he come to Buffy to rub her face in it? No. He came because he trusted her, respected her ability, and needed help in something that he considered a mutual goal.

Of the three boyfriends to date, Riley Finn is the one most worthy
of respect.

Let me offer a quote from Patricia McKillip's excellent *Forgotten Beasts
of Eld*, not just to be literarily pretentious, but because it's so true: "I
am a child because I did not care what either of you did, only that I
loved you."

A child's love is undiscerning. Adult love is not. Unconditional love
is something that every child wants—and often unreasonably so. Most
adolescents want it as well, although they call it something different.
They want to be special. They want to *feel* special. And if someone

who can't give the time of day to anyone without kicking their shins somehow doesn't kick yours, you often do feel more valuable. The idea that they'll one day be kicking your shins when the novelty wears off is counter-romantic, and doesn't bear thinking about. So it's often either unacknowledged or unconsidered.

Riley Finn was the type of person whom you could go home to at the end of the day. Where Angel was willing to let Buffy face the Harvest alone after their very first meeting, Riley would not.

Riley tried to communicate. He tried to talk. He tried to figure out a way to make things better. He was willing to *compromise*.

Live with Angel? Mr. pouty? Arg. Live with Spike, Mr. I Know What You Like, Come Live In The Depths Of Self-indulgent Despair With Me Because You Don't Deserve Any Better? Arg. Live with someone who respects you and treats you well and is decent enough to help other people, gosh, even strangers, and also *has* a job? Boring.

I gnash my teeth.

Whether or not this makes good television is not the nature of this discussion, although perhaps it should be; let me get to that now.

I think that more people would have accepted Riley with less open hostility had there not been so much visible sex. Tara and Willow, for obvious reasons, were handled with so much more class and subtlety; much was left to our imagination, and perhaps, conservatives that we often are, this appealed to us. The very little left to our imaginations in the Buffy/Riley bedfests were probably mandated by television censors.

Riley, outsider, pushed aside the Scooby siblings, splintering the group onscreen, and arguably depriving some of the cohort of their screen time. This is entirely realistic, but again, breeds hostility.

James Marsters once said in a interview that to get screen time you either had to be kissing Buffy or kicking her butt. Riley was chosen as the kisser—but the screen time shared was Buffy's; he didn't diminish what others had, because he had become the focus of her life at that time.

When Spike took his place, this was considered interesting, daring, innovative, dark. That there were whole episodes with very little of the rest of the Scoobies was hardly decried at all.

But Riley was an outsider. He was normal. He was well-adjusted. He was Mr. Clean. All the little endearing neuroses that defined Willow or Xander, or even the laconic Oz, were missing, as was the more comedic, over-the-top venom of Cordelia.

It occurs to me that I've implied that teenagers all loved Angel and Spike, and that older people liked Riley—and this is just plain wrong. There were quiet teenagers who did like Riley quite a bit, and vocal adults who hated the very sight of him. Experience strikes and changes us at different times and with different imperatives.

Would you rather fantasize about Spike? Probably.

But what I liked best about Buffy is her struggle to find and hold a moral compass in a world that had so much danger and so little belief for her. I liked best that fact that the early seasons of the show did not verge into the angst and the soap opera of so much television drama. Look at "Prophecy Girl" (1-12), one of my all-time favorite episodes. In it, Buffy is finally forced to acknowledge Xander's huge crush, and her rejection is short, honest, and uncomfortable; his graceless acceptance of it is also short, honest, and uncomfortable. Whedon's humor was evident throughout—and a clear signal that the humor came from pain. But everything about that situation was believable, and none of it was self-indulgent.

Spuffy—as Spike/Buffy are often called—changed all that.

Riley Finn *didn't*. And had the writers carried through, above the thunder and din of unhappy fandom, I think it would have made a stronger statement and offered a stronger vision for the inevitable change from the rebel who fights just beneath the radar of authority to the woman who must *become* it if she's to survive.

Riley, you're missed.

Michelle Sagara West was born in 1963 and lives in Toronto. She was a finalist twice for the John W. Campbell Memorial Award for the Best New Writer in 1991 and 1992. Michelle has since published numerous fantasy novels consisting of the Book of the Sundered series (five titles), The Sacred Hunt series (five titles) and The Sun Sword trilogy. Her latest book is volume three in The Sun Sword trilogy and is called The Shining Court.

Justine Larbalestier

A *BUFFY* CONFESSION

I love this essay. I can relate to Justine Larbalestier as she loses her scholarly detachment to become obsessed with a television show that so many dismiss as teen silliness. I can relate to her frustration and defensiveness with fans who insist on being critical ("Don't they want to enjoy the show?") and her joy in the creation of Buffy festivals of every stripe. Most of all, I can relate to her overwhelming fear that the next show, or the next season, would be terrible, and that the magic of Buffy would end . . . a fear that's built over the years to the point that the announcement of the series' end was almost a relief.

I AM A *BUFFY* TRAGIC. I have been an avid follower and, of late, scholar of *Buffy the Vampire Slayer* since the first season. It's the first television show I've ever been obsessed with, the first time I've found myself in the role of a fan. A particularly strange shift for me because I've spent a large part of my scholarly career writing about fans without actually being one. Now I am. I watch the show. A lot. I read and write about it online, in magazines, fanzines, journals, books. I've lectured about it. I've been interviewed about it for Australian TV, radio, and print media.

There's a long list of reasons why so many people love *Buffy*. Reasons that have been given by fans and scholars and reviewers and others consuming vast tracks of the Internet and print in the form of articles and reviews, poems and stories. *Buffy the Vampire Slayer* captured me in the first place because it was a genre TV show that took the rules of the genre seriously, understood them, was metaphorically resonate, cared about continuity and consistency, engaged in fabulous world-building, was intelligently written and acted, and had a sassy self-awareness that was not sly or annoying. It is both funny and sad, often at the same time.

My obsession involves watching the show repeatedly, devouring DVD and other commentary by the writers, particularly Joss Whedon, and thinking long and hard about the show. This intense engagement with a set of interlocked texts as complex and as well-executed as *Buffy* is extraordinarily pleasurable.

My increasing obsession and professional engagement with *Buffy* has found me frequently called upon to defend the show. Not to the large unwashed hordes out there who will never watch or understand the show (and frankly, who cares about them?) but to other *Buffy* fans. Ever since the fourth season, when Buffy and the Scoobies left Sunnydale High behind, there has been a vehement rain of *Buffy* fan backlash.

Like relationships with other human beings, fan relationships with TV shows sometimes thrive on a mix of love and hatred, none more so than *Buffy*. For the past few seasons, my role of defender has meant I haven't always admitted to my own dissatisfactions with *Buffy*. I love *Buffy the Vampire Slayer* more than I've ever loved a TV show (hell, more than quite a few people in my life) but there are times when I hate it too.

DEFENDING *BUFFY THE VAMPIRE SLAYER*

...I read occasionally that people haven't been as happy with this year (actually, I hear that every year), show's not the same . . .

Posted by: Joss Whedon May 22, 2002, 2:15 A.M. UPN.com linear board, www.cise.ufl.edu/~hsiao/media/tv/buffy/bronze/upn/20020522.html

I loathe defending *Buffy* to other fans. I feel like I'm defending a close relative. I want to tell them, "If you can't say anything nice, then shut up." I am not rational about it. While defending the show I will say anything, no matter how illogical. I will frequently contradict myself. I don't care. If a particular writer is attacked I will dredge the record for good episodes or lines they've written. I will airily wave aside complaints about plot holes as a clever play with the tropes of the genre. I'll make stuff up: "That was not a crap line. It was a direct reference to Cansino's last film, *The Widow in the Shadows*, made for RKO just before he was blacklisted. Had a limited release in 1962. Nope, not available on DVD. Though apparently there's a French bootleg video."

I cannot stand fans being so narkily and pickily critical of the show. Don't they understand how tight the TV-land budget of time and money is? Don't they understand that certain actors aren't always available? Don't they *want* to enjoy the show? Anyway, why does everything have to be about whether each episode or season was good or not? Don't they realize that you can't possibly decide that until you've watched it at least five or more (often *way* more) times? I wish they would embrace proper criticism, that mystical process whereby you can write thousands of words about the object you dissect without once revealing whether you like it or not.

Of course, I also can't stand fans who (like myself) defend *Buffy* against all criticism no matter how just. Or who like it for the wrong reasons. The show is not perfect. There have been bad episodes. I know that. I just can't stand to hear others say it.

The first murmurs of "They've lost it" and "*Buffy*'s going down the toilet" began with Angel's return at the beginning of season three. He was dead. How could they bring him back? What a cheap gimmick. Like some trashy afternoon soap opera. When a character's dead they should stay dead. (Hmmm, I pointed out, you mean like Buffy's death in "Prophecy Girl," 1-12?) His return from Hell, the critics muttered, undermines the tragic arc of the second season. Of course, by the end there was far less murmuring about bringing Angel back, and many fans now believe season three is the best ever.

Buffy had been criticized by fans before, but only for less-than-great episodes. "Out of Mind, Out of Sight" (1-11), "Bad Eggs" (2-12), and "Beauty and the Beasts" (3-4) had all been slammed, but season four was the first time a sizeable number were trashing a whole season. What was it about season four? I have friends who say it was Angel's departure. These same people prefer *Angel* to *Buffy*. As they are clearly insane, I'll discount them. (They also think "Once More, With Feeling," 6-7, is the worst *Buffy* episode ever, so you can rest easy with my dismissal of their opinions.)

Most of the criticism boiled down to unhappiness with the Scoobies leaving high school. The show, many said, just doesn't work once the central literalized metaphor—high school is hell—is lost. When the Scoobies are in college or working various odd jobs, or unemployed, there's no easy overarching metaphor that binds the show together. Being a young adult, trying to find yourself; life after high school is more complex. But it *does* resonate. The Scoobies' search for adult lives and adult identities is certainly more emotionally real than any number of so-called realist shows about everyday life, such as *thirtysomething*.

Another criticism aimed at season four is its preponderance of arc episodes. I have a friend who is convinced that more arc episodes than stand-alone means that a show is "decadent." *Buffy*, he says, has been irretrievably decadent since that dreaded fourth season. The references to previous incidents, once clever and witty, now overwhelm the show, making it an indulgent exercise playing to the in-crowd. *Buffy* is so dependent on internal references, this friend maintains, that it is now a soap opera.

I disagree. Strongly. Or maybe I don't. Maybe it *is* a soap opera, but one screened in prime time with brilliant writing, fabulous acting, and far less than sixty pages of script filmed a day.

Some other criticisms of the show I've had to deal with:

None of Buffy's lovers since Angel have been worthy of her. He was her one true love. My response is to try not to roll my eyes. Angel is, in fact, my least favorite of Buffy's partners. Even Riley is better (despite the writers apparently not knowing how dodgy it is for a T. A. to sleep with one of his freshman students). Their relationship was particularly interesting toward the end, when Riley's doing the whole vampire drug/sex thing. Ah, sweet tragedy. Buffy mooning after the wooden Angel was tedious, overdone (a big uggh to their theme music), and lasted way too long. It only became interesting after he became Angelus. The more compelling (with way better dialogue) season two relationships were between Spike and Drusilla and Cordelia and Xander.

They've neutered Spike. He hasn't been a decent character since season two. Oh, how many ways can I disagree with this one? I love Spike with a chip. I love Spike with a soul. I adore him tragically in love with Buffy. "Fool for Love" (5-7) gives every Spike episode an extra layer—oh the fun of looking for William (I-may-be-a-bad-poet-but-I'm-a-good-man) in badass Spike.

All the villains have sucked ever since the Mayor was toasted. Why does no one remember how lame the Master was? Worst villain ever. (And unfortunately he had the same name as the villain in *Doctor Who*, who was way less lame.) The Initiative was a great idea. Glory is underrated. The Trio was mostly silly but had many interesting moments.

The writing has just gotten worse and worse (also known as the why-can't-Joss-write-every-episode complaint). There are just as many shithouse, badly written episodes in the early seasons. "Out of Mind, Out of Sight" (1-10), anyone? Or "Inca Mummy Girl" (2-4)? (Can't help with the Joss complaint. I wish Joss wrote and directed every episode too, although with the proviso that I don't think every episode he writes on his own is pure gold. "Lie To Me" 2-7, "Anne" 3-1 and "Family" 5-6 are nowhere near the level of "Prophecy Girl" 1-12 or "The Body" 5-16. One episode Whedon co-wrote is amongst the worst *Buffy* episodes ever: the aforementioned "Out of Mind, Out of Sight.")

Season four was going to be hated even before it first aired. *Buffy* tragics (like me) sat down to watch the first broadcast of "The Freshman" (4-1) with a great deal of fear in their hearts. Would the show be as good as it used to be? Is it all over? That fan fear has remained. Can the best TV show of all time stay good after so many seasons? Every episode is watched with an eye for evidence of decline. And every *Buffy* fan I know has turned to me to prove to them that the end isn't pretty seriously nigh.

The fear is in my heart, too. In my position as defender of *Buffy* to the once faithful, I watch each new episode with mounting terror. Is it a crap episode? Is it a crap season? Should I be heckling along with everybody else? Is Buffy's inability to kill Spike a sign of decadence? Is Willow's evil turn amateurishly handled, and her recovery even more so? Are they lamely recycling villains? Am I ever going to be able to watch a new episode of the show and simply enjoy it?

BUFFY MINI-FESTIVALS,
OR HOW DVDS SAVED MY LIFE

No, I will never again enjoy an episode the first time through. I'm too nervous, too absorbed with anticipating criticisms and how to respond to them. I'm not capable of enjoying an episode until I've watched it several times. And it doesn't become pure pleasure until the DVD set comes out and I've watched said episode in the context of the whole season (including all the writer/director commentaries) in the space of two or three *Buffy*-packed days.

Oh the glories of DVDs. Episodes that I hated when I first saw them are transformed. "Ted" (2-11) turns out to be a chillingly good episode, not the dreaded movie-of-the-week number I remembered. Even less-than-great episodes like "Some Assembly Required" (2-2) with its spectacularly lame plot—boy reanimates dead sports hero brother (with his high-school-science know-how) and then builds him a mate out of spare dead-girl parts—turns out to have wonderful arc development and priceless exchanges between the Scoobies. It's a rare episode that doesn't have at least a moment of fabulous dialogue or a gorgeous setup for events a season or more later.

Joss Whedon's commentary over "The Body" (5-16) confirms every worshipful thought you have ever indulged about the guy's writing and his attitude to making the show. The creators think about what they're doing:

> JOSS WHEDON: "Buffy" is made by a bunch of writers who think very, very hard about what they are doing in terms of psychology and methodology. We take the show very seriously. We are perhaps the most pompous geeks of them all. When somebody says there is a philosophy behind "Buffy" that is the truth. When they say there is symbolism and meaning in what we're doing, that's true too. (Joss Whedon AOL Chat, 10 November 2002 *www.geocities.com/soporjoe77/josschat.html*)

Although watching a whole season back-to-back is excellent, there are stomach-tightening moments when horrible suspicions about a given episode or story arc are confirmed. Yep, it is as bad as I feared. But there is a solution—a beautiful one, which has salved the wounds suffered while watching and defending *Buffy*. I create my own *Buffy* mini-festivals! I recommend it as the very best way to ensure your *Buffy* viewing is stress- and anxiety-free.

All that's required is some judicious episode selection. Start with the obvious, say a series of relationship festivals: Spike & Buffy (first "School Hard," 2-3; next "Halloween," 2-6; and so forth), or Cordelia and Xander ("What's My Line, Part 2," 2-10; "Ted," 2-11; "Bad Eggs," 2-12; and "Innocence," 2-14; etc.). Or you could have a Jonathan festival ("Inca Mummy Girl," 2-4; "Reptile Boy," 2-5; etc.) Or a Ripper retrospective ("Halloween," 2-18; "Band Candy," 3-6; etc). Then you can graduate to the less obvious: the Anya's-Afraid-of-Bunny-Rabbits festival, the Conveniently-Located-Axe festival, and the Slutty Clothes festival.

Here are some of my favorites:

THE PERFECT BUFFY FESTIVAL

There's at least one perfect episode of *Buffy* every season. Watching them together gives me a happy. The following are my current choice of most perfect from seasons one to six:

"Prophecy Girl" (1-12): What is so fabulous about "Prophecy Girl" is not that Buffy beats the tedious arch-villain but that she does it with the aid of the entire ensemble cast. The episode is the distilled essence of everything that had been keeping me watching the show up to that point: the fabulous sharp dialogue between the characters ("You're looking at my neck," says Xander to Angel on the way to rescue Buffy), the rip-roaring plot that barely lets up, the beautifully drawn friendship between Buffy, Willow and Xander, the tragedy of sixteen-year-old Buffy walking knowingly to her death. All the promise of the season comes to fruition. Before "Prophecy Girl," I thought *Buffy* was a pretty cool show with some great moments, way better than anything else on the box. In its wake, I was an obsessive *Buffy*holic.

"Innocence" (2-14): the episode where the Buffy and Angel romance finally got interesting. I adore the moment when you *really* know Angel is bad: not simply because he bites into the woman's neck, but because he blows out a plume of her cigarette smoke. Angel's smoking. He's a villain now. This is a perfect arc episode, because it turns the action up to eleven.

"The Zeppo" (3-13): By season three, the fans were completely familiar with the standard *Buffy* plot, so clearly it was past time for the creators to mess things up a bit. They did so delightfully. *Buffy* deconstructs itself by making the A plot into the B plot. Angel and Buffy snatch a moment alone together, the music swells up, Xander walks in, the music goes away. It's the first time the writers really played around with the structure of a *Buffy* episode, and it's, well, perfect.

The perfect episodes of seasons four through six are, of course, a no-brainer: "Hush" (4-22), "The Body" (5-16), and "Once More, With Feeling" (6-7).[1] Not just perfect *Buffy* but perfect television.

---

[1] See the coda at the end of this article for feelings about season seven.

WILLOW & TARA FESTIVAL

Okay, this is a pretty obvious festival, but I adore these two, and their relationship illustrates one of the many things I love about *Buffy the Vampire Slayer*: it endlessly builds on itself. Casual dialogue from early seasons start to become more resonant in the light of later events. "Willow's not looking to date you," Xander says to Buffy, "or if she is she's playing it pretty close to her chest" ("Prophecy Girl," 1-12). Then, two seasons later, in "Doppelgangland," (3-16), vamp Willow comes on to Willow with the traditional face-licking method. "I think I'm kinda gay," says Willow, somewhat perturbed by the whole experience.

Seeds are planted and then they grow. It's glorious to watch. Especially when they grow into Tara and Willow having the best metaphoric sex ever shown on television. When these two women do spells together, then *whoosh*. From the hand-holding vending-machine propelling of "Hush" (4-10) to the unbelievably sexy spell of "Who Are You?" (4-16): Tara's thumb to Willow's forehead, lips and sternum, they begin to chant, they start to breathe heavily, their hands touch, their breathing becomes even heavier, they glisten with sweat, their eyes half-close, a magical circle rises around them, they stare into each others' eyes, Willow falls back gasping. Oh my. But there's more to come: the superlative "You Make Me Complete" scene from "Once More, With Feeling" (6-7). Sigh.

ALL-CHARMING-PRETTY-BOYS
WHO-AREN'T-VAMPIRES-ARE-BAD FESTIVAL

I always knew that, but thanks to *Buffy* for proving it over and over again. Watch Tom in "Reptile Boy" (2-5), Ford in "Lie to Me" (2-7), and Parker Abrams in "Living Conditions" (4-2), "Harsh Light of Day" (4-3), and "Beer Bad" (4-5). They're all variations of the same guy and they're all bastards. But cute bastards.

DREAMING *BUFFY* FESTIVAL

I love the way the show uses dreams. Instead of the gorgeous though not especially informative *Twin Peaks*' dream sequences (nicely referenced with the red curtains in "Restless," 4-22) *Buffy*'s dreams are not merely beautifully done but provide acres of plot and character exposition. In fact, the very first time we see Buffy, she's in bed dreaming about the season's villain the Master ("Welcome to the Hellmouth," 1-1). Turns out, Buffy dreams a lot and those dream sequences just get better and better. The moment when Giles suddenly turns to strangle Buffy while Willow and Xander sit by obliviously ("When She Was Bad," 2-1) startles the viewer and instantly conveys just how much Buffy has *not* recovered from her ordeal with the Master. The predictive dream sequences of "Surprise" (2-13) and "Graduation Day, Part 2" (3-22), with its references to Dawn's arrival in Sunnydale two seasons later, are the beautiful seeds that grows into the all-dream episode of "Restless" (4-22). How much do I love "Restless"? My love is bigger than the ocean. I cap off this festival with the mostly delusional "Normal Again" (6-17). Delusions, dreams. Same thing.

TRAGIC *BUFFY* FESTIVAL

I love the sheer heart-wrenching pleasure of tragedy, and *Buffy* is the most tragic show on television. Hours of joyous pain and many damp tissues. A single line of dialogue can set me off, from Buffy's plaintive "Giles, I'm sixteen years old. I don't want to die" ("Prophecy Girl," 1-12) to Jonathan's speech when he presents Buffy's Class Protector Award—"Most of the people here have been saved by you" ("The Prom," 3-20). "The Prom" makes me tear up no matter how many times I see it. So does "Innocence" (2-14); "I Only Have Eyes For You" (2-19), with its haunting use of an already creepily haunting song; and "Seeing Red" (6-19) with Tara's death. Of course, "The Body" (5-16) and "The Gift" (5-22) ("Don't do it Buffy, let the brat jump!") make me howl.

Buffy's life (like those of Hamlet and Odysseus) is one continuing train wreck that affects everyone around her. At the end of season six, there's not a cast member who is not in some way a tragic figure. I love it.

But, as I've mentioned several times, there are times when I hate *Buffy*. Here are two festivals that show why:

"ACTUALLY, THEY'RE ALL STUPID" FESTIVAL

Unfortunately, there are a handful of episodes where the Scoobies seem to have collectively or individually lost all claim to even the intelligence of a gnat. Most don't involve some spell that explains the idiocy away. Buffy spends most of "Triangle" (5-11) crying in an unconvincing, vaudevillian, over-the-top way. What the hell was that all about? I bought that kind of acting in "Something Blue" (4-9) 'cause, well, there was a *spell*.

Worse still are the episodes when the entire cast, director, and writing team are rendered moronic. "The Inca Mummy Girl" (2-4) has an even lamer plot than "Some Assembly Required" (2-14), with no cool Scooby dialogue or arc plotting to save it. It's ineptly written, directed and, sad to say, acted. The story could have been lifted from a *Goosebumps* book. Kids go to museum, scary mummy comes to life. The plot holes are large enough to drive an eighteen-wheeler through. The South American exchange student is staying for two weeks with the hugest trunk you ever saw—conveniently big enough to stash a body in. Everyone keeps doing things purely for plot reasons. There's dead time. When Xander picks up the Incan mummy girl from Buffy's place there's an endless, pointless filler conversation between them and Joyce and Buffy. It's like watching *As the World Turns*. The dialogue between the Scoobies is awful: "Do we have to speak Spanish?" asks Xander. "Cause I don't know much besides 'Doritos' and 'Chihuahua'."

"A VERY SPECIAL BUFFY"

This is the worst of all possible festivals, suitable for viewing only by the very brave. I hate it with a fiery, burning passion when an episode of *Buffy* turns into "a very special *Buffy*," something Whedon has explicitly promised would never happen. In these episodes, some kind of heart- (or rather stomach-) wrenching problem comes up and is dealt with and we learn a lesson. You know what, kids? Domestic violence is wrong ("Beauty and the Beasts," 3-4). Sick kids are sweet ("Killed By Death," 2-18). Death is sad ("Help," 7-4). These episodes are vile. I have to pinch myself. Am I watching some horrible cross between *Charmed* and *7th Heaven*?

"Help" (7-4) does appallingly badly everything that "The Body" (5-7) did brilliantly. We're supposed to care about some kid we've never seen before who talks in breathless meant-to-be-wise-beyond-her-years psychobabble. Die already. The penultimate scene consists of the Scoobies sitting around discussing their tragic loss as heart-tugging music swells around them. (Whedon specifically didn't use music in "The Body," because it's too easy; he didn't want to let the audience off the hook.) Buffy says she wished she'd saved the kid: "She was special." Yeah, the kid's horrendous teenage-angst poetry sure was special. In the last scene Buffy is back in her counselor's office. Gee, kids, looks like even our superhero Buffy can't save everyone. Though, hang on—isn't that the lesson learned from Joyce's death? The last two scenes of "Help" are just like the wrap of some sitcom or *Touched by an Angel*. It was all I could do not to throw up.

But even worse is the "very special *Buffy*" arc of season six: Willow's magic addiction. Or, gee, could it be a metaphor for drug addiction? Just in case you haven't caught on, there's a poster-boy drug dealer with hippy clothes and long hair called Rack, who talks slow, and lots of scenes of Willow being all spaced and, ooh, kind of stoned-looking. The sight of Willow in "Wrecked" (6-10) (which gets my vote for worst *Buffy* episode ever), in the junkie waiting room causes me physical pain. Drugs are bad, man. Just say no. I wished I'd been stoned watching it, which would have at least eased my pain. Man, the *Buffy* metaphors used to be a tad more clever and emotionally resonant. As in, you sleep with your boyfriend and overnight he turns into a monster.

I hate Willow's becoming Dark Magic Queen all the more because the writers blew it. The setup for Willow's descent goes all the way back to her first tentative steps with magic in season one. They did not need to belabor the drug addiction metaphor with Rack and Amy and Willow's AA (or is that MA?) total abstinence. (Especially as Giles's approach at the beginning of season seven seems far more sensible.) I have rewritten that arc in my head a hundred times. First I put together a mini-festival of Willow's use of magic which includes Giles's angry remonstration with Willow after she brings Buffy back ("Flooded," 6-4), and Willow's chilling speech to Dawn in ("Two to Go," 6-21). In the versions in my head, Willow's complete descent into blind grief, rage, and madness, does not turn her into an after-school-special villain mouthing ludicrous lines like "There's no one in the world who has the power to stop me now!"

WAY MORE LOVE THAN HATE

Ultimately, the brilliance of *Buffy* makes the occasional falls from grace that much harder to stand. Knowing that every episode of *Buffy* could be a work of genius on the level of "Who Are You?" (4-16), or "Restless" (4-22), or "Once More, With Feeling" (6-7), makes the occasional sub-*Charmed*-level hour a stab to the heart. Why can't *Buffy* be produced like *The Sopranos*, with time and money to burn?

Buffy is both good and bad; wonderful and excremental. Even the very worst episodes have moments of gold (well, okay, *almost* all do). And, even a few good episodes have a cringe-worthy moment or two. A great deal of criticism and other writing about *Buffy* has gotten caught up in dichotomous thinking: it's good or it's bad, it's feminist or it's misogynist; it's racist or it isn't. *Buffy* is all of these.

Buffy is certainly obsession-inspiring. That's why I fervently hope that season seven is the last season of *Buffy*. Frankly, I can't take any more. I pray that the show will end. I want to watch television without a stomach full of knots. Seven seasons is plenty. More than enough to keep me happy with endless reprogramming of my *Buffy* festivals. If it all stops at the end of this season, then I can rule out the possibility that there will ever be an entire bad season that is nothing but episodes like "Killed by Death" (2-18), and "Wrecked" (6-10), and "Help" (7-4). I want a finished, no-longer-unfolding text. I don't want there ever to be a set of *Buffy* DVDs that I can't do anything with.

CODA: WAY MORE HATE THAN LOVE

The balanced, temperate words above were written only a short way into season seven, before I realized how horrifically *Buffy the Vampire Slayer* had gone off the rails. It's many months now since I have made any attempt to defend the show. Instead I have taken to bitterly muttering about how much better it would have been if they'd finished in the sixth season, making "Normal Again" (6-17) the final episode. I'm now one of those people I used to defend the show against. There is no one more bitter than an ex-true believer. Color me narky and picky.

I'm writing this coda a week after the season finale and to be honest I'm still in shock. On the one hand, I've gotten my wish: season seven is the last season of *Buffy*. On the other hand, I've also gotten what I most feared: a set of *Buffy* DVDs I can't do anything with.

Everything I write in this coda is flying in the face of my assertion that you really can't have a coherent opinion about a *Buffy* season until it's come out on DVD and you've seen it at least five times. I'm not saying I won't change my mind, but right now I'm looking forward to watching season seven on DVD about as much as I look forward to a 24 hour plane ride in cattle class.

Season seven was a nightmare. Only three episodes I would describe as good (forget about looking for any works of genius—a "Once More, With Feeling", a "Hush"—there weren't any): "Selfless" (7-5), "Conversations With Dead People" (7-7), and "Chosen" (7-22). Each of these episodes had problems. "Selfless" added all sorts of resonances to Anya's character, setting up exciting possibilities for future development. None of them went anywhere. The rest of the season trundled along as if "Selfless" had never happened. The rationale for Tara's not appearing to Willow was lame in the extreme. Why would Willow be persuaded, even for a second, by the annoying ditz from "Help"? "Chosen" felt exactly like what it was: an episode butchered to fit its hour time slot. Everything except the tedious Spike & Buffy love story was short-changed (I sure wish Faith and Robin Wood had gotten a bit more of that screen time). Anya's death, which should have been tragic (especially in light of the groundwork laid down in "Selfless"), managed to elicit little more than a "bummer, man" expression from Xander. Hardly anyone else even noticed.

No episode of season seven made me cry. Well, okay, except for tears of disbelief that the show could possibly have become so bad. The worst failing of season seven has been the writing. Overall it's been shocking. The humor was forced, and the characters all developed multiple personalities, none of them believable. The Buffy and Spike relationship become as wet and annoying as that of Buffy and Angel. Since when was Buffy a humorless bitch? Had the Scoobies learned nothing that they would so easily turn against her yet again? Since when did these people speak in a series of tedious speeches:

Buffy to Faith: "Don't be afraid to lead them. Whether you wanted it or not, their lives are yours. It's only gonna get harder. Protect them, but lead them" ("Empty Places," 7-19).

And yet, after all, it is *Buffy*. This is the nasty divorce, but we may in a year or two become friends again. There's always a chance that those DVDs will work their magic and I'll be able to come up with a whole new set of *Buffy* mini-festivals. (I can't help noticing that "Selfless" is the perfect end to the Anya's-afraid-of-bunny-rabbits festival.) Right now, though, I'm just so relieved it's over.

Justine Larbalestier is a Sydney-born researcher and writer. She has written a radio show about the end of relationships, a short film about the Midas legend, and extensively on American science fiction culture, particularly in the 40s and 50s as well as Buffy the Vampire Slayer. *Her first book is* The Battle of the Sexes in Science Fiction *(Wesleyan University Press, 2002).*

Jennifer Crusie

DATING DEATH

How does Joss do it? How does he, in the midst of horror, action, and comedy, manage to create love stories that ring true, that touch us, time and time again? For the answer to this question we look outside the SF genre and turn to a leading romance novelist, Jennifer Crusie.

ROMANCE WRITERS TEND TO LOVE *Buffy the Vampire Slayer* because it's the only show on TV that gets the dynamics of falling in love right most of the time. Whedon and his writers seem to have an instinct for the messy part of romance, the off-the-wall, over-the-top, why-am-I-doing-this? insanity that makes love such a pain in the neck, whether somebody's biting you there or not. The reasons for this are many and varied, and all the more telling when the people at Mutant Enemy get it wrong. Watching *Buffy* is an education in how to write romance.

A look at how Buffy Summers meets and mates gives the first part of the answer as to why *Buffy* makes the best love on TV. Buffy has had three loves in her seven-year fight against the Hellmouth, and three of these relationships followed the basic psychological progress—assumption, attraction, infatuation, and attachment—which is why they all felt true emotionally, even if some viewers were less than pleased with Buffy's choices.

The first move in establishing a relationship is assumption: gauging, consciously or unconsciously, if this person is somebody desirable, somebody it is possible to love. Is the object of potential desire physically attractive? Smart? Strong? Funny? These are all clues that the object is genetically a catch, physically and mentally healthy; it's DNA shrieking "Pick that one, I want to live forever!" Since Sunnydale is populated almost entirely by beautiful, verbal teenagers, this is not a difficult stage for the Scooby Gang, their angst notwithstanding. But Buffy as Mythic Heroine is going to need more than just a knee-jerk jock of the week, so Whedon ushers in Angel, the Heathcliff for the turn-of-the-millennium. He's strong (he can hold his own with the Slayer), he's smart (he knows the evil world she must learn about in order to fight it), he has a mordant sense of humor (even more effective because Angel is not a happy man), and he's physically attractive, or, as Buffy puts it after she first meets him in "Welcome to the Hellmouth" (1-1), "dark, gorgeous in an annoying kind of way."

Once assumption is made, the second stage, or attraction, begins: finding out if this is somebody who *should* be loved. Friends and family play a huge role here, along with physical and emotional connections. Buffy's peer group sees Angel as attractive (even Xander's jealousy is backhanded approval since he rates Angel a threat), her mother less so, perversely making him even more desirable because he's outside the bounds of parental control. Also in the mix are physical cues: he falls into step easily beside her, they fight beside one another in sync, and they share long, deep looks (known to the psych trade as copulatory gazes). And then there are the emotional cues: he's the only one who understands the darkness in her, she's the only human he's connected to in two hundred years. Everything is in place for Angel and Buffy to believably fall in love.

But for attraction to turn to infatuation, there have to be physiological cues—joy, or pain, or both. Joy is physical pleasure or emotional connection, great kisses or moments when eyes meet across a room in perfect understanding. Pain is stress, danger, jealousy, the reason for war romances and office affairs. (There's a reason there are so many love stories in Sunnydale; it's Pain Central.) The more of these cues that are present, the faster the relationship will move into the giddiness of immature love. And both joy and pain cues are all over the place in the Buffy-and-Angel story, climaxing in their first kiss, a physical thrill so great it provokes his vampire side, the part of his story he'd forgotten to mention ("Angel," 1-7). The revelation that he's her destined enemy would be enough to kill infatuation. But something has happened before the reveal: Buffy has moved past immature love to a recognition of who Angel is besides the hottie who loves her. She has moved into mature love.

The question "Is this real love or just infatuation?" misses the point: it's all infatuation in the beginning, infatuation (or immature love) is the stage everyone passes through on the way to mature love. Erich Fromm in *The Art of Loving* makes the distinction between the two, pointing out that infatuation is about the person doing the loving, the lover, but true love is about the person who is loved, the object. Infatuation is about conditional love: I love you because of what you do for me, because you're funny, you're loving, you're sexy, you're smart, you're not a vampire, etc. But what happens when the object stops being funny and sexy? What happens when he turns into a vampire? "I love you because" is conditional love, based on what the object does for the lover; the "You complete me" statement that sounds good but is really a threat: "Complete me or lose me, it's all about me." Mature love goes beyond that and says that it doesn't matter whether the object is wonderful or not, the love is just there, like the air we breathe. So Angel vamps and Buffy screams and rejects him, but when she has the opportunity to kill him, fulfilling her destiny as a vampire slayer, she deliberately misses, and Angel saves her from the woman who made him a vampire, symbolically killing his old life to enter a new one with Buffy. Their love is unconditional, the season ends, the love story is finished. Unless, of course, it's playing out in Sunnydale.

Buffy's choice to spare Angel in the first season is not based on blindly unconditional love; she has plenty of clues in that story arc that he is on her side. The second season brings the real test: in one of Whedon's blatant, powerful metaphors, Buffy loses her virginity to a loving, sexually skilled Angel and wakes up with the murderous beast, Angelus. It's easy to love Angel, he meets all the conditions for it, he completes Buffy. Loving Angelus is the antithesis of that, nobody could rationally love a vicious demon who rapes and murders without compunction. In the same way, it's easy to love Buffy-the-Savior if you're Angel, impossible to love her if you're Angelus.

And yet they still love each other, much to their mutual disgust and despair. Angelus is riddled with love for her, and because of that he is driven to destroy her. The loathing he feels for her is as deep as the love he fights; as he tells Spike in "Innocence" (2-14), "To kill this girl . . . you have to love her." Buffy is stuck, too: she cannot bring herself to kill Angelus until he gives her no choice by opening the portal to hell. But she kills him as a sacrifice to save the world, not as an execution to punish and reject him, something that Whedon makes clear by transforming Angelus into Angel before she strikes ("Becoming, Part 2," 2-22). When he comes back from Hell, tortured for a century until he is only slightly above a beast, he still loves her and saves her instinctively, just as she loves and protects him even though his mind is gone ("Beauty and the Beasts," 3-4). The power of their love is larger than life not because they're larger-than-life characters, but because it is implacably and completely unconditional.

Their final act of love is their great sacrifice at the end of the third season. Angel leaves her to free her and Buffy lets him go: He's protected her until she's graduated into adulthood, she's stood by him until he believes in himself again, and now unconditional love recognizes that they have to move on with only the hope of their promise at the end of the series that they'll be together again some day. It's brilliant storytelling that gives Whedon the opportunity to move the series to a different level, but it's also brilliant romance writing, a love story of mythic proportions.

Following that love story was going to be tough in any case, so Whedon pulled his punches and introduced Parker, the embodiment of the dangers of infatuation. Buffy makes the Parker Mistake because she wants to fall in love with an everyday human being more than she wants Parker in the specific. Zipping through the assumption and attraction in a rush to get to normal and loved, Buffy misses the cues that would have told her he was a shallow, not very bright user, and pays the price. Parker adds to Buffy's experience with men, but mostly he serves as foil and foreshadowing for Buffy's next big romance, Riley Finn.

The assumption phase for this romance is automatic: Riley and Buffy are both beautiful, blond, athletic college students. When they discover in "Hush" (4-10) that they're both superhuman demon fighters, attraction goes wild, fueled by copulatory gazes over dead demons and hot hand-to-hand combat. In fact, combat is the foreplay for their first sexual encounter, one that leads to frequent, healthy, sweaty, well-lit intercourse. But a gulf opens between them when Riley discovers that his superhuman strength comes from drugs that are killing him, which forces him to return to being just a strong human. If he truly loved Buffy unconditionally, Riley would accept their differences as fact and not as a comment on his inadequacy. Instead, he sees Buffy only in relationship to himself, a reproach to his own lost power, and punishes her by finding sexual solace with the enemy as a vampire addict, a tacit admission that all that safe, bouncy lovemaking was a sham. Buffy fails him just as badly by turning from him when she discovers his addiction, betrayed because he isn't the hero she needs him to be. Real love is unconditional, and they don't have it.

There's also another factor at work: by the time the fourth season ends, Buffy is no longer a wisecracking teenager. She's an adult, increasingly aware that the line between good and evil is more of a smudge, and she knows that Riley's matter-of-fact, Manichean view of the universe is too simplistic. The fifth season codes this in the form of the two men vying for her: Riley the Impossibly Good and Spike the Unspeakably Evil, an ostensibly easy choice. But it slowly becomes evident that while the noble Riley's love is selfish and conditional, the murderous Spike's love is without qualification.

At first glance, assumption plays no part in Buffy and Spike's relationship. They meet as mortal enemies, trying without hesitation to kill one another. But their first interactions are, in fact, strong cues for assumption, and although she dismisses him as just another vampire, and he sees her as pretty much the third notch on his Slayer-killing belt, they surprise each other. He's much more powerful than she realizes, and she's much more complex than he can fathom. Adding to the attraction is the fact that, from the beginning, their conflict is sexual. In their first real physical confrontation in "School Hard" (2-3), he knocks her to the ground and straddles her, saying, "I'll make it quick. It won't hurt a bit," and she says, "Wrong. It's gonna hurt *a lot*," foreshadowing the next five seasons of mutual violence. It's a coded erotic beginning to a complex hate/hate relationship that takes an abrupt turn when Spike is forced to choose between Angelus's plan for the end of the world and his own enjoyment of life. Stuck between Angelus and Buffy, he chooses her, and starts irrevocably down a path that leads him to unconditional love, not only of Buffy but of life ("Becoming, Part 2," 2-22).

Caught in a dynamic so strong neither can break away, Spike and Buffy continue to ignore what viewers can see plainly: they're meant for each other. But when Buffy is injured and forced to confront her own mortality, it's Spike she goes to for answers in "Fool for Love" (5-7). When she asks him how he killed two Slayers, he gives her the key she doesn't want. "Every Slayer," he tells her, fixing her with a copulatory gaze, "has a death wish," and then he rephrases it in sexual terms: "You know you want to dance." It's in this scene that their erotic attraction becomes clear: They're tied to each other in a heated, perverse symbiosis that fuses all the elements of attraction: they're beautiful, strong, smart, funny, and forbidden, and they're the only two people on the planet who can understand each other. They're the ultimate aphrodisiac: they know each other to the core.

Swamped by emotion and lust, Spike moves into infatuation much more readily than Buffy, because he's the true romantic, the real fool for love. In that, he's smarter than Buffy, who keeps trying to fall in love with Good instead of finding a partner who not only understands her but also values her for what she is. Spike might have gone on loving her hopelessly forever, except for a major plot move: Buffy dies to save the world. If Spike's love were immature and conditional, that would finish things, and he'd return to his old life. Instead, he stays in a life that doesn't fit him, helping her friends and protecting her sister, knowing that he'll never see her again and still loving her hopelessly. When she comes back from the dead and claws her way out of the grave, he's the only one who understands what's happened, and his calm handling of her crisis is one of the best demonstrations of real love ever filmed. When she asks, "How long was I gone?" and he says, "Hundred and forty-seven days yesterday . . . one forty-eight today," he speaks volumes about how much he loves her ("Afterlife," 6-3).

And Buffy knows it. He's the only one she can trust with the truth about her "rescue," the only one she can talk to without anger or guilt, the only one who accepts her absolutely. But her love isn't based on those things; like Spike's, it's also unconditional. Although she finally ends their affair, she stands by him through stupid crimes (selling monster eggs?), attempted rape, and insanity, refusing to kill him again and again even though he crosses her moral line, rejecting his offer to leave when it appears that the First Evil plans to work through him, telling him "I'm not ready for you not to be here" ("First Date," 7-14). Even throughout a very uneven sixth season that swings between brilliant episodes and stories that are appalling world and character violations, Spike and Buffy's love story stays true because Spike, like Angel before him, loves Buffy unconditionally, sacrifices for her, endures torture for her, almost dies for her, finally does die for her, and, much against her will, Buffy reciprocates, risking her life to save him, forgiving him the unforgivable, telling him at the end that she loves him because he's earned it.

But there's another dimension to *Buffy*'s love stories beyond the psychological accuracy, a dimension that makes them even deeper, the ever-present knowledge that while falling in love can be devastating, consummating that love can be lethal. A quick run-down of Love's

Greatest Hits on *Buffy* shows that love in this world really is a matter of life and death.

Buffy sleeps with Angel who turns into a demon and tries to kill her with a short time-out when they're possessed by the spirits of a murder-suicide love match ("I Only Have Eyes for You," 2-19). When she tries to date within her species, she ends up with an ex-boyfriend who tries to feed her to vampires ("Lie to Me," 2-7), a nice guy with a death wish ("Never Kill a Boy on the First Date," 1-5), a groping loser who turns into The Creature from the Swim Team ("Go Fish," 2-20), and another nice guy whose best friend tries to kill her as Sunnydale's Mr. Hyde ("Beauty and the Beasts," 3-4). After that, she falls for a man whose jealous mentor tries to send her to her death ("The I in Team," 4-13) and a vampire who's tried to kill her so many times he's practically the Wile E. Coyote of Sunnydale.

Buffy's friends aren't doing any better. Willow's hopeless crush on Xander leads her to accept a stranger's invitation to a nice walk in the dark and almost gets her killed in "Welcome to the Hellmouth" (1-1). After that she gets a crush on an Internet pen pal who turns out to be a demon-infested robot ("I Robot, You Jane," 1-8), falls in love with a werewolf who tries to rip her apart ("Phases," 2-15); and finally finds a haven with Tara, who is shot to death as she's standing in Willow's bedroom, making a sexual advance. Or there's Cordelia Chase, who almost gets vamped by her dance partner ("The Harvest," 1-2), dates a fraternity boy who tries to feed her to a giant lizard ("Reptile Boy," 2-5), is kidnapped by a Frankenstein football player who wants to cut off her head so they can be together forever, and falls in love with Xander who betrays her, which results in her impalement on a rebar ("Lover's Walk," 3-8). Buffy's family doesn't fare any better. Her mother has two boyfriends in the entire run of the show (not counting her candy-inspired interlude with Giles on the hood of the police car), a homicidal robot ("Ted," 2-11) and the nice guy who sends her flowers the morning she dies ("The Body," 5-16). And Buffy's little sister, Dawn, goes on her first date and gets her first kiss from a guy who turns into a vampire, pins her down in the missionary position, and offers to make her immortal, after which she stakes him.

But it's not just Sunnydale's women who are mauled by the metaphor. Whedon's universe offers equal-opportunity death to men. Angel is human until a pick-up date named Darla murders him in an alley and makes him a vampire. He manages to make it through the next two hundred years and then meets Buffy, his one true love, who runs a phallic sword through him and sends him to hell. Spike's story is similar: He meets Drusilla when she finds him weeping in the street after rejection by the woman he loves; she comforts him by making him a vampire. He loves her for the next century until he falls for Buffy, someone even more lethal than Dru, and finally dying spectacularly in the series finale to save her and defeat his kind. Giles, Buffy's Watcher, falls in love with a fellow teacher and then, on the night they plan to consummate their love, finds her dead in his bed ("Passion," 2-17). But the real champ in the Sex-Is-Death sweepstakes is Xander, who ignores nonlethal and therefore nonsexual Willow to lust after a substitute teacher who invites him to her house for a study date and turns into a praying mantis ("Teacher's Pet," 1-4), an undead exchange student whose kiss causes death ("Inca Mummy Girl," 2-4), and Cordelia, who wishes him into an alternate universe where he's a vampire staked by Buffy ("The Wish," 3-9). When he tries to be proactive and use magic to make things work, hordes of women attack him, ready to love him to death ("Bewitched, Bothered, and Bewildered," 2-16). He loses his virginity to deviant Slayer Faith, who tries to strangle him when he comes back for seconds, and proposes to Anya the Vengeance Demon who does her best to eviscerate him by proxy when he leaves her at the altar. Then his rebound date strings him up above an ancient symbol and penetrates his abdomen with a spear so that his blood will unleash the undead ("First Date," 7-14).

Still, the most interesting sex-as-pain-and-death relationship in this series is Buffy and Spike. Their frequent physical fights grow more and more sexual, so that when Spike finally tells Buffy he loves her, and she tries to track back to where she went wrong, she decides it's the pain: "I do beat him up a lot. For him, that's like third base" ("Crush," 5-14). The foreplay for their first sexual encounter is a knockdown fight, during which Spike tells her, "I wasn't planning to hurt you, much," right before she hits him and then kisses him and then hits him again ("Smashed," 6-9). It's important that Buffy doesn't sleep with Spike until she knows the prophylactic chip in his head does not work for her, because it means that in the heated proximity of the rough sex they become addicted to, they're both easy to kill, each knowing that the "little death" of orgasm can, at any moment, change from symbol to reality, and the fact that the sex is violent simulates this. They're miming death over and over again, practicing the moment they both assume they're hurtling toward, the moment they fulfill their roles as Vampire Slayer and Slayer Assassin. That erotic risk coupled with their repeated demonstrations of unconditional love makes their twisted relationship one of the most powerful ever written, a fitting climax to a series in which "dying for a kiss" isn't just a figure of speech, at least not for Spike.

But Whedon's greatest love story doesn't stop there. He takes it down another layer, to the metaphor that fuels the series and raises the romances of *Buffy* to the level of myth: Buffy as the Slayer is unconditionally, inextricably, erotically tied to Death.

Angel's transformation into a vampire after their first kiss in the first season is the only incident in the series in which sexual arousal is directly linked to becoming the monster, but it ties into the long tradition of oral eroticism that the vampire story has represented since Bram Stoker's *Dracula*. Buffy screams when confronted with the truth, but it's a truth that she needs to face. She can't remain an innocent and save the world, too, just as she can't remain sexually innocent and become a mature woman. That metaphor is reinforced when she makes love with Angel for the first time and wakes up with Angelus, a move that at first glance seems only to symbolize "all men are beasts," but comes to mean that all lovers are dangerous when Buffy proves to be just as lethal as Angelus. When Buffy refuses to destroy Angelus, she protects death; when she sacrifices Angel to save the world, she sacrifices love.

The power of this metaphor also explains Buffy's failed relationship with Riley. Yes, their love is conditional, but what really undercuts their relationship is a much deeper failing: Riley is the wrong metaphor. As the corn-fed farm boy, Riley represents the Beautiful American, light and peace and wholesomeness, and Buffy wants to connect to him because she wants to be Good's Girlfriend. But the relationship feels wrong: Riley wears a milk mustache while Buffy's hands drip blood. His appreciation of her as the Slayer seems to stem from the fact that she's really athletic and great at covert ops, just like one of the guys. He never seems to understand what Angel and Spike know instinctively, that Buffy has a heart of darkness. As Buffy comes to understand this herself, the series darkens but it also deepens, becoming much richer as each season adds more layers to the metaphor, so that in the last three seasons Whedon connects directly with this paradox at the core of Buffy, the complexity that made the series so irresistible from the beginning: Our savior is a murderess, and she's infatuated with Death.

The clearest embodiment of that is her relationship with Spike. Everything in their interactions reeks of sex and death, from the moment in "Fool for Love" (5-7) when Spike tells her that he's waiting for her to get tired of the struggle and come to him to be taken. He looms over her, phallic pool cue in hand, whispering in her ear that all he needs to get her is "One. Good. Day," and becomes the symbol that eroticizes Buffy's dark side. This makes it all the more perplexing that the Mutant Enemy writers see their relationship as one-sided and harmful. In what was evidently one of the great botched metaphors in the history of storytelling, Buffy and Spike consummate their relationship and demolish a derelict mansion in their throes. Houses are a common symbol for people in stories (think of Roderick Usher's mansion in "The Fall of the House of Usher" or Emily's decaying home in Faulkner's *Rose for Emily*), and this one seems to clearly represent Buffy's once rich but now derelict past life. She has died in one life and been resurrected into a new one, but she's clinging to the past, living in the decaying shell of her former existence, an old life that must be rejected before she can live fully in the new world. When she embraces Spike, she embraces the dark side of her destiny, an adult rejection of the simplistic good/evil universe of her childhood, freeing herself to move into the future and defeat the worst enemy of all, the First Evil. Their consummation takes them to their deepest levels, both symbolically and literally as they fall into the basement, and leaves Buffy standing in a shaft of light in the morning, reborn. As metaphoric scenes go, it's one of the most powerful in the history of the series.

Except that's evidently not what the writers had in mind, since they insisted in interviews that the wreck symbolized the relationship as a bad choice. If Spike and Buffy wreck her cheery little bungalow home, that's bad. If they dismantle a church, that's bad. If they demolish a deserted, derelict mansion, that's urban renewal. The continued insistence throughout season six that this relationship is wrong, unhealthy, symbolic of something evil and immoral is not only inexplicable but annoying, which is probably why so many viewers are unhappy with the direction the series takes in the sixth season: they were reading a different metaphor than the writers intended.

But in the seventh season, Whedon brings the story back to its roots by taking it down one more metaphoric layer, to the beginning of his myth. In "Get It Done" (7-15), Buffy travels back to the beginning of the slayers and discovers that the first Slayer was created when a council of men chained a helpless girl to be raped by a demon in order to imbue her with supernatural powers that would protect them. The concept of the Slayer has always been a violation of free will, from the very first episode in which Buffy is forced back to her role as Slayer against her wishes to the last season populated by bewildered and frightened Potentials who would rather just go home. In "Get It Done" (7-15), the image of a chained Buffy penetrated both orally and vaginally by the creeping black vapor of the demon, symbolizes this violation at the center of the myth, the rape of free will that every Slayer represents. As defined by the council, the creation of the Slayer was a violent sexual sacrifice to death, a sacrifice that is destined to be repeated in every generation.

But the myth of *Buffy the Vampire Slayer* has never been the myth of the Slayer; it's the myth of Buffy Summers, the Slayer who is different. Instead of obeying and dying like her predecessors, season after season, she has rejected the male power hierarchies that have tried to control her. She defies Giles in the first season and makes him treat her as a partner in decision making. She fires the council in season three, and when they come back for season five, she defeats them and forces them to work for her. In season seven, she goes back to the beginning and defies the original council, resetting the power structure at the heart of myth and taking back her story, and refusing the rape and its sexual-submission-as-power ploy, saying "You think I came all this way to get knocked up by some demon dust?" ("Get It Done," 7-15). She is the Slayer who is different, the lover who embraces death on her own terms, the blonde who goes into the alley and comes back with patriarchy's head, and she does it not as a virginal, powerless Joan of Arc (even if she wistfully christens herself "Joan" in "Tabula Rasa," 6-8), but as a fiercely sexual, passionate woman who knows exactly what she's doing when she opens her arms to darkness.

In a world where any attempt to find connection results in pain and death, love is an act of unbelievable courage. That *Buffy the Vampire Slayer* explores that dangerous act in so many forms on so many levels through so many characters is the most compelling aspect of the series. But first among equals, it is Buffy in her passion and in her blazing, defiant sexuality that most defines the myth. Buffy, the great feminist icon as warrior, lover, and finally mature woman. She's our Ishtar who aced the SATs, our Morrigan with a snarky sense of humor, our Kali with a better fashion sense, and the complexity of her myth, the depth of her metaphor, and the truth of her love stories makes her a great romantic heroine and *Buffy the Vampire Slayer* one of the great romances of our time.

Jenny Crusie began writing fiction in 1991 as part of her doctoral dissertation research at Ohio State. When the fiction turned out to be vastly more interesting than the research, she switched to the MFA program. She sold her first book in 1992 and followed that with fourteen more novels including five for St. Martin's Press that have earned her New York Times *and* USA Today *best-seller status. She thinks* Buffy the Vampire Slayer *is the best thing that ever happened to television, and Joss Whedon is God.*

Marguerite Krause

THE MEANING
OF *BUFFY*

Marguerite Krause reveals the meaning of Buffy and along the way discusses Buffy's relationship with her mom, possible romance between Buffy and Giles (yuck), Cordelia's self-love, and other fascinating topics.

ANYONE WHO HAS WATCHED more than a few episodes of *Buffy the Vampire Slayer* quickly figures out that this television program isn't really about a gorgeous young woman who kills blood-sucking monsters. Sure, most of the episodes contain pivotal scenes of vampire staking or demon decapitation—but they're not what the show is *about*. In fact, at its core, *Buffy* isn't even about any of the obvious metaphors that the whole mythology (heroic champion of the innocent battling monsters) might suggest, such as high school as a living hell, or the eternal battle of Good and Evil.

From the very first episode of the series to the final story, on the most consistent, fundamental level, *Buffy* has been about relationships—how to create them, and how to sustain them once you have them. Not just any relationship, either, but the kind that is strong enough and deep enough to provide answers to life's ultimate questions (why am I here? where am I headed? what does it all mean?).

The opening scenes of "Welcome to the Hellmouth" (1-1) establish dramatic themes and plot patterns that reverberate throughout the rest of the series. When Buffy Summers arrives in Sunnydale, the last thing she's thinking about is vampire slaying. Buffy has one and only one subject uppermost in her mind: her relationships with the people around her.

The first example we're shown is the mother-daughter relationship. Although we clearly see their affection for one another, there's a lot of strain between Buffy and her mother Joyce because of Buffy's past behavior and because of the fact that she must keep secret a critical area of her life—her activities as the Slayer. Her need to resort to secrets and deceptions underlies another of the recurring themes of the show: the isolation of the individual.

Once the basic parameters of the Buffy-Joyce interaction are established, "Welcome to the Hellmouth" (1-1) moves on to show Buffy exploring another kind of relationship: friendship with her peers. Much of this first episode is devoted to Buffy's efforts to determine her place in the social structure of Sunnydale High. Who will be her friends and allies, who will be her enemies, and how can she tell the difference?

The creation and development of relationships is not restricted to the first episode of *Buffy*, or the first few episodes, or the first season. In every episode, no matter what else is happening in that specific story, relationship issues are never far from the surface.

This quest for meaningful relationships lies at the core of the phenomenon that is *Buffy*. With that as the heart and soul of this remarkable television series, is there one relationship that stands out from all the rest? One exemplary pairing of characters that represents the ideal to which all the others aspire? One couple who embodies the answer to the question of the meaning of life in the *Buffy* universe?

Let's examine the likely suspects.

We've already touched on the mother-daughter relationship. Buffy and Joyce interact in mostly healthy, supportive ways, but in the vast majority of episodes, Buffy has to deceive her mom about crucially important events in her life. This forms an insurmountable barrier between them, made up of lack of communication, mistrust, and outright lies. Given the circumstances, they have a remarkable relationship, but it remains fundamentally flawed. Even after Joyce eventually learns that her daughter is endowed with supernatural powers and involved in a never-ending battle to protect the world from Evil, the tension between them never completely goes away. Joyce and Buffy each yearn to protect the other from danger and unhappiness, and this clash of priorities cannot be resolved. Their fears and doubts put them at odds with one another for the rest of Joyce's life. Buffy loves her mom, but she—and therefore we, the audience—can't find complete comfort or a fundamental meaning of existence within the context of that relationship.

What about the father-daughter relationship? Buffy seems to feel affection for her father, but he's completely disconnected from her daily life. For all practical purposes, as far as the series is concerned, they don't *have* a relationship. Instead, Buffy has Giles. At the beginning, Buffy fights the whole idea of being part of a Slayer-Watcher team, but strong bonds of mutual reliance, trust, and affection soon begin to grow between them. Buffy learns that even when other aspects of her life are a shambles, she can rely on Giles. He is her moral compass, a rock of certainty, a dependable touchstone in the often confusing and conflicting labyrinth of dreams and responsibilities, wishful thinking and harsh reality that Buffy has to negotiate week after week.

From one perspective—that of the Watchers' Council—there is no question whatsoever that the entire meaning of Buffy's existence is defined by and fulfilled in her partnership with Giles. After all, she is the Slayer, and nothing can be more important than her ongoing quest to successfully save the world from destruction. By that argument, the next most important person in the world has to be her Watcher. First, he is the brains to her brawn, providing the factual information and strategic advice she needs in order to win her battles. Second, he possesses a degree of maturity and wisdom that enable him to guide Buffy when the ethics of a situation are unclear and facts alone aren't enough to determine the best course of action. Third, Giles provides essential emotional support, reassuring Buffy when she has doubts, encouraging her to face her fears and triumph over despair.

Yet, in spite of all these logical reasons that Buffy's relationship with Giles should be the philosophical center and emotional heart and soul of the show, it never pretended to hold that position. As mentor, advisor, and friend, Giles played an important role in many of the stories. But the true meaning of *Buffy* cannot be found in the Slayer-Watcher relationship.

There is no doubt that Buffy and Giles feel deep affection for one another, but the instances in which they openly express or share emotional closeness are fleeting. Giles is a father figure, but *only* a figure, not the real thing, which automatically puts him at a disadvantage in his interactions with Buffy. Because he isn't really Buffy's father, they cannot achieve *and maintain* the depth of intimacy that is the ideal in family relationships. Because he is not one of her peers, they can't share the emotional closeness that is possible in a relationship of equals.

Could Giles and Buffy *become* equals? After all, over the course of the series, Buffy has turned eighteen and met all the criteria that normally identify a fully mature, independent adult—going to college, running a household (after Joyce's death), becoming part of the staff at Sunnydale High. Some fans love imagining that a mature, romantic relationship could develop between Buffy and Giles (or has already happened, hidden in subtext and "between the lines" of the aired episodes). For most people, though, the possibility is too awkward to contemplate for long. Too many episodes, especially in the first three seasons of the show, emphasized the high-school environment and the recurring theme of Buffy's childhood innocence in conflict with the demands of her responsibilities as Slayer. To put Giles, with his status as parental stand-in and undeniable authority figure, in a romantic relationship with Buffy smacks uncomfortably of incest.

Whether you find such speculations intriguing, disturbing, or incomprehensible, they're also outside the scope of the present discussion. Exploring all the "might have beens" in the series opens up far too many variables. If we stay strictly within the boundaries of events and character interactions presented in the episodes as broadcast, it's clear that Giles and Buffy interacted sometimes as father and daughter, sometimes as mentor and student; no matter their precise roles, their attempts at mutual understanding were often awkward and imperfect.

The shining example of a healthy, successful relationship in the *Buffy* universe has to be sought elsewhere.

Throughout the series, Buffy's strongest relationships are with her peers. Most are fellow students, including Willow, Xander, Cordelia, Oz, Tara, and Riley. Other characters are not literally Buffy's peers— they aren't exactly her age or facing the same social circumstances— but still have to be considered peers in a broader sense. These include her sister, Dawn; her true love, Angel; troubled Faith; sometime-demon Anya; and, in later seasons, the unbelievably confused and confusing Spike.

One word can sum up Buffy's relationships with each of these people and, just as important, their relationships with one another and Giles: complex. Early in the series, Buffy loved Angel, Xander loved Buffy, Willow loved Xander, and Cordelia loved . . . well, Cordelia. Everybody hated Spike, except for Dru, who loved him—that is, until she was distracted by Angelus, and eventually demonstrated that she was too self-involved to *really* love anyone. The farther the series progressed, the more complicated and contradictory the relationships among all of the characters became. The ever-changing nature of these relationships makes for utterly fascinating storytelling, but far from satisfying lives for the characters themselves. Whatever they think they know about the person standing next to them one week may be irrelevant, or dead wrong, the next. The ignorant, cruel, completely self-absorbed Cordelia of the early episodes evolves into a helpful member of the Scooby gang and, eventually, Xander's affectionate girlfriend. Angel changes, quite literally, from romantic hero to despicable monster and back again. Even a despised enemy like Spike becomes a valued ally under the right circumstances and by the climax of the series finale, "Chosen (7-22)," a true champion. Early in the seventh season, relationships among Buffy and her friends are so thoroughly convoluted that Nancy in "Beneath You" (7-2) is justified in asking, "Is there anyone here who hasn't slept together?"

Sometimes an unlikely, transient relationship is played for comic effect, as when Joyce and Giles succumb to their inner teens in "Band Candy" (3-6). In "Tabula Rasa" (6-8), the idea of Giles and Spike as father and son was absurd and perfect at the same time, but other of the humorously scrambled relationships in that story had a poignant undertone, such as Xander assuming he belonged with lifelong friend Willow, or Anya and Giles struggling to understand the nature of their connection. An interesting aspect of this episode is which of the *real* relationships made themselves felt despite the power of Willow's spell of forgetfulness. Note that Buffy and Dawn quickly realized they were sisters, Spike made an emotional connection with Buffy, and Tara and Willow were inexorably drawn together.

A common thread runs through almost all of the character relationships in the *Buffy* universe: eventually, on one level or another, they fail. All the way back in the first season, at the end of "I Robot, You Jane" (1-8), Buffy and Xander try to make Willow feel better for having fallen in love with the demon Moloch, disguised as cyber pen pal Malcolm. They joke and laugh about Xander having loved the praying-mantis teacher and Buffy loving a vampire. Buffy says, "Face it, none of us are ever going to have a healthy, normal relationship," and Xander replies, "We're doomed." At that, their amusement fades, and the episode ends with all of them looking distinctly worried. With good reason: as future stories prove, one initially promising relationship after another is destined to go down in defeat.

The love between Buffy and Angel is the first of what becomes a depressing pattern of interpersonal relationship failures. Buffy and Angel may be soul mates, deeply, passionately, and sincerely in love with one another, but time and again any hope of meaningful, lasting happiness is sabotaged by their inability to communicate fully with one another. They are weeks into their relationship before Buffy learns that Angel is a vampire, and he continues to keep most of the details of his past secret from her for the rest of their time together. Their favorite method for coping with uncomfortable subjects is to not talk about them. This makes it easier for Buffy to concentrate on her feelings for Angel the man, and avoid thinking about Angelus the demon, but it doesn't help at all when it comes to building a foundation for a lasting relationship.

Lack of communication damages Angel's and Buffy's relationships—as a couple and as individuals—with all of the other characters, too. Buffy hesitates to describe the true depth of her feelings for Angel, or the reasons she trusts him, to Giles or any of her friends, leaving them to conclude that any of her decisions regarding Angel are clouded by adolescent passion and therefore not to be trusted. Jenny Calendar fails to share her suspicions about the gypsy curse and its possible consequences with Giles or Buffy, which leads to the loss of Angel's soul and the resurrection of Angelus. After Angel's soul is restored and he survives banishment to Hell to return to Sunnydale once more, his ability to communicate with the Scoobies is even more severely restricted than before. They can't distinguish between Angel and Angelus, and for the most part don't even make an effort to try. Without their trust and forgiveness, Angel can't form meaningful relationships with Buffy's companions.

Some of the factors that stand in the way of Buffy and Angel finding happiness together are outside their control. Angel can't stop being a two-centuries-old vampire, and Buffy can't stop being the Slayer. Ultimately, however, their relationship fails because of the choices they make. Each wants what's best for the other, but wanting something and being able to imagine a way to achieve it are two very different things. Buffy, with the innocence of youth and the desperation of someone deeply in love, seems willing to try to fit Angel into her life, but Angel sees only the risks involved. The Mayor sums up Angel's dilemma for him in "Choices" (3-19), when he says, "What kind of a life can you offer her? I don't see a lot of Sunday picnics in the offing. I see skulking in the shadows, hiding from the sun. She's a blossoming young girl and you want to keep her from the life she should have until it has passed her by. My God! I think that's a little selfish. Is that what you came back from Hell for? Is that your greater purpose?"

The final episode of season seven, "Chosen," offered the possibility that Buffy and Angel's relationship could change for the better, someday. As Buffy says, "In the midst of all this insanity, a couple of things are actually starting to make sense . . . I'm not finished becoming whoever the hell it is I'm going to turn out to be . . . Maybe one day I'll turn around and realize I'm ready. . . That'll be then. When I'm done."

However, with the end of the series, such speculation is mere wishful thinking. During the seven seasons of the show, without the ability to conceive any hope for the future, Angel's relationship with Buffy is doomed.

All of these elements—failure to communicate, lack of trust, inability to envision or create a viable future—disrupt the course of true love for couple after couple. Buffy and Riley are constantly hiding from one another, first literally, then emotionally. Oz can't maintain his relationship with Willow because he can't trust himself. Anya has no trouble at all expressing her true feelings, but Xander does, to the point that he doesn't even admit them to himself until the day of their wedding, when it's far too late. Giles and Buffy, for all their ties of duty and affection, and for all of their good intentions (Giles only wants what's best for Buffy), reach a point of such fundamental disagreement on how (or whether) their relationship needs to change that they can't even live on the same continent any more. Even after Giles returns to Sunnydale in "Bring on the Night" (7-10), he remains a mostly peripheral figure in Buffy's life. He and Buffy barely connect or communicate, a major factor in his decision to have Spike killed in "Lies My Parents Told Me" (7-17). Although they take the first steps toward reconciliation during "Chosen" (7-22), the details and stability of their new understanding are unclear.

There is only one exception to this pattern of relationships that fail: Willow and Tara.

On the surface, Willow and Tara face many of the same obstacles that we've seen before. But there are strong indications, from the earliest phases of their friendship, that Willow and Tara's relationship is different from any other explored in the show.

For the other characters, secrets and deceptions tend to take on a life of their own, with one lie leading to another until dishonesty becomes a habit and misunderstandings inevitable. When the truth is finally, reluctantly revealed, resentment and anger block attempts to repair the damage that's been done and move on to a new stage in the relationship. Buffy and Riley, for example, never fully come to terms with one another's mission in life. Even when their relationship is at its most mutually supportive, they don't seem to completely understand one another. Riley can't seem to come to grips with the reality of magic; Buffy can't understand how he can be so focused on "killing monsters" and miss the larger, more complex issues that are often at stake. As for Buffy and Spike, she's so ashamed of their relationship that she spends most of the sixth season unwilling to admit to her friends, Spike, or herself that it even exists. Xander and Anya keep whole lists of secrets from one another, as revealed in their song-and-dance number in the sixth season's "Once More, With Feeling" (6-7). When Xander commits what Anya perceives as the ultimate betrayal—abandoning her at the altar in "Hell's Bells" (6-16) —she can't forgive him, and the relationship, like so many before it, fails.

Not so for Willow and Tara. Their relationship breaks all the previously established rules. From their first encounter, at the Wiccan meeting in "Hush" (4-10), Tara offers unqualified, unselfish support to Willow. In that episode, Tara takes the risk of sharing her true self—her magical skills—with Willow without any sign of hesitation or doubt. And Willow accepts her offer to combine their power and work together with similar, unquestioning trust. The early stage of secret-keeping and deception, a guarantee of lasting trauma as far as all the other characters are concerned, barely happens between Willow and Tara. Although Willow demonstrates a measure of circumspection during her earliest conversations with Tara—admitting that she has some other friends she hangs out with, but not going into detail—Tara accepts her discretion as perfectly normal. What matters most to her is that Willow be comfortable in their friendship.

By the time of "Who Are You?" (4-16, six episodes after "Hush"), it's clear that Willow shares everything with Tara, and has told her all about Buffy and the Scooby gang. She hasn't told them about Tara yet, but not out of shame or fear or uncertainty: she's just so happy to be Tara's friend that she wants to savor the feeling in privacy for a while. When Willow finally does get a chance to introduce Tara to Buffy later in the same episode, it's a completely relaxed, positive experience (even though, early in the story, Faith disguised as Buffy was horrible to Tara). When Willow and Tara's friendship deepens and they become lovers, Buffy initially is a little freaked ("New Moon Rising," 4-19), but she quickly gets over the surprise. As she reassures Riley later, speaking as much about herself as about his reaction to Willow having dated Oz: "You found out that Willow was in kind of an unconventional relationship, and it gave you a momentary wiggins. It happens." From that point on, Tara gradually becomes a respected part of the Scooby gang.

Tara does keep one secret from Willow for a time but, instead of driving a wedge between them, its revelation draws them even closer to one another. In the fifth-season episode "Family" (5-6), Tara's father, brother, and cousin arrive in Sunnydale and try to convince Tara to come home with them. Her father insists—and Tara grew up believing—that she has magic abilities because she is part demon, a curse theoretically passed down through the female side of their family. Tara reluctantly prepares to abandon the life she's built for herself in Sunnydale, rather than risk having Willow and her friends learn her "dark secret." However, before she is whisked away by her relatives, Spike proves there is no demon in her, and cleverly guesses the truth: "It's just a family legend, am I right? Just a bit of spin to keep the ladies in line?" The Scoobies prevent Tara's father from taking her away; when he challenges their right to interfere, Buffy's response is short and to the point: "We're family." Their support mirrors Willow's unconditional acceptance. Instead of feeling threatened or betrayed by the fact that Tara concealed an important part of her background, Willow understands and sympathizes with her fears, and states her admiration that, despite everything, Tara has overcome her difficulties to become the warm, open-hearted woman Willow loves.

This brings us to a crucial question. Why does the Willow-Tara pairing succeed when all other relationships in the *Buffy*verse fail? Part of the credit must go to Willow. Of all the members of the Scooby gang, she seems the most sympathetic and supportive of her friends and the least prone to holding a grudge. When she does make a mistake—as in "Something Blue" (4-9), where her inadvertent curses of her friends start her down the path to becoming a vengeance demon—she recognizes it, apologizes sincerely, and does what she can to make amends. Still, all of Willow's sterling qualities can't sustain her relationship with Oz. There has to be another factor at work—and that factor is Tara.

In her early appearances, Tara didn't make a strong impression on most people (either the other characters, or the audience watching the show). She was shy and self-effacing. Under the least bit of social pressure, she blushed and stuttered and ducked her head as if she were not only afraid to speak up for herself, but convinced before she started that it wouldn't do any good to try. To outside observers, she seemed to be no more than an appendage to Willow—a friend and, later, lover who made Willow happy, and a moderately talented magic user who could help the more powerful Willow realize her full potential. But that was all.

Such surface impressions, however, don't do justice to Tara's true personality. Beneath the shy, quiet exterior lay untapped reserves of moral courage and emotional strength. In her first episode, "Hush" (4-10), she braved the dark, silent campus and the threat of capture by The Gentlemen to bring Willow information that might enable them to break the spell of silence that had crippled the town. In "Who Are You?" (4-16), she provided the knowledge Willow needed to search for Buffy's essence, and an anchor to guide Willow back when her search was complete. In "New Moon Rising" (4-19), Tara was prepared to stand aside and let Oz resume his place as most significant person in Willow's life, if that was what would make Willow happy. Again and again, as the series progressed, Tara consistently acted with Willow's welfare uppermost in her mind.

This doesn't mean that Tara and Willow's relationship was completely lacking in conflict or challenges. However, although they occasionally disagreed with or disappointed one another, they both knew how to give and accept apologies. Most important of all, they knew how to forgive.

Willow's addiction to magic in the sixth season strained her relationship with Tara to the breaking point. By the end of "Tabula Rasa" (6-8), when Tara moves out of the Summers house and, for all practical purposes, out of Willow's life, it looks as if they've been defeated by the Sunnydale Curse: too many lies culminating in an unforgivable betrayal.

But then something unprecedented happens. Instead of resenting the fact that Tara left her (or simply retreating into self-pity as she does after Oz's departure in "Wild at Heart"), Willow soon takes responsibility for the damage she did to their relationship, and resolves to set things right. After reaching the low point of allowing her thirst for magic to endanger Dawn's life ("Wrecked," 6-10), she finally accepts the advice Tara gave her in "Tabula Rasa" (6-8), and gives up magic entirely, and then sticks to her resolve even when events in such episodes as "Older and Far Away" (6-14) and "Normal Again" (6-17) tempt her to regret her decision. Tara's reaction to Willow's efforts are most significant of all. Although she left Willow for entirely justifiable reasons—Willow lied to her and manipulated her perceptions and memories—she doesn't abandon her completely. Even though she has been betrayed in the most personal ways possible, Tara acknowledges the betrayal, accepts it . . . and moves on. Her anger and disappointment don't prevent her from continuing to love Willow. Tara's inner strength, patience, and commitment give Willow the time she needs to regain her self-control and self-esteem. By the time of "Entropy," (6-18), Willow has done her best to overcome her magic addiction and make amends for the harm she has caused, and at that point Tara is willing to not only support her but also *forgive* her and build their relationship anew. Together, they learn from their mistakes. Together they are stronger, happier, better people than they ever could be separately.

After Tara's death in "Seeing Red" (6-19), Willow forgets what she had learned, for a while. But not forever. Xander can't take Tara's place, but he can force Willow to remember what she had learned with Tara. In the end, the fact that Willow and Tara's relationship was cut short by Warren's careless cruelty doesn't change the fundamental nature of that relationship, or its ultimate success.

Buffy the Vampire Slayer isn't about killing monsters. *Buffy* is about the search for meaning in life. Again and again, that meaning is found in reliable, balanced, loving partnerships between individuals. Saving the world is all well and good, but any accomplishment is hollow without someone to share it with at the end of the day. All of the characters have stumbled in and out of relationships, some lasting longer than others, with friends, family, and lovers—all, with one exception, have failed. Some of the relationships, admittedly, weren't given the chance to achieve their full potential. Giles and Jenny Calendar, for instance, showed signs in "Becoming, Part 1" (6-21) of being on the brink of achieving a level of trust, communication, and forgiveness that might have overcome their initially rocky start. In season seven, Willow begins a romance with Kennedy, one of the potential Slayers, but it lacks the depth and intensity of her relationship with Tara. Granted, in the final episodes, little time is available for developing personal relationships. However, that doesn't entirely excuse the essential shallowness of Willow's and Kennedy's interactions. Perhaps, given time, they could become equal partners in a rich and complex relationship. Kennedy finds Willow attractive. Willow, who struggles with indecision and self-doubt throughout the crisis with the First, relies on Kennedy for strength and support. If there is anything more to their love, we're never given the opportunity to see it.

But we don't have to rely on what ifs or might have beens to find our model for ultimate meaning in *Buffy*. Tara and Willow showed all of us—their friends and the audience—how to achieve the highest standards of love. Honesty. Communication. Acceptance. Encouragement. Support. Commitment. Conviction. Forgiveness. Determination to never give up.

And *that* is what *Buffy* is all about.

Marguerite Krause's favorite activities involve working with words. In addition to writing, she works as a freelance copyeditor, helping other writers to sharpen their skills, and for relaxation loves nothing better than to curl up with a good book. She also has a master's degree in music and performs with a local symphony orchestra, and has held a variety of jobs over the years: short-order cook, day-care provider, ice-cream packer, and driver for a courier company. She is married to her high-school sweetheart; they have two children. Her two-part epic fantasy novel, Moons' Dreaming *and* Moons' Dancing, *cowritten with Susan Sizemore, will be released by Five Star (a Gale Imprint) in Fall 2003.*

Sarah Zettel

WHEN DID THE SCOOBIES BECOME INSIDERS?

I know, I know, season four was flawed and season six was depressing, but I don't care. Every season of Buffy works for me; I love them all. Every season has its brilliance, its joy (OK, less so in seasons six and seven), its intensity. But I have to admit that something is different about the later seasons — not worse, I won't concede that, but different. But I could never put my finger on what it was. Sarah Zettel can, and does.

ELLO. MY NAME IS SARAH and I'm a *Buffy the Vampire Slayer* fan. (*Hi, Sarah.*)

I've been crazy about the concept of *Buffy* since a friend of mine brought over the original movie one Halloween. When I heard they were making a series, I was actually *worried*, because I wasn't sure they'd be able to match the quality of the film. Needless to say, I got over that in a hurry.

I'm writing this shortly after the season seven finale, the series finale. Looking back across seven years of Buffy, I think I've found the series' essential underpinning. It's somewhere in most, if not all, of the stories. It's certainly been explored at one time or another with each of the regular characters, and most of the incidental characters as well. It's the idea of the outsider. Who is an outsider? What does it mean that they are "outside"? When is it better to be an outsider than insider?

But there's been more to it than that. At the beginning of the show the heroes were energized by their status as outsiders. Being distanced from the norm gave them their ability to see clearly, to move freely and to empathize with others. Insiders, those with power and popularity, were portrayed as shallow, self-centered, or blinkered, where they weren't actually evil.

Once they left high school, however, the status of the main characters changed from all being outsiders to that of being insiders. They are the only ones in possession of the truth about Sunnydale and its demons. They alone have a clear understanding of how these dangers must be dealt with.

But despite this fundamental change in the portrayal of the characters, the portrayal and consequences of being insiders did not change. Now the heroes are becoming, well, shallow, self-centered, or blinkered, where they aren't actually evil.

In the beginning, there was the word . . . okay there was the Library. There was also Buffy, alone in a new school and desperately trying not to be who she is. There was Willow, awkward and ostracized and pining after Xander who in turn was awkward and ostracized and pining after . . . anybody pretty (except Willow). They were three outsiders who shared a secret that pulled them even further outside of the everyday life of school, friends, and family.

It wasn't just the three young heroes who were outsiders in the first three seasons. Giles carries the weight of secrets as well as duty, on top of being a librarian in a California town *not* noted for its intellectual aspirations, not to mention being an Englishman in America. Then, of course, we had Angel, who couldn't be true to either part of his nature, and couldn't be fully trusted. Still later, we got Oz, with his aspirations to be a true musician, and the relapsing-recurring handicap of being a werewolf.

But it was this outsider status that was the source of their strength, and their unity. Their friendships, their secrets, their true lives pushed them out of a mainstream that didn't have room for them, and didn't particularly want to make room for them. Our gang not only had their other worldly enemies, personified by Principal Snyder, but the continuous, everyday enemy that was high-school and Life. This pair pounded them with lousy relationships and personal disappointments. It was the fight, the thing that dragged them the farthest outside "normal" life that gave them their rare moments of triumph and a sustaining friendship. If Buffy and the other heroes had ties to pull them away from world-saving, they would not have become so good at it so quickly. They also would not have become such good friends.

The best example of the strength outsider status is Cordelia. Cordelia is directly and repeatedly affected by Sunnydale demonic nature. She, however, is extremely reluctant to join in the fight. Her life is too good as it is. She does not want to change, or to risk the status quo. Cordelia does not become a truly effective member of the team, or a fully-likeable person, until she decides to assert her independence and come out of the closet with her relationship with Xander. In so doing, she becomes an outsider herself and scomes into possession of the personal qualities that are truly important and praiseworthy.

With the arrival of Faith, we get an ongoing example of the dangers of wanting too badly to be an insider. When she feels excluded by the Gang and overshadowed by Buffy, Faith goes looking for approval and inclusion on the other side. The Mayor offers her love and praise that she could not find with the heroes. Unlike Cordelia, who has too much to find her way as an outsider, Faith has too little. Her neediness leaves her vulnerable to the predations of the ones who want to use her (of course, the Mayor really did love her, but that's another essay).

The defeat of the Mayor and their emergence from high school brings about the reversal of the Scoobies' status from outsiders to insiders. The Big Bad of season four, the season that covers Buffy's first year of college, is inherently different from all the other villains we've seen. The Initiative and Professor Walsh are not extra-knowledgeable about the situation they've entered. Unlike the Mayor, Spike, Dru, and Angelus, or even the Master, they don't have any special experience or insight. The Initiative's ignorance is what makes them dangerous. The Mayor understands precisely what he is doing when he seeks to become a demon, and he's looking forward to it. Professor Walsh, however, has no real understanding of what she's starting when she creates Riley, let alone Adam. She and the Initiative ignore the reality of magic and the particular logic of the supernatural. As a result, they become the proverbial bull in the china shop, and come very close to smashing what they are seeking to save, namely, the world.

In this season, it's Buffy and the others who have the true understanding of who they are and what is happening around them, and it is their understanding that enables them to stop Adam and his creators.

The character development that best exemplifies the overall shift from outsider to insider in season four is Willow. The pagan group at UC Sunnydale she seeks to join has no idea of the reality of what being a witch means. It's Willow who knows the truth. By forming a friendship with Willow, Tara is brought inside the secret and from there, into her real life.

In season four, we also get the return of a character who, like Faith, clearly illustrates the dangers of wanting to be an insider. Jonathan. Like Faith, inclusion and acceptance become more important to him than morality or independence. He cannot accept being an outsider, and, as with Faith, this brings about his downfall.

At first, Jonathan is nothing more nor less than a high-school nebbish who falls into an extreme form of the despair many of us who were outsiders in high school felt. I'm never getting out of this. I'm never going to have friends, love, any kind of life. Nobody understands. I might as well be dead.

Jonathan feels even more excluded from normal life than the heroes. He, out of all the students, recognizes Buffy as an insider rather than an outsider. It's not an accident that it's Jonathan who gives the speech naming Buffy as class protector, or that he's in the thick of the fight at graduation, along with Larry (another outsider who got very comfortable with his true self, thanks to Xander).

But in the season-four episode "Superstar" (4-17) we find that instead of being cured of the worst of his troubles by Buffy's intervention, Jonathan is still longing for inclusion. So much so that he's willing to take a dangerous magical shortcut to get it. As the Superstar, he not only knows all about the demons and the vampires, he's better at fighting them than Buffy is. To be fully inside and on top of the world, he's got to know all that the Scoobies do, and then some. At the end of it, himself once more, and saved from himself once more by Buffy, he's contrite and, it appears, on the road to recovery. Surely by now he's going to accept that he's an outsider and build his life the slow, hard way, as our heroes had to do when they were outsiders.

Fast-forward to season six and we see that's a no-go. Jonathan is still longing for inclusion, and inclusion once again involves doing the Scoobies one better. He believes that secret knowledge of magic and the demonic will give him the life that he wants. This is the knowledge and power that the Scoobies possess in depth, and he knows it. In joining up with Warren and Andrew, he not only gains inseparable comrades, like Buffy has, he gets to use what little he knows about Sunnydale, to gain, he hopes, power and prestige—again, like Buffy has, in his view. The Scoobies are the measure of what Jonathan wants to be. He just doesn't understand how to get there.

We see this again at the beginning of season seven when he returns to Sunnydale. He doesn't seem to really want to save the world, or that's not all he wants to do. He wants to make things up to Buffy and the others.

In season six, instead of being the ones to avoid, the Scoobies have become the ones to beat. By season seven, they are the powers to appease and emulate. Andrew, like Jonathan longing for acceptance, actually manages to become an insider through his status as a semi-scooby.

Another character whose appearance throws Buffy's status as insider into sharp relief is Dawn. Here is someone Buffy had to protect and keep secrets from. In effect, she had to exclude Dawn from the real life of Sunnydale as she herself was once excluded from the real life of high school and adolescence. The result is a jealous Dawn who desperately wants to come inside the secret world and be on a par with her Slayer sister.

While Buffy was in high school, the other citizens of Sunnydale actively avoided seeing what was going on around them much of the time, accepting what comforting lies they could. Even Joyce did not really want to see the truth. When Dawn is introduced, however, Buffy's secrets are being actively sought out. She is in possession of desirable, even vital, truths that make her not isolated or outcast, but special and superior.

Even the Watcher's Council are shown to be outsiders compared to Buffy in season five. In "Graduation Day" (3-21, 3-22), Buffy tells the Council what to do, rather than the other way around, because Buffy is the one with her finger on the pulse of the situation. Like the Initiative before them, the Council's ignorance of Sunnydale's hazards and complexities make the situation worse than it has to be. They must learn the truth of the matter from someone on the inside—in this case, Buffy.

By seasons six and seven, what were isolating secrets have become deeper truths. The powers and the knowledge of the Scoobies draw them further into the dark and unpleasant reality of life on the Hellmouth. Instead of being the outcasts, our gang are now the Secret Masters of Sunnydale. This culminates in the season seven finale, in which Buffy one-ups the ultimate insiders—the ancient magicians who created the Slayer line itself. This shift from outsiders to insiders created a serious problem for the ongoing story.

Never mind that now that the Mayor is gone, one has to suspend disbelief on a much stronger hook, because no one seems to be working to hide Sunnydale's secrets anymore (at least until everyone inexplicably leaves town). The foundation of the show is about outcasts and the status of being outcast, and that it is more important to do the right thing than it is to be included (witness what happens to Riley when he asserts independent thought instead of just going along with the Initiative). The status of the main characters has changed from weak outsiders to powerful insiders, but the overall story's depiction of the damaging consequences of what it is to be a powerful insider has not changed. Now that the heroes are inside and are the heavy players in the power game, they become continually more damaged and inflict more damage. Xander, rather than constantly being rejected, has the power to reject Anya, and the costs are huge. Willow, who has gone from the weak self-deprecating nerd to cool and powerful witch, nearly destroys the world. Buffy's attempts to cast herself out of life once she's been forced back into it nearly succeed, which probably would mean the end of the world, because she's already defeated all the easy Apocalypses (what *is* the correct plural, anyway?).

In addition, we have the ongoing problem that because they are so powerful and knowledgeable, our heroes must continually be made weak in order for there to be genuine conflict with whatever Big Bad has come along. The way Buffy and the others have been made weak since the beginning is some personal, emotional damage. The storyline necessitates that our powerful insider heroes be repeatedly emotionally hamstrung, because otherwise they are like Superman without kryptonite—invulnerable. So, there's not only no end to the evil Sunnydale inflicts, there doesn't seem to be a bottom to its despair either.

I miss the triumph. Back when the Scoobies were outsiders, there was a respite at the end of each adventure, a sense of "Whew! We did it. Good job." But for seasons five and six, even the final triumph has left the heroes measuring the deep cost, especially in blood and bodies. It does make you wonder why they don't seriously consider getting the heck out of Dodge. Except then the world would end, because they weren't there to stop it, and that really would get the guilt going.

Whistler tells Buffy that in the end she was always alone. Except that's never been true. There's always been help. The circle expands, and Good, or at the very least a lesser Evil, chips in. Buffy goes alone to fight Angelus, but she's still got Spike and Willow backing her up.

When the Mayor's ascension threatened the whole of Sunnydale's graduating class, Buffy and the others reached out. They found help among their peers and they all fought the good fight together. Not only that, but the good side of Faith, or some Good posing as Faith, gave Buffy the cornerstone to defeat the new-made demon.

But now that they are on the inside of Sunnydale's secrets, they seem unable or unwilling to reach out. There are no new good characters to come to their aid, no force of Good made manifest beyond them (unless you count Spike, and he's more of someone who needs saving that someone who will help save them). Good, when it shows, just dumps more responsibilities, like the Key, on the heroes, and vanishes.

I miss the idea that there is Good in the world beyond the main characters, that there is help, that there are resources they can call on beyond themselves. The beleaguered, weakened *loneliness* of them being the thin red line between the world and The End when they are flawed and tired and burdened by power, is becoming exhausting.

Our heroes, once the consummate, creative, energetic outsiders have now been walled up on the inside and do not seem able to find their way back out. For a series that once declaimed the triumphant power of friendship, independence and self-acceptance, it's a disappointing end.

Sarah Zettel was born in Sacramento, California. Since then, she has lived in three states, ten cities, and two countries. She has been writing fantasy and science fiction since she could pick up a pen. Her latest works are A Sorcerer's Treason *and* The Usurper's Crown.

Charlaine Harris

A REFLECTION ON UGLINESS

Award-winning author Charlaine Harris has a bone to pick with Joss Whedon. (I'll just get out of the way . . .)

I F YOU'VE WATCHED as many episodes of *Buffy* as I have, you've probably noticed an interesting phenomenon.

The monsters are all ugly. The good guys are all pretty.

Oh, I've had moments of disgruntlement with the *Buffy*verse.

For example, I'm a round person myself, and I've noticed Sunnydale doesn't exactly cater to the overweight. Well, okay. Probably living over the Hellmouth would make you so nervous you wouldn't eat much. And I've noticed that most of the Sunnydale populace is hardly what you would call racially diverse. Dawn has an African-American friend, and the villainous Mr. Trick is black. Mr. Wood, the last season's ambiguous principal, is black, and does finally emerge (mostly) on the side of good. But with those few exceptions, and the rare black vampire, the population of the town is pretty bleached. Okay . . . maybe the Hispanics and African-Americans were smarter than the WASPs, and got the hell out of Sunnydale. In a way, that absence of color is almost complimentary.

But ugliness is a different issue. If you're ugly, you're evil.

Think of it, if you haven't already. Buffy herself is lovely, of course. Her clothes are always cute. Her shoes never have scuff marks. Buffy's hair and makeup are perfection. That's understandable. She's the hero!

Willow, Xander, Giles, Cordelia, Oz, Dawn, Angel, Riley, Spike—all variations on hotness.

You'd think that *Buffy the Vampire Slayer*, of all shows—the only television show to ever acknowledge openly that high school is Hell and dating can be fatal—would show a little more sophistication in this department. But . . . no.

The tricky part is, some monsters aren't *always* ugly; that is, not one hundred percent of the time. (Well, trolls and goblins are; and demons, most often.) But Glory, the god, is beautiful most of the time. Even Ben, the male whose body she sometimes inhabits, is a very attractive young man. And Anya, the former vengeance demon, is cute enough in her human form to pass as just another coed at Sunnydale High. Angel and Spike are indisputably fantasy figures for millions of teenage girls—and some boys, too.

Corrupted humans—that is, those who started out good—get to keep their ordinary looks. Think of Faith, the Slayer who turns to the Dark Side in a major way, until season seven. Ethan Rayne, Giles's old college friend, is quite attractive, too, and evidently he was a barrel of fun when he and Giles were in their early twenties: but somewhere along the line, Rayne, too, felt the lure of Evil. The Mayor, Mr. Trick's boss, is looking forward to his transformation into pure Evil for much of his residence in Sunnydale, but he gets to retain a passable human form until then; and the same is true of Faith's evil Watcher, Gwendolyn Post, who seems like a perfectly proper woman at first.

But what happens when the completely transformed monster's true evil nature comes to the fore? Angel's forehead bulges, his fangs elongate, and he gets that squinty-eyed look. (Even though Buffy kisses him when Angel's transformed, he's definitely showing his ferocious side.) Ditto for Spike—when he's ready to attack, he bulges to the north and sprouts fangs to the south. Vengeance-demon Anya gets the cracked complexion of a snickerdoodle. Glory is simply monstrous. Seth Green, so adorable as Oz, makes a pretty nasty werewolf. In the first season, the four bullying high school students who are feared by the whole campus turn into hyenas—is that a great metaphor, or what? And they're really, really hideous.

You'll notice that, of these, Glory is the only one who has no Good side, or even normal side, to justify her pretty face. She is unique among Buffy baddies. Of all the monsters who have a physically attractive aspect, she alone has no redeeming features.

The rest of the monsters don't even give "cute" a nod.

The two gray-faced murdered children in the episode where Joyce tries to burn Buffy at the stake? They twine together to reveal their true form, a hideous German demonic figure.

Adam, the "perfect man" created by Dr. Walsh, handsome Riley's secretly demented boss in "The Initiative" (4-7)? Well, "perfect" Adam is intelligent, logical, and ferociously strong—but he's mad, and bad, and conscienceless. And, needless to say, completely hideous. Dr. Walsh, herself, I don't classify as evil. Dr. Walsh does not believe that of herself, and would only acknowledge that she was acting for a higher Good; and she retains her ordinary, middle-aged woman looks.

The serpent Glory sends after the Key, the serpent who can identify Dawn as being the object that Glory wants more than anything. Well, it's a twenty-foot-long serpent with a face. Need I say more? Ditto for the snake god Mikusa who lives below the fraternity house in *Buffy's* second season.

Glory's minions are "hobbits with leprosy," as Xander describes them—and that's pretty accurate.

Count Dracula—sure, he's supposed to look seductive. But he's whiter than a toothpaste ad (much whiter than the other vampires), and his hair is frizzy.

Principal Snyder? Malignancy embodied in a small man with snaggle teeth and bat ears, his face contorted in a permanent sneer.

And the eerily gliding monsters of "Hush" (4-10), whom I find most frightening of all—they're hideous in an almost classical, terrifying way. They're truly children's nightmares, with their silent smiles.

So why are the monsters almost invariably ugly?

I know that lots of different people wrote the scripts, but I assume they all had to follow a certain set of guidelines. I think the bad guys were doomed to be ugly. I think this may be Joss Whedon's way of telling us we all have an Evil side; that when we allow our darker side to dominate our behavior, we become ugly all the way through. This is a powerful thought, though not exactly an original one, and if it was a predetermined goal of the show, it's worked.

But, in my opinion, if this is Whedon's tactic, it's also misguided. Buffy makes lots of mistakes, while still remaining a hero. Lovable Xander, loyal Willow, literal Anya, intelligent Giles—all of them have faults and failings. And, like these *Buffy* characters, we all know that we're less than perfect.

Wouldn't we learn a more graphic lesson if the monsters retained their more attractive aspects even as they showed their most monstrous behavior? Evil is not so clearly denoted in the real world.

Maybe that's one of the reasons why we love *Buffy*. We know who's evil. The bad guys and gals *look* evil when they're *acting* evil. Not only that, in many cases we're forewarned. We get a clear signal that their worst nature is coming to the fore when they *turn* ugly (i.e., the vampires, Oz). Of course, this makes the villains easy to spot, so they're easier to fight and defeat.

Surviving in this world—even just surviving high school—would be a cinch, if villains all operated according to Sunnydale rules.

There have been signs that Whedon's view is growing more sophisticated. In recent years, the archenemies have become more attractive . . . or, at least, more mundane. Warren, for example, looks the same all the time—nerdy. Maybe it's no coincidence that Warren and his sidekicks Jonathan and Andrew are the least satisfying opponents beautiful Buffy has faced. Warren is a great illustration for the "the banality of Evil." When he originally entered the lives of the Scooby gang, it was as the despicable—but understandable—inventor of a beautiful robot, a robot who indignantly insisted that she was created to be a girlfriend, not a sexual toy. Warren programmed this robot to believe that a good girlfriend doesn't cry, a good girlfriend is always sexually available, and a girlfriend only speaks when she's spoken to. Furthermore, she always wants to do what Warren wants to do.

In creating a completely loving and yielding woman, Warren has created his own monster. Soon, he is bored with the poor thing, while she lacks the capacity to change her feelings toward him. This robot is the central sympathetic figure of an excellent episode, while her human creator, Warren, emerges as a creep. He's managed to connect with a real, flesh-and-blood girlfriend (and we wonder how, when we get to know Warren better in future episodes), and the robot has been abandoned in Warren's dorm room. When she tracks Warren down, she finds she's been betrayed. When her anger at this rejection leads her to violence, she's allowed to run down. But she's beautiful to the end; she's no real monster but a created artifact.

Warren, on the other hand, yields to more and greater Evil, in a rather unbelievable descent from a nerdy guy who wants a cute girlfriend to a brainy and amoral creep. Yet he still looks like the college kid next door—at least if you live in a white, middle-class town like Sunnydale. But in the end, even the human and average-looking Warren becomes a hideous monster, although not because he becomes some supernatural being. His inner ugliness is revealed by force when Willow flays him alive. Finally, Warren's outside matches his inside in horror.

Unlike most of the vampire cast, Angel and Spike have good sides, and those good sides predominate the longer the characters last in the series. The more the two vampires behave well, the more we are allowed to see them in their handsome personas. It's no coincidence that the Good side of their nature is manifested in their love for Buffy Summers, the Slayer. Buffy, though no intellectual, is pretty, strong, brave, and loyal. Her flaws (invariably picking the wrong man, being too quick to judgment) only make her more appealing.

The only episode I can recall in which Buffy even looked disheveled is the one in which she drank a lot of beer—beer that had been treated with magic. She and the cute guys she's drinking with (Buffy is going through one of her periodic attempts to be a normal girl) all turn into Neanderthals. (The boys end up looking gross. Buffy doesn't, though she's sloppy and her hair's a wreck.) The lesson's clear here: drinking turns you into a primitive and unpleasant creature, stupid and brutal.

And ugly.

It's pretty unfortunate that Whedon uses physical unattractiveness to signal moral decay. It's too simple a code. No one would ever believe the Master was up to any good, or the hammer-wielding troll that goes after Willow and Anya. I think today's audience could figure out the Bad Guy, even if he (or she) was most attractive. Glory, in her human guise, was a step in that direction, and Warren, Mr. Average, is even further along the trail. But both Glory and Warren took that last step.

They became ugly.

And Ugly, in *Buffy*, is Bad.

Charlaine Harris, who writes one conventional mystery series and one humorous/vampire/romance/adventure mystery series, lives in southern Arkansas with a husband, three children, a ferret, two dogs, and a duck. The duck stays outside. Charlaine won the 2002 Anthony Award for Dead Until Dark, *the debut novel of her vampire series. Almost needless to say, she loves Buffy.*

Jacqueline Lichtenberg

POWER
OF BECOMING

Is Faith hot? Is Angelus more fun than Angel? Is Dracula a master-bator? Is Buffy great literature? Acclaimed author Jacqueline Lichtenberg explores these questions (OK, actually just the last one) and along the way explains Buffy's magical initiation, the evolution of television, and the fundamental flaws in the Willow-Tara relationship.

*B*UFFY, THE VAMPIRE SLAYER is not "just" a television show. It is part of the process whereby television as an artistic medium is finally coming into its own in the world of Great Literature.

So what is Great Literature? As we learn in our first high-school literature courses, to qualify as Great Literature the events of the story must cause the main character to change inwardly, emotionally, either to be shattered or strengthened by the events. The characters learn lessons and become different people.

Great Literature is also identified by the effect on the reader—that the reader feels the characters' emotions and understands the impact of the lessons on the character—understands inwardly how it comes about that this kind of person becomes that kind of person because of the events in the story. Thus the work is memorable. The characters' journeys of becoming are indelibly stamped upon the reader's mind.

Beyond that, to be labeled "Great Literature" the piece has to contribute some distinctive evolutionary change to its field of literature and out-last its contemporaries.

Buffy's field of literature is the television dramatic series, and I believe I already see evidence that the show is contributing to a process whereby television is becoming a medium that can support Great Literature.[1]

In the 1960s commercial television discovered that the shows that made the most money were the ones that were "anthology series"—with the episode constructed so that at the end of the episode the ongoing characters are restored to the same emotional and physical condition they were in at the beginning. This allowed the individual shows to be aired in random order in reruns and still be understood by a new viewer. Thus the stories that could be told were disqualified from being called "literature" at all—never mind "great"—because the characters must not learn, grow, change, or become.

Gene Roddenberry often explained that *Star Trek: The Original Series* would not have been aired, or survived to go into reruns, if it had not been an anthology series. Hollywood was bewildered by the effect that *Star Trek* had on the teens of the 1970s, and tried many other things to capture that enthusiastic audience again. They fumbled for twenty years, but in the 1990s they finally got it.

I suspect the Internet allowed the producers very close contact with fan opinion, and they finally began to listen to what fans were saying. And some of them had been fans!

J. Michael Straczynski hung out with his fans via the *Babylon 5* (pilot 1993, first episode January 1994) newsgroup and really listened. *Babylon 5* was not the tremendous commercial success it needed to be to complete its five-year mission, but it broke new ground. It was successful in creating intricate characters whose personal stories affected the course of history, and it broke out of the anthology-series mold and used the story-arc format (pioneered in prime time by *Dallas*) to tell an SF/F story. It treated telepathy, time travel, reincarnation, supernatural beings, and alien mysticism as pragmatic elements of reality.

The *Buffy The Vampire Slayer* feature film came out in 1992.[2] Joss Whedon has indicated he wasn't able to materialize his vision of Buffy in that film, and is widely quoted as saying the director "ruined it." But in 1997, when the *Buffy* TV show aired, he had more artistic con-

---

[1] The second-season finale is titled "Becoming" (3-21, 3-22) and marks several pivotal points in becoming. Angel opens Hell by pulling the Sword of Acathla; Willow becomes a witch when she restores Angel's soul; and Buffy becomes a mature figure when she sacrifices her personal happiness, sending Angel to Hell.

[2] I enlisted the aid of two television experts, fan Cherri Muñoz and the scriptwriter/journalist Anne Phyllis Pinzow to verify the following timeline.

trol. Of course, that's partly due to moving from film to television. But what happened between 1992 and 1997 in television to prepare the way for *Buffy*?

Forever Knight (pilot August 1989, first episode May 1992), with the vampire as good guy. *Quantum Leap* (1989–1993), an anthology series using the SF-premise as a vehicle to tell a personal story of change. *Highlander* (1992–98), a hero with monogamous tendencies and a sense of honor. *Lois and Clark* (pilot September 1993), again a hero with monogamous tendencies and a serious attitude toward wielding power. *X-Files* (1993), introducing not just UFOs but the supernatural to the mass audience. *Hercules: The Legendary Journeys* (1994–99) and *Sliders* (1995), introducing alternate realities, dimensional gates, alternate history. *Xena: The Warrior Princess* (1995) and *Star Trek: Voyager* (1995)—the woman as hero and authority figure. *The Stand* by Stephen King (1994), introducing the elbow room that the horror format can give to serious drama. *La Femme Nikita* (1997)—at last a young female hero, tough as nails, forced into an untenable position and doing something about it, carefully, wisely.

Each of these (except Stephen King's of course) was marginally successful, appealing to a small but seriously dedicated audience. Each has spawned fanfic on the Internet and anguished write-in campaigns at cancellation. Each marginally successful show gets Hollywood moguls thinking about what element caused that success and what caused failure, and how to extract the successful part and combine it with something else to create a blockbuster. And they always measure themselves against a blockbuster like *The Stand*.

The WB network launched in 1995, countering the earlier launch of the UPN network. The WB deliberately targeted the lucrative demographic teen group and gathered more affiliate stations than UPN.

Joss Whedon brought The WB an idea that combined the vampires which had dominated children's books in the 1980s, a successful film, and a universe in which magic is blatantly real rather than disguised as science. *Buffy* might have been pitched as *Forever Knight* meets *La Femme Nikita* in a Lovecraftian world that would leave King in the dust.

He gave The WB the strong female lead that had made *Xena* popular and that *Star Trek: Voyager* had chosen to emphasize with Captain Janeway, the first woman to captain the *Enterprise*. And don't think The WB didn't know in 1996 that USA Network was incubating *La Femme Nikita*. But Whedon gave The WB a young hero, young enough to grab the huge audience that had grown up on children's vampire books and a strong female lead character who could kick ass as neatly as Hercules.

He started with a very clear cut, uncomplicated, emotionally pristine conflict—Buffy vs. the Undead. She can smash and destroy with all her might and she is not committing murder. Walking horrors attack her and she doesn't have to stop and worry about ethics, she just stakes them. You don't have to be a teen to appreciate the clarity of these moments.

But then Whedon adds Angel—and suddenly things aren't clear anymore. Suddenly our powerful hero, Buffy, has an internal conflict. Suddenly this show is elevated to the level of adult drama and we have family entertainment, not a kiddie-show. Here is a teen confronted with an adult's problem, and nobody can help her with it. She is on her own—as any hero must be.

All great literature explores the depths of human nature, the source of our evil impulses, the source of our noblest aspirations, and the synthesis of Good and Evil that is the dynamic balancing act called Personality, the fuel for all relationships.

But until the commercial-driven business of television found that their most lucrative audience is 14–30-year-olds, we've never had Great Literature in the performing arts developed specifically to depict the process of "Becoming" as teens experience it. Well—maybe *Romeo and Juliet* but they didn't make it to adulthood.

And overall, through all its seasons, that is what *Buffy* is about— "Becoming." It wasn't just the title of a magnificent two-part cliff-hanger episode—it is the theme of the entire show. The characters change character, change personality, change relationships year after year as they "become." And it's that process of change, of becoming, that is the key identifying characteristic of Great Literature—but who would think that you could have Great Literature about teens?

One of many illustrations of *Buffy* as Great Literature can be found by comparing Buffy and Willow.

Buffy herself was barely a teenager when she acquired enormous Power—magical Power, physical Power, and the Power that comes from being Unique. She isn't "a slayer"—she is "the Slayer." We've watched her become a woman, surviving a series of classically text-book-perfect magical initiations.[3]

She's had to learn to use her power without it using her. She has sent

---

[3] "Helpless" (3-12) aired 1/19/99. This was the ultimate initiation. On Buffy's eighteenth birthday, the Council of Watchers ordered Giles to give Buffy an injection that would take her powers away. She is then faced with a psychotic vampire where she must kill using only what she has learned in her years as the Slayer. At the end, we learn that it's not only her initiation but Giles's too.

her vampire lover to Hell to save the world ("Becoming, Part 2," 2-22).

She went into a symbolic Hell in "Anne" (3-1)—the symbolism of the tar-black rectangle she had to dive into to rescue the slaves from that Hell dimension is perfect for a ceremonial magical initiation. When she returns, she's become Buffy again because she confronted her worst fears. This shows that the initiation took root deep within her psyche where it will grow. In the seventh season we have seen the results as Buffy accepts her identity as the Slayer and nurtures her possible successors. The traditional Initiate must train a successor, and Buffy has tried.[4]

The magical power of her love is focused through the silver love-token[5] she divests herself of while mourning Angel, separating from him—letting go, coming to terms with the consequences of her decisions and actions ("Faith, Hope, and Trick," 3-3). That magical focus allows Angel to breach the dimensional gate and return from Hell. Remember the magical power of silver.

Angel later revealed that the power had let him go. The being wanted Buffy and the world to suffer and the being thought more suffering could be created by sending Angel back to Sunnydale ("Amends," 3-10).

Buffy, as most young people, has to leave home to confront her identity and returns having become someone else, forever changed. She met the First Slayer and came into possession of her full power, again forever changed ("Restless," 4-22).

She has buried her mother ("Forever," 5-17), torn by regrets that can never be mended—learning the meaning of regret. She has sacrificed her life to save Dawn ("The Gift," 5-22) and the universe, a decision made out of all these changes she has undergone. She was dragged back from Heaven by her best friends ("Bargaining," 6-1, 6-2)—completing the death initiation, one of the highest degrees in ceremonial magic.[6] And she sacrificed her uniqueness to give all potentials the power that she has—and did not regret it.

---

[4] Name changing or taking on a new name is a necessary part of Initiation. The use of a disregarded middle name qualifies as a name-change.

[5] Angel gives her a claddagh ring in "Surprise" (2-13). Angel says "The hands represent friendship. The crown represents loyalty. And the heart . . . well, you know. Wear it pointing toward you. It's a sign that you belong to somebody."

[6] The candidate is led into the ceremonial hall in near darkness, placed in a coffin with the lid closed, and left in this sensory-deprivation chamber for a long time. When the coffin is opened, sometimes by the candidate's own efforts, the candidate arises with a new name. These ceremonial initiations are designed to replicate the psychological processes we go through in real life, telescoping seven years of hard living into a few hours. But the most effective Initiations are those lived through life. Every Ceremonial Initiation, to be effective, must be followed by a recapitulation of the lesson life-events. Then the ceremonial "Death" initiation is followed by massive lifestyle changes. In the language of "Death –"Birth."

In any other TV series (except possibly a soap opera) each of these events would have been the whole of a five-year series run.

But through the high-pressure rapidity of these events, we have watched Buffy evolve. She has matured faster than the mere years could account for. She has become harder, more self-reliant, more accustomed to wielding power—and more daring. The power she carries does not make her happy, or even relieve her of pain. It doesn't create joy, either.

This is Buffy's story—the hard, harsh, demanding, arduous life of the magician-in-training, which is closely parallel to the training of a martial-arts master.

One of the well-known characteristics of a magical initiation[7] is that after an Initiation, before the year is out, the Initiate's life falls apart. We've seen this happen to Buffy repeatedly.

She arrives in Sunnydale and is rejected by those she considers her social peers ("Dead Man's Party," 4-2). She lost Angel, acquired a mysterious sister and lost her only-child status, lost her mother, and even lost Giles ("Once More, With Feeling," 6-7).

She dropped out of college with no profession that can earn money—having no visible means of support is the hallmark of the High Initiate. She has even acquired an inner planes master (the First Slayer)—a demanding ancestral presence lurking on the astral plane pushing and guiding toward wisdom.

If you've read the books by Carlos Castaneda on the Yaqui way to power (an American Indian Tradition),[8] you will see that Buffy's life does put her through the series of initiations Castaneda is put through by his Yaqui teacher.

Willow on the other hand has not been treading the initiatory path while she's been learning how to do magic.

So, by comparison, Willow's life has been relatively (only relatively)

---

[7] *The Training and Work of an Initiate* by Dion Fortune is a good place to start learning about the Western Ceremonial Initiatory tradition. As *Star Trek* drew upon Shakespeare and other great literature, *Buffy* draws upon Ancient Greek, Kabbalistic, and Egyptian sources. Besides studying mythology, anthropology, and archeology, the curious student should investigate the traditions behind the magical systems alluded to in *Buffy*. For the beginner, the best place to start is Fortune's book *Psychic Self-Defense* (various publishers over nearly a century, look for a cheap current paperback) and my own *Biblical Tarot: Never Cross a Palm With Silver* (Toad Hall Inc.), both of which can be found on *amazon.com*. Or read my award-winning SF/F review column from *The Monthly Aspectarian* which examines what can be learned about magical initiation by reading science fiction novels: www.simegen.com/reviews/rereadablebooks/

[8] *Teachings of Don Juan: A Yaqui Way of Knowledge* by Carlos Castaneda, Pocket Books; ISBN: 0671600419; Reissue edition (June 1985)

stable. She lost Oz ("Wild at Heart," 4-6), but went on. She acquired Tara—truly a surprise though not a shock to discover she's now gay,[9] an identity change, though not creating any self-loathing or rejection by her peers.

But Tara, as odd as her family is, is not the same kind of challenge for Willow that Buffy faces when falling in love, or lust, with a vampire or a soldier who hunts demons.

Willow has not had an easy time of it. She has suffered. She has dared. And she's failed ignominiously a few times. But Willow's response to any failure is to acquire more knowledge and more power.

Buffy's response to stress, strain, trials, tests, grief, and failure is to look within, to question who she is, to fight against the destiny of the Slayer ("I want a normal life!") and to reconcile herself to the sacrifices her destiny demands ("I'll do what I have to do.") In contrast, Willow tends to look at these same kinds of events as entirely external problems to be solved, or opportunities to gain knowledge or power.

Willow has steadily acquired magical power but without going through the mystical symbolic initiations that have tempered Buffy. She has been able to bring up enough power to solve the group's problems—and always magic provides an easy and definitive, external solution to the problem of the day.[10]

Her value to the group lies in her knowledge and power. She can find out anything and fix anything.[11]

Lured, seduced by such rewards, she has reached for more and more power—and at last acquired more than she can handle. Why? What's the difference between Buffy and Willow?

Buffy, we have seen from the very beginning, has a robust sense of self-esteem. Though her mother is divorced, and refuses to notice Buffy's oddities, she has provided the kind of nurturing that has allowed Buffy to develop self-confidence and an inner strength.

Willow, on the other hand, shows through body language, tone of voice, use of eyes, style of dress, hairdo, and social awkwardness that she does not have that kind of inward self-confidence.

---

[9] "Doppelgangland" (3-16)—Vamp Willow crosses over from a different dimension. Our Willow dresses in Vamp Willow's dominatrix black outfit so she can rescue Oz and the others in the Bronze. Willow is distressed by Vamp Willow. Later she talks about Vamp Will, stating, "And I think I'm kinda gay."

[10] Willow gives Angel's soul back ("Becoming, Parts 1 & 2," 2-21, 2-22). Willow casts a spell so Tara doesn't see her use magic ("Tabula Rasa," 6-8).

[11] "Halloween" (2-6). Willow is a ghost but she's still trying to hit the books so she can help solve the problem. Only thing, she can't turn the pages because she's a ghost.

We aren't told why—her parents are not visible enough for analysis. We do see that Willow hardly ever mentions her family, and the bare glimpses we've had of her mother[12] only reinforce the notion that her parents aren't part of her life and haven't been for a long time.

But it doesn't matter why Willow starts out as the quintessential geek, buried in her computer, with razor-sharp intellect, cutting right through all her schoolwork without noticing it's there. She takes to Giles's books like a duck to water, and remembers what she reads (and reads at blazing speed).

Given that much sheer brain power, how could Willow not have the easy social presence and confident manner that Buffy has? Because the product of her intellect (good grades, etc.) has never solved whatever emotional problem lurks at the depths of her personality.

This is a very common situation—in fact to some extent anyone can relate to this problem. We all have some talent, some power, some attribute that we develop early in life to execute our "coping strategy."

In psychology, "coping strategy" is the term for how we deal with challenges, difficulties, and "life." For example, when confronted by bullies, some people run away, some retreat without turning their backs, some bluster and shout to intimidate the bullies, and some wade right in and kick ass. When confronted by an abusive spouse, some people appease and blame themselves for the other's behavior, and some just leave.

Generally, what a person does in response to a challenge is determined by what has worked well for that person in early childhood. In the teen years, coping strategies are developed, honed, practiced, and mastered to the point where the twentysomething people don't even realize they have them. It just seems like the only right response.

Buffy is an ass-kicker—that's her coping strategy. When she was the social queen of her school, she out-dressed, out-insulted, out-clique-gathered, and out-flirted everyone. When she became the Slayer, she out-punched, out-staked, out-kicked, and out-sassed the vampires. The smart remarks are the holdover from her social-queen days, a brilliant piece of writing.[13]

---

[12] "Gingerbread" (3-11). Willow's mother helps Joyce with the MOO campaign and later helps Joyce capture the girls so they can burn them at the stake for being witches.

[13] When Willow was trying to keep Sunnydale safe while Buffy was away, she tried to imitate Buffy by writing and saying puns. They usually fell flat ("Dead Man's Party,"3-2). Even years later, Willow still didn't have the art of punning down. Remember, the puns she programmed into Warren's Buffybot also fell flat ("Bargaining, Parts 1 & 2," 6-1, 6-2).

Willow is a conflict-avoider and, as some self-help books would term it, an appeaser. In the very first episode, when Buffy introduces herself to Willow, Willow's first thought is that Buffy wants her seat, and she is prepared to give it to her.

Typically, the appeaser personality tends to be preoccupied with issues involving status, and power, and the idea that power confers status, which releases one from the need to appease someone who is more powerful. For example, Willow says "I'm not your sidekick" in a tone that indicates a sidekick is someone with less status or power.

When confronted with an angry person, Willow tries to soothe them. When confronted with a problem, she does research. Her power is intellectual. In high school, she avoided social situations, stuck with the boy-next-door for a friend, and gravitated to Buffy's crowd because they valued her intellectual abilities.

Willow is a person who thirsts for an external acknowledgment of her value, but fears that acknowledgment as well. Although this is built into every episode from the beginning, it is verbalized finally in season six. Willow actually tells Buffy she only feels useful when using magic. Without the magic, she's simply an ordinary human who is only in the way.

The pain of that conflict was not assuaged by her intellectual abilities, so when she was offered a plum of a scholarship, she turned it down to stay in Sunnydale with Buffy, fighting vampires and demons.

At that point, she was in the midst of developing a new coping strategy, or rather a refinement of the one that had always worked for her. Willow was feeling the awakening of her magical powers, which depend on the ability to concentrate—an ability she had honed to perfection hiding from life within her computer.

Most likely, Willow was unaware of why magic was so alluring to her subconscious mind. It was a renewed hope that here at last was the tool she could use to become self-confident, to find her self-esteem, to define her identity, to cause the world to accept her—or at least stop forcing her to appease.

When she entered college, she had already had a taste of wielding magic, but she knew she didn't have access to the information she needed. So she was drawn into investigating witchcraft. She found a very ordinary college group and a woman even more shy than herself,[14] someone who didn't have to be appeased, but who would do the appeasing—at least at first.

---

[14] "Hush" (4-10) is the first episode where Tara is credited, but Willow meets her prior to this.

When Willow discovered that, in addition to being more shy than herself, Tara was the genuine article—a real magic-user schooled and trained in the craft—Tara became the instant love of Willow's life. It was not a healthy relationship from the very beginning.

How can that be? How can the most beautiful and perfect relationship on this show be unhealthy at the core?

Tara had knowledge and skill in magic, but apparently lacked the training to be an initiator. She was still very much a student and not qualified to be a high priestess. She could not lead Willow to self-confidence because she had none herself. She became Willow's tool in the relentless pursuit of power for power's sake.

She appeased Willow—which melted Willow into total adoration—and very often that appeasement was done by allowing Willow to have access to Tara's knowledge, and, through joint rituals, directly to her personal power—much more power than Willow was prepared to channel.

In other words, this relationship is unhealthy because it is a prime example of a codependent[15] relationship. Willow supplies Tara with the confidence of belonging to a peer group, thus allowing her to avoid tackling her shyness. Tara supplies Willow with magical power to augment her intellectual power, so Willow can repeat the unsuccessful coping strategy of her childhood—using her intellectual power to gain acceptance. This time she substitutes magical power for intellectual power, as if that would make a difference.

Tara comes to wisdom first, however, possibly because of her family background. When she saw Willow becoming addicted to using magic, she practiced "tough love" and left Willow[16] in spite of how much it hurt both of them. If you study the psychology of addiction and the process of breaking addiction—where the term "tough love" is used extensively—you will find that such a leaving is absolutely the final, last resort to help a person come to their senses. There is no act of love more convincing than tough love. It is Tara's initiation of sacrifice.

But, from Willow's point of view, this separation was only provisional—"just until you get a grip on yourself"—not the absolute, total

---

[15] *Codependent No More: How to Stop Controlling Others and Start Caring for Yourself* by Melody Beattie—you'll find this on *amazon.com* also.

[16] In "Tabula Rasa" (6-8) Willow uses magic to erase Buffy's memory of Heaven, but instead everyone's memory is erased. When memory is restored at the end of the episode, Tara realizes the magnitude of the danger to Willow and does the only thing she knows how—she leaves Willow. Note that Willow's horrible mistake is completely fixed when they get their memories back. She does not suffer a consequence of her actions—except that Tara leaves.

and irretrievable loss that Willow so needed at that point to begin her Becoming—to begin her initiatory path.

By applications of intellect or magic, Willow has been able to avoid the consequences of her actions time and again. She needs the initiation of confronting the whole, total, irreversible, irretrievable, consequence of her choices.

Buffy had to choose to send Angel to Hell. And she had to live through the consequences of that choice. When Angel returns from Hell, he lurks awhile, and then leaves permanently. She chose not to cling to Riley—and by the time she changed her mind it was too late. When Buffy makes a decision about fighting the monsters, it changes the world, permanently. Her actions have irreversible consequences and she's learned to live with that.

Willow had Oz walk out on her—but again, it's only temporary— only because he needs to get a handle on his shifting and his beast. We all expect to see him come back. Willow had Tara walk out on her, but again, only until Willow gets a grip on her problem. Now Tara is dead— but not as a direct consequence of a free will choice that Willow has made. In all these critical instances, the situation Willow is in has been caused by someone else's choice, not Willow's.

This kind of a life pattern does not equip one to handle great power. It makes one the victim of power, should it ever materialize — as money, position, weaponry, or even magic.

Though Willow's friends are supportive of her attempt to cope with her addiction, they see Willow's condition as similar to that of an alcoholic. Nothing could be further from the truth.

For a magician, the breath is the power. Life itself is power. Every thought, every emotion, manifests in far-reaching ways. A magician cannot take a step without the earth trembling. It is like physical strength. A very strong man has to turn a door handle very, very gently so as not to break it off. A magician must tread lightly through the world, leaving not a trace, for the alternative is to leave a swath of destruction behind.

Willow is not addicted to magic. Willow is addicted to the surging hope that this deed or the next or the next will finally assuage her inner pain.

The cure is to find that inner pain, penetrate it to the underlying fear, confront that fear, find the little person inside the fear (the child within) and love that little person.

Willow has to learn to accept herself, accept her own inadequacies, her intellect, and her talent for magic and by the series finale, she apparently does.

To achieve that, she had to have her standard, tried and true coping strategy of appeasement destroyed, and be left naked before the world with no way to cope.

The death of Tara has the potential to do this for Willow because it is permanent. Willow's first move upon finding Tara dead was to appeal to a god who could restore Tara as Buffy was restored. She did everything she could to appease that great power, and it didn't work.

Left with no one to turn to, no one to appease, and all that power burning holes in her soul, Willow finally surges forth into a more mature and aggressive Willow.

But typically for an appeaser who has so much power that she becomes the one who must be appeased, she fastens on the motive of revenge. She has the power to kill a human being, and she proceeds to do so without mercy.

Many fans see this as Willow's character changing, but that isn't what's happened. The seeds of this moment have been there since the first time we ever saw Willow. In that moment of murder for revenge,[17] Willow's character has come to full maturity.

And that is incontrovertible evidence of a master craftsman at work on this show, making it truly Great Art and Great Literature.

We never saw this coming—never expected Willow to pull in all her magic and focus it on revenge. It is so out of character for Willow as a person!

Yet, now that we've seen it actually happen, now that we think about Willow as a human being, not a character in a story, it is so absolutely inevitable, so perfectly right and correct, we can only stand in awe of the writer who has spent seven years developing this before our eyes without our seeing it.

Magically, at the end of the sixth season Willow faced the greatest initiation. She was in full, direct confrontation with the consequences of her own weakness. She had been used by her power—she had become the victim of her own power.

She has used magic to commit murder, and it didn't help her feel any better. She just went on to attack her very dearest friends. Giles and Xander saved her by touching her emotions, but as the seventh

---

[17] In "Villains" (6-20), Willow tortures Warren to death.

season opened, we had no reason to expect that the power that is within her won't grab her and use her again.[18]

In season seven Willow, fresh from a sequence of Magical Initiations in England, faces the requisite tests following any Initiation. She is confronted with opportunities to use her Power and must judge each situation for herself. Because of the intimate ties to her friends and her ability to be emotionally honest with them, she finds she now has the strength to resist the temptation to use Power for personal gain, and thus has more strength to use it for the good of all.

She had to go entirely back to the Dark-Haired Willow and climb out of that trap by her own Will. This is also very typical of the aftermath of Initiation. What has been done within Ceremonial Initiation must be manifested in the life.

During the last episode, "Chosen" (7-22), Willow is still unsure of herself. She has to perform Magic to unleash the power of the slayer to all potential slayers. Her fear is that darkness will overpower her and she will lose control once again. Buffy tells her that she is confident in Willow, possibly because Buffy recognizes the changes in Willow as being akin to the changes she has undergone which allow her to control her Power.

Willow uses the sickle to perform the needed magic and turns white (a first). The expression on her face tells it all. She has 'become.'

So now the show has ended. With the exception of Spike and Anya, the Scoobies are safe and Sunnydale is no more. The Hellmouth is closed. Both the demons and the humans abandoned the city long before its destruction. The potentials are Slayers and have become the ones who must find the other potentials and instill that confidence of becoming in the ones who never made it to Sunnydale for the ultimate sacrifice.

Now think back to Buffy's Becoming and compare it with Willow's Becoming—notice how all the other characters have lived, loved, laughed, and touched both Willow and Buffy? And each of them has "become" as well. When one changes, they all change.

What is the power that changes them? What makes them become?

The power that binds this group in a dynamic process of becoming is

---

[18] In the first few episodes of the seventh season we see that Willow has undergone some heavy ritual initiation at the hands of a coven in England—people qualified to initiate Willow. We see her with a changed attitude, but ritual initiations can't be completed without manifestation in Life—without tests to be passed where the stakes are real. Now, if the initiatory pattern is to be completed, Willow's life has to fall apart.

emotional honesty. They suffer together, they heal each other's wounds, they move in together and shelter each other. They accept Dawn even though she was inserted into their lives, and pitch in to raise her as best they can. They change because of what they feel for each other.

Joss Whedon has been writing a perfect example of a new genre I call "Intimate Adventure"[19]—where the real adventure demanding courage is on the field of relationships, not action. Note that the "action" in *Buffy* is routine, repetitive, and unoriginal—face the monster, get beaten to a pulp, vanquish or kill the monster. But each season there are new relationships, new emotional complexities, and new challenges to emotional courage.

Buffy has allowed characters to grow, change, learn, and evolve because of the pain, the angst, the loves, losses, and emotional battering they take standing between us and the Hellmouth Spawn.

And what is the hallmark of Great Literature that was lacking on television up until the 1990s? Character maturation due to the power of intimate relationships. And that's what we see in *Buffy*—a trait that was forbidden to televised SF/F when *Star Trek* first went on the air. Close friendships and love change the characters before our eyes, so that the next time they face a challenge, they tackle it with a different coping strategy—step by step evolving a more mature coping strategy until they face major challenges.

How many characters on other TV shows do we learn to know, understand, and love before they commit deliberate murder?

Murder is something only bad guys do. The import of what Willow has done is not in the murder itself, but in the wellspring of personal emotion—the deep and terrible love for Tara, the vast and unstoppable pain of that loss, and the righteous rage that loosed her magic to take over and rule her. She used her power for personal gain—the gain being entirely emotional.

And in the end, she learned that she could master the Power and not be used by it when she had a task to perform for humanity. This time she sought nothing for herself, not even self-confidence or the high regard of others.

We all understood why, at Tara's death, Willow went for revenge in the one way that violated the covenant between her and Tara. And so

---

[19] Intimate Adventure—*Publishers Weekly*, November 10, 1989, p.22. Defined and explained at *www.simegen.com/jl/intimateadventure.html* where you will find links to the complete article "A Proposal for a New Genre," reprinted from *The Monthly Aspectarian* (*www.lightworks.com*)

did all the other characters. We understood because we had lived their intimate adventure with them.

The hallmark of Great Literature is that the reader understands how the events cause the character to become someone different. Our understanding of Willow indicates that *Buffy The Vampire Slayer* is Great Literature.

But look again at the sequence of shows beginning between 1989 when I first mentioned intimate adventure in *Publishers Weekly*, when *Forever Knight* first appeared—and today.

Every one of those shows has a following producing fan fiction and vast amounts of e-mail. Every one of those shows touches the creative core of millions of people, just as *Star Trek* does. When I started writing *Star Trek Lives!* in 1972 to explain why people like *Star Trek*,[20] I only hoped that Hollywood would eventually figure it out.

And now we have *Buffy, Enterprise, Farscape*, and *Smallville*, and more SF/F than one person can watch and still do a day's work.

Buffy is not the end product of this process of becoming that television is undergoing. It has made a major innovation by adding dimensions of relationship to the *Babylon 5* breakthrough of story-arc structure. But most important of all, *Buffy* has given us evolving characters—characters who are significantly changed by the traumas and emotional anguish they have to live through.

In *Buffy*, all the characters Become. And in that Becoming lies their power to change television, and perhaps SF/F as well.

Great Literature is about the process of Becoming, of growth and learning through hard lessons. It explains the human condition, shows us how our own unique experiences are related to common human ones familiar to everyone. Great Literature changes its field, opens new avenues, explores new venues and is copied or emulated. *Buffy* appears to have all three of these key traits.

Romantic Times Award-winning author Jacqueline Lichtenberg is the primary author of Star Trek Lives!, *the Bantam paperback that revealed the existence of* Star Trek *fandom and its fanzines and touched off the explosion of fannish involvement in the television show.* Star Trek Lives! *presents her theory of why fans love* Star Trek *so much that they write stories about*

---

[20] Jacqueline Lichtenberg biography and bibliography can be found at *www.simegen.com/jl/*.

it. *Her first published novel,* House of Zeor, *the first novel in the legendary Sime~Gen Universe now in print from Meisha Merlin Publishing, Inc., proved her theory has merit. In addition to her series of vampire short stories, she has a vampire romance published by BenBella Books, titled* Those of My Blood. *She has two occult/SF novels in print,* Molt Brother *and* City of a Million Legends. *Jacqueline has spent more than 25 years as a tarot and astrology practitioner and teacher. She is author of* The Biblical Tarot: Never Cross A Palm With Silver, *and is the SF/F reviewer for the Occult/New Age publication* The Monthly Aspectarian. *www.simegen.com/jl/ will provide more details.*

Kevin Andrew Murphy

UNSEEN HORRORS & SHADOWY MANIPULATIONS

Here's a disturbing thought.What if the Buffy we know and love is not the pure thing, not straight from the mind of Joss, but rather has been meddled with by forces of evil too awful to contemplate.The very brave Kevin Murphy takes on this horrific idea, and lays out the cold, hard truth.

O N TELEVISION, Buffy and her gang must contend with unseen horrors, unspeakable evils, and the dark and shadowy manipulations of secret organizations bent on reshaping the world in their own image. In reality, the writers, producers, and cast of the show contend with much the same.

The names are different, of course, but the objectives and methodologies are remarkably similar—as are the tools at their disposal, the main ones being censorship and pressure. Censorship to remove thoughts and images they find offensive, and pressure to incorporate ones they deem desirable. The degree of success in achieving these goals depends on the power of the entity.

Starting with some of the most powerful beings, in the *Buffy*verse, the Powers of Darkness are opposed by the mysterious Loa, the Spirit

Guides, and the Powers That Be—benevolent entities that guard, protect and shepherd, but not to be trifled with lightly. In the real world, there are the various corporate sponsors, whose advertising dollars pay the bills of commercial television, keeping shows safe from the dreaded cancellation. Both rarely speak, but when they do, the pronouncements are dire.

As Joss Whedon remarked in an interview with *Zap2it.com*, "Double Meat Palace was the only thing we ever did to make advertisers pull out. They did not like us making fun of fast food." Consequently, Buffy got a new job for season seven and the Double Meat Palace storyline was scrapped.

At the same time as the advertisers would have been making their displeasure known, there's an exchange in the "Loyalty" (3-15) episode of *Angel*, where Wesley goes in supplication to an icon of the Loa, only to find it's a human-size anthropomorphic hamburger. The fiberglass statue grows and animates, then hits Wesley with a lightning bolt, crying, "Your insolence is displeasing!" Wes responds, under his breath, "Try chatting with a cranky hamburger . . ."

It's hard not to read this as a commentary on Joss Whedon's company, Mutant Enemy, dealing with the burger advertisers.

Of course, the Loa, the Spirit Guides, and the Powers That Be (and the related corporate sponsors) are not the only entities our heroes must contend with. Buffy and the Scooby gang also deal with the Watcher's Council, which is also generally benevolent but is interested in the Slayer only as she is of use to it. Whedon and crew? The network executives, again with a similar relationship.

Television networks censor and pressure in service to their financial needs and corporate ends, not the artistic needs of an individual show or the wishes of its fans. For example, the much-anticipated kiss between Willow and Tara had to wait until another show on the WB, *Dawson's Creek*, showed a kiss between Jack (Kerr Smith) and Ethan (Adam Kaufman, who also played Parker that same season on Buffy). This quick peck was a television landmark, a gay kiss in a teen show, but the WB chose to give it to another show—not because it was necessarily better for *Dawson's* than it was for *Buffy*, but because it was better for the network. It would be another season before a lengthier gay kiss on *Dawson's* and the even longer and more comforting kiss between Tara and Willow in "The Body" in season five. And even then, it is something that the network is still sensitive to.

As reported by Nicholas Fonseca in *The Crass Menagerie* article "Foul

Language. Raunchy Sex. Gore galore. On TV?,"[1] "*Buffy* exec producer Marti Noxon says UPN censors have more qualms about Willow's romance with Tara (Amber Benson) than the show's campy violence or ravenous (straight) sex scenes—including that racy interlude last winter in which Gellar's Slayer offered oral pleasure to Spike. Laughs Noxon, 'Yeah, that one was pretty dirty.'"

A more significant example of network censorship occurred in season three, with the suspension of the episode "Earshot" (3-18) in the wake of the Columbine High School shootings. "Earshot" (3-18) dealt, in part, with the possibility of a school shooting, and the following interchange was viewed as something too sensitive to be aired in the United States only a week after the murders:

WILLOW: We have a list of the people in the cafeteria. I'll do some computer work, match it against the FBI mass-murderer profiles. We can rule some people out.

XANDER: I'm still having trouble with the idea that one of us is just gonna gun everybody down for no reason.

CORDELIA (sarcastically): Yeah, 'cause that never happens in American high schools.

OZ: It's bordering on trendy at this point.

Canada, however, was not as traumatized by the US high school shooting, and in certain areas, "Earshot" (3-18) aired as scheduled, leading to a rampant bit of tape-trading between US and Canadian fans, and, even more significantly, the rise of Internet bootlegging of copies of the episode in MPG file format. This only increased as the WB decided they would also delay the second half of the season finale, "Graduation Day, Part 2," (3-22) for fear of being held liable if any violence happened anywhere during a high school graduation ceremony.

Thankfully, only Sunnydale had its mayor turn into a giant snake and attempt to eat the graduating class, so there was no spontaneous use of flamethrowers and crossbows from high schoolers across the United States. What there was was an unprecedented rise in file-trading and tape-swapping, much to the chagrin of the WB. Especially after series creator, Joss Whedon, told *USA Today*, "Okay, I'm having a Grateful Dead moment here, but I'm saying, 'Bootleg the puppy.'"

---

[1] EW.com—posted June 2, 2002.

In the end, the WB could only put a stop to the file-trading—and their own projected loss of revenues for a couple million-dollar episodes—by finally airing both of the "forbidden episodes," as they were dubbed by Joss in one of his postings in the Bronze, the *Buffy* posting board:

> It's nice to see how much people care about seeing the ep—although there were threats made against WB execs, which is, uh, most creepy. Look to poor Britain, who gets it in clumps, out of order, on different networks or not at all. All we have to do is wait a couple of months. Besides, now they're the FORBIDDEN EPISODES, and isn't that a treat in itself. And to be slightly SPOILERISH, all this fuss over the graduation scene means the scene at the end of act one just slipped right by 'em. La la la . . .

Then, of course, there is self-censorship on the part of the writer, because they know what will sell with the network, and there are only so many outrageous things one can do at once. As Joss said to *Entertainment Tonight* on March 31, 2000, "The censors aren't really a problem for me, because I'm not really big into gore." This, for the WB, was a selling point, as reported by A.J. Jacobs in the April 25, 1997, *Entertainment Weekly*: "'It's the least bloody violence on television,' boasts The WB's Garth Ancier." Thankfully for Joss, this was a stricture he could work with, responsible for gore-free vampire dustings, as well as the following quote in the same article: "As far as I'm concerned, the first episode of *Buffy* was the beginning of my career. It was the first time I told a story from start to finish the way I wanted."

A popular argument goes that since the networks own *Buffy*, all of this is not, in fact, censorship, merely editorial control. Nevertheless, editorial prohibitions and pronouncements—especially ones which the creators do not agree with—are censorship all the same. They are merely called something different for internal politics and to separate them from *government* censorship, which is, in principle at least, prohibited in the US by the First Amendment of the US Constitution.

Buffy, however, is global, and the First Amendment only protects the freedom of those who own the presses, not the freedom of those who work for them. Studios are free to make whatever edits they want, subject to their agreements with the artists, and television networks are free to "edit for content" (censor) for rebroadcast, subject to their own agreements with the studios.

Beyond the networks themselves, there's the industry-sponsored Television Parental Guidelines Monitoring Board. This industry ratings board is appointed by the networks to regulate their shows, and is roughly analogous to the late unlamented Principal Snyder, whose final words before being eaten by the Mayor were "This is not orderly. This is not discipline! You're on my campus, buddy! And when I say I want quiet, I want . . ."

Like Principal Snyder, the bureaucrats of the ratings board are often clueless, unable to deal with things that don't conform to standard expectations. ("You. All of you. Why can't you be dealing drugs like normal people?") While policing episodes for George Carlin's "Seven Words You Can't Say on Television" (excepting "piss," which has been used multiple times on *Buffy*), they miss obscenities that aren't part of the American idiom. For example, Spike continually flips a two-fingered gesture that means the same thing in Britain that flipping a one-fingered gesture with the middle finger means in the US. Then there are interchanges such as the following from season five's "The Gift":

> BUFFY: Remember: the ritual starts, we all die. And I'll kill anyone who comes near Dawn.
> SPIKE: Well, not exactly the St. Crispin's Day speech, was it?
> GILES: We few, we happy few . . .
> SPIKE: . . . we band of buggered.

And this speech from Spike's first appearance in "School Hard" (2-3):

> SPIKE: You're that Anointed guy. I read about you. You've got Slayer problems. That's a bad piece of luck. Do you know what I find works real good with Slayers? Killing them. A lot faster than nancy-boy there. Yeah, I did a couple Slayers in my time. I don't like to brag. Who am I kidding? I love to brag! Yeah. He's the big noise in these parts. Anointed, and all that. Me and Dru, we're movin' in. Now. Any of you want to test who's got the biggest wrinklies 'round here . . . step on up. I'll do your Slayer for you. But you keep your flunkies from tryin' anything behind my back. Deal?

"Buggered," "wrinklies," and "nancy-boy" are all exceedingly vulgar. Not that the censors have noticed, or at least cared. Even Harmony, in "Fool for Love" (5-7) has had more of a clue:

HARMONY: How are you going to kill her? Think. The second you even point that thing at her you're gonna be all . . . (Spike imitation) "Aaah!" and then you'll get bitch-slapped up and down Main Street unless she's had enough and just stakes you.

SPIKE: This is different. Move.

HARMONY: No! And then you'll come back to me and stomp around and swear a bunch of weird English curses.

SPIKE (losing patience): Harm . . .

HARMONY: What is a "bollock," anyway?

Of course, what is vulgar there is simply weird here. However, in other countries, editorial control from networks and censorship boards is responsible for the deletion of segments, scenes or even entire episodes, depending on the local laws and the whims of the censors. In the UK, this problem is compounded by the fact that, so far as the BBC is concerned, science fiction and fantasy shows are children's fare. As such, they are thus given the "teatime" slot, before the eight- and nine-o'clock prime-time viewing hours. However, as the Broadcasting Standards Commission (BSC) in the UK ruled against *Buffy*, in one of many instances, "In relation to the sex scene, it considered that it had exceeded acceptable boundaries for broadcast at a time when young children could be watching." Shows are therefore edited to be "appropriate for children," with the sex and violence toned down or removed entirely.

This has predictably led to outcries from fans, later showings (yet after prime time), subscriptions to the pay network Sky One (which gets *Buffy* and *Angel* only three months after the US), and of course brisk sales and rentals of uncensored videos and DVDs (though local ratings make it so that no one under eighteen may purchase copies of *Angel*).

Of course, corporate decision-makers and ratings boards are not the only censors on the block. There are also government censors, and, worse yet, government propaganda agencies. In season four, Buffy becomes romantically involved with Riley and is drawn into the government-sponsored agenda of The Initiative. During the same season, *Buffy*'s network at the time, The WB, got into bed with the ONDCP, the White House Office of National Drug Control Policy.

As reported by Daniel Forbes of *Salon* Magazine (*salon.com*) in his article "Prime-time Propaganda," the ONDCP came to an agreement with the various television networks (including The WB, *Buffy*'s network at the time) such that the government would waive its rights to various slots of advertising time. They had bought these for anti-drug and -alcohol messages a few years before, during a depressed television market, as part of a congressionally mandated two-for-one sale—which now had the networks less than pleased, since season four was in the middle of the dot.com boom and advertising rates were at an all-time high. In exchange for the government waiving its rights to these highly lucrative advertising slots, the ONDCP wanted the networks to incorporate anti-drug and -alcohol messages into their shows. The networks agreed, The WB even printing a press release bragging about this, though in many cases did not inform the writers or producers of why the network brass were requesting such stories, or that the scripts were being vetted at the White House.

Early on in season four, viewers were treated to "Beer Bad" (4-5), arguably one of the lesser episodes of the season, featuring enchanted beer that makes frat boys (and Buffy) turn into Neanderthals, but a hilarious parody when watched as what happens when an independent-minded crew of writers are ordered to write anti-drug and -alcohol propaganda. In particular, this exchange:

> XANDER: Well, I cut her off before the others so I don't think she had as much to drink.
> GILES: I can't believe you served Buffy that beer.
> XANDER: I didn't know it was evil.
> GILES: But you knew it was beer.
> XANDER: Well, excuse me, Mr. "I Spent the Sixties in an Electric Kool-Aid Funky Satan Groove."
> GILES: It was the early seventies and you should know better.

Fortunately, the ONDCP's "Prime-time Propaganda" program has ended (for the moment) and they've gone back to the more traditional anti-drug messages in regular advertising slots. Then again, the dot.com boom is over, so there isn't as much incentive to free up advertising space either.

Of course, agencies of the United States government, real or fictitious, aren't the only groups who believe in social engineering through the manipulation of television. There are many others, most of them formed by well-meaning private citizens with an axe to grind.

In "Gingerbread" (3-11), Joyce forms MOO (Mothers Opposed to the Occult) in order to protect the children of Sunnydale from the dangers posed by witches and witchcraft (even if she has to burn Buffy and Willow at the stake to do it). In reality, the Parents Television Council (*parentstv.org*) lists *Buffy* at #1 on its "Worst" list of programs unacceptable for children and family viewing, mostly because of sex and violence, but also citing concerns about the occult. Their specific criticisms:

> Offensive language has included uses of 'bitch,' 'bastard,' 'hell,' 'damn,' 'ass,' and 'piss.' Violence on *Buffy the Vampire Slayer* is not only frequent, but also very graphic. In past seasons, episodes included vampires being aroused by biting their victims, Buffy being stabbed, and Dawn's wrists being slit. In the 2001 season finale, Buffy committed suicide, jumping to her death to save the world. The 2001–2002 season premiere showed her decayed corpse regenerated and resurrected through witchcraft.

Strangely, the sitcom *Sabrina, the Teenage Witch* was listed as #3 on their "Best" list, despite the occult theme and Salem occasionally trying to take over the world. However, unlike MOO, the PTC goes about burning the shows it doesn't like in a more figurative sense, organizing letter-writing campaigns and petition drives to bombard the networks, producers, and advertisers, as well as the FCC. This sort of pressure from the PTC—and earlier groups in the same mold, such as the Moral Majority—has resulted in the death of a number of television shows, including the occult-themed *Friday the 13th: The Series* and the landmark comedy *Soap*, which not only made occasional forays into the occult, but was among the first shows to deal with gay issues.

Critics and self-proclaimed morality police wield much power, but sometimes the most vehement would-be censors are the fans themselves. Like Cordelia's cruel clique, the Cordettes, as quick to turn on Cordy as praise her, the fans of *Buffy* and *Angel* praise things one day and decry them the next. As reported on *E! Online*'s "Watch with Wanda" grill, gossip and gripe, May 3, 2002, at the end of the article "Buffy Creator Joss Whedon Talks Climaxes, Criticism and Angel's Fate:"

> Q. *Buffy* and *Angel* fans seem to be more critical than ever this season. Does that affect you?
> A. It always affects me. At the same time, I need to give them what they need, not what they want. They need to have their hearts broken. They need to see change. They hated Oz, and then they hated that he left. These things are inevitable. If people are freaking out, I'm good. If people are going, "Hmmm . . . well, that was fine," I'm fucked.

Fan response to Oz was at first negative, then positive as Joss wrote an episode to endear him to the viewers. A similar situation occurred with Tara, the episode "Family" (5-6) exploring her character (and increasing her likeability), but the most freaking out by the fans has been over the issue of Willow's sexuality, which, after protests from fans who did not wish Willow to be gay, elicited this response from Joss on the bronze posting board:

> I realize that this has shocked a lot of people, and I've made a mistake by trying to shove this lifestyle—which is embraced by, maybe, at most, 10 percent of Americans—down people's throats. So I'm going to take it back, and from now on, Willow will no longer be a Jew.

This response drew high marks from gay fans (and others enjoying good sarcasm), but not forever. Gay issues continue to be a concern on *Buffy*, and not just with MOO and the PTC. For example, in a strange parallel to the scene in "Hush" (4-10) where we first meet Tara, and Willow must contend with the politics of the campus Wiccan group—which preaches blessing and empowerment while at the same time using ridicule and scorn to silence criticism and divergent views—in reality, similar tactics are used by the Kittenboard (*kittenboard.com*), a Willow/Tara lesbian-relationship-focused fan and activism board.

To be allowed to enter the Kittenboard inner forum, "The Kitty and Buffy Season 7," one must fit the following criteria:

> 2. They must have never have said a bad word about the kittenboard or kittens in general anywhere.

To join in the regular discussions on the Kittenboard, one simply has to subscribe to the following doctrine (from the Kittenboard FAQ):

> 19. Is Willow gay or bi? or Will Willow date boys again?
>   She's gay. Everyone, writers, actors and the show has said she is gay. Don't ask the question or post a thread about it. The answer to the second question? She's gay, no boys in the future for her, that would mean Oz as well.

Mention of anything outside this accepted doctrine results in the deletion of one's post. The discussion and thoughts of the group are strictly controlled by the moderator, which has resulted in members defecting, rather like Willow and Tara did from the campus Wiccans, to create the more moderate "Plan C" (*pub78.ezboard.com/bplanckittiens*) and "Blood of the Banned" (*pub78.ezboard.com/bwillowandtarastuff*) boards.

As explained in the "Blood of the Banned" FAQ:

> Why the "Blood of the Banned"???
>
> It all became with a joke made at the Plan C. And it has nothing to do with Willow and Tara.
>
> Mods of the Plan C and I have been banned from a third board, who call themselves the "only W/T board."
>
> We've made some jokes about it and I decided to rename the board "Blood of the Banned." Then Paul and I decided that Plan C and our board will be sister sites. So here we are.
>
> No people, you're not the only Willow and Tara board. We're here too.
>
> Ange.

Contrast these tactics with the following exchange by the Wiccan group in "Hush" (4-10):

> WICCA 1: We come together, daughters of Gaia, sisters to the moon. We walk with the darkness, the wolf at our side, through the waterfall of power to the blackest heart of eternity. I think we should have a bake sale.
> WICCA 2: I don't know
> WICCA 1: You guys like a bake sale right? I mean we need money for the dance recital and you know I do an empowering lemon bundt.
> WICCA 2: The most important thing is the Gaian newsletter. We need to get the message of blessing out to the sisters. Also who left their scented candles dripping all over my women-power shrine?
> WILLOW: Well, this is good. I mean, this is all fun ya know, but there's also other stuff that we might show an interest in, as a Wicca group.
> WICCA 1 (hesitantly): Like what?
> WILLOW: Well, there's the wacky notion of spells. You know, conjuring, transmutation . . .

WICCA 2 (giggling): Oh yeah, then we could all get on our broom-sticks and fly around on our broomsticks.
WICCA 1: You know, certain stereotypes are not very empowering.
TARA: I think that . . .
WICCA 2: One person's energy can suck the power from an entire circle. No offense.
TARA: Well, maybe we could, uh . . .
WICCA 2: Yeah, Tara. Guys . . . quiet. Do you have a suggestion?
Tara just shakes her head and looks down, but then she looks at Willow.
WICCA 2: Okay, let's talk about the theme for the bacchanal.

The certain stereotype that the Kittenboard feels is not very empowering is generally referred to as "The Myth of the Dead Lesbian," or "The Lesbian Cliché" for short, which basically boils down to the following motif: One lesbian dies; the other becomes evil. Or, as explained in the Kittenboard's Lesbian Cliché FAQ:

> 2) What specifically is the "Dead/Evil Lesbian Cliché"?
> That all lesbians and, specifically lesbian couples, can never find happiness and always meet tragic ends. One of the most repeated scenarios is that one lesbian dies horribly and her lover goes crazy, killing others or herself. (Sound familiar?)

The parallels to Tara's death and Willow's subsequent murderous rampage at the end of season six are obvious, and more elaborate descriptions of this motif and essays examining it can be found at the Kittenboard, along with listings of prior instances in literature and film. Discussions can also be found, though, of course, overly divergent opinions will be deleted by the moderator.

For a private group, this is standard, and, to a certain degree, expected. Those who do not agree with a group's policies are free to go off and form their own groups, as with Willow and Tara leaving the campus Wicca group, and Plan C and Blood of the Banned splintering off from the Kittenboard.

However, just as the campus Wiccans wished to publish the "Gaian Newsletter" to get out the "message of blessing" to their sisters, the Kittenboard is also into advocacy. And one of the things they advocate, in a strange parallel to the conservative Christian Parents Television Council, is censorship.

At the 2002 World Science Fiction Convention, a track of *Buffy* panels were created by author Seanan McGuire, who was also moderator for the panel *The Dead Lesbian Myth—Buffy and the Death of Tara.* During the course of the discussion, Seanan made the following statement:

> I ended up really liking Tara, to the point where I went over the course of a season, from . . . A magazine I write for I started an article with, "I think I should tell you right up front that I would like to see Tara boiled in applesauce and fed to hogs." I went over the course of less than half a season from that viewpoint to sobbing hysterically on the couch, going, "Those bastards, those bastards, how dare they make me care . . ."

This statement was then buzz-clipped in a panel report by Rally, the main Kittenboard member covering the convention, as:

> "Tara should be boiled in applesauce and fed to wild pigs."— Seanan McGuire—Moderator of the Buffy and The Death of Tara Panel

Though a lesbian herself, Seanan was also reported as a homophobe. This report elicited much shock and outrage from the membership of the Kittenboard, followed almost immediately by cries for PTC-style letter-writing campaigns and pressure on convention organizers to no longer invite any of the panelists to future conventions. For example, from the Kittenboard thread, *World Science Fiction Convention W/T the cliché & the lie*:

> Bob said, "I think copies need to be made and sent to a great many people . . ." Starting with EVERY SAN FRANCISCO and SAN JOSE PAPER AND TV STATION. Let the convention organizers hear from these towns and that homophobic conventions are not welcome. I want a retraction for the convention and an apology. Members of this board offered to be on this sham of a panel and were refused. Instead, they put little miss Anita Bryant jr. up there . . . as the MODERATOR!

Thankfully, after a number of days, Rally transcribed her tapes of the panel discussion so that Seanan's remarks could be read in context, though likely not before a number of letters had gone out.

Of course, Seanan McGuire was in many ways taking the heat for the true focus of the Kittenboard's ire, Joss Whedon, who has been receiving a huge amount of pressure for his decision to kill Tara. As he responded on the Bronze board:

over the gay thing, revisited
Posted by: Joss—May 22, 2002, 2:27 A.M.
   Thought I was out, but . . . had one more thing to add. I killed Tara. Some of you may have been hurt by that. It is very unlikely it was more painful to you than it was to me. I couldn't even discuss it in story meetings without getting upset, physically. Which is why I knew it was the right thing to do. Because stories, as I have so often said, are not about what we WANT. And I knew some people would be angry with me for destroying the only gay couple on the show, but the idea that I COULDN'T kill Tara because she was gay is as offensive to me as the idea that I DID kill her because she was gay. Willow's story was not about being gay. It was about weakness, addiction, loss . . .the way life hits you in the gut right when you think you're back on your feet. The course of true love never did run smooth, not on my show. (only Dennis Franz has suffered more than my characters.) I love Amber and she knows it. Eventually, this story will end for all of them. Hers ended sooner.
Or did it . . .?
Yeah, it did.

This was not accepted by the Kittens and has led to the writing of letters to writers and producers, a call for a boycott of episodes taking place after the death of Tara, and calls to not buy *Buffy* video tapes or DVDs. There's even an interesting web site that takes this as a title, *Sex, Lies & btw.: Don't Buy Their Video Tapes!* (*www.puk.de/ivanova/ toaster_neub.html*) with links to the Kittenboard's Lesbian Cliché FAQ and an interesting comparison of quotes from Joss and the other shows writers, many of them in response to the pressure they have been receiving, ranging from the sad—

It's the first time that we've gotten public outcry where I really can't even read some of the letters, they hurt so much. It's very indicative of how underrepresented gay people feel in the culture. Because the kinds of letters we've gotten have been so emotional and so personal and so deeply felt, you realize that every single instance of a positive portrayal of gay love on television means so much to people. (Marti Noxon, *Advocate*, July 2002)

to the angry—
In characterizing Tara's death as yet another in the string of cliched lesbian deaths, you indicate that you do not see Tara as anything but a lesbian, you do not see her as the unique character she was, but rather just as a woman who had sex with women, and, in doing so, you reveal your own homophobia, your own prejudice and, more than anything else, your own lack of understanding of what we did with that character. (Drew Z. Greenberg, *Bronze Beta*, Oct. 15, 2002)

At the date of this writing, the lesbian drama still continues: Willow now dating Kennedy, Tara not yet returned—even as an incarnation of the First Evil, though this is more due to reported contract negotiation difficulties with Amber Benson, who portrays Tara, than with a decision by the show's writers.

Then again, members of the Kittenboard have claimed that Amber has said she would not return, out of respect for her fans. But given that Plan C was named after a (joking) plot for Amber Benson to be kidnapped by women in kitten ears en route to a Canadian *Star Trek* convention, it is possible that Amber's respect for her fans is tempered by fear:

(Excerpt from planc.bravepages.com/aboutus/manifesto.html)

[. . .]Plan B: Kidnap Amber.
We stealthily take over the hotel at AmberCon (forget TorontoTrek, it was AmberCon, dammit), disguise ourselves in kitten ears, kill the lights, kidnap Amber in an Amber-sized bag tied with velvet rope (no chafing), and escape in a fanboat outside. Due to the large number of kittens involved, some would have to ride outside the craft and thus flutterkicking was practiced.

Then we realized that there would be geeks in Klingon costumes in the hotel, some probably carrying batleffs, and as we are a non-violent group, didn't relish the idea of having to fight our way out.

And so was born . . .

Plan C.

1) Border guard (with kitten ears) instructs Amber that the path to Toronto is under "construction" and recommends a detour that will get her there faster. [. . .]

After all, an unbalanced fan killed singer Selena Perez, and another killed actress Rebecca Schaeffer. Benson, talented as both, can hardly miss the parallels, especially since her character has already been kidnapped (by Glory) and murdered (by Warren). And death threats have already been sent to executives of The WB, who are far less recognizable and don't have to make convention appearances to further their careers.

If this is the case, then the fans, in their intensity, have been responsible for an even greater change in the show, the voluntary exclusion of an actor. Which, overall, is far more significant than the dropping of a minor subplot, such as the Double Meat Palace storyline. Tara was the conscience of the show, the hamburgers were a joke.

Finally, Sarah Michelle Gellar has elected not to renew her contract, thus ending the series, at least in its current form. Fans are free to speculate as to her reasoning for this, but it's fairly certain that all the pressures did not go on the plus side of the scale. And so the story ends . . . for the moment.

The manipulations continue. *Buffy* is over, but *Angel* and the gang will continue to face threats and horrors, fighting them, dealing with them, making workarounds and compromises in untenable situations, and even occasionally being beaten. And the same will be true of the cast, crew, and the writing staff of any future shows in the continued mythology.

A native of California, Kevin Andrew Murphy writes novels, plays, short stories, poems, and games. His most recent works are the novels Fathom: The World Below *(a novelization of Michael Turner's Fathom comics) and* Drum into Silence, *a posthumous collaboration with the late Jo Clayton, concluding her* Drums of Chaos *trilogy, as well as a novella, "With a Flourish and a Flair," in* Deuces Down, *the latest volume in George R.R. Martin's* Wild Cards *series. He has poems upcoming in Vox13's humorous H.P. Lovecraft anthology* Hastur, Pussycat! Kill! Kill! *and the mainstream* Poets Against the War *anthology. White Wolf will be publishing his World of Darkness novel* Penny Dreadful, *and he's currently working on a role-playing game adaptation of* Wild Cards *for the Theatrix system. More of his works may be found at www.sff.net/people/Kevin.A.Murphy.*

Carla Montgomery

INNOCENCE

What's Joss got against sex? As one who can relate to Xander, I've been cheering him on from the beginning, from Bug Lady to Mummy Girl to Faith (now that was a coup), but it never goes well. Nor does the rest of the Scooby gang do much better. Carla Montgomery explores this phenomenon, focusing on the most ill-fated sexual encounter of them all.

A WEREWOLF. A demon. A witch. A vampire.

What do these supernatural icons have in common other than appearing on your doorstep every Halloween demanding candy? Answer: All of them have been, at one time or another, the primary love interest of a main character on the *Buffy the Vampire Slayer* series. As followers of the show, we all know that dealings with the dark side are a given around the Hellmouth. For Buffy and company, they are a way of life. And, affairs of the heart, or various other parts of the anatomy, are obviously not exempt from the dangers of associating with Evil and those that are under its sway.

Throughout the series, the writers of the show haven't flinched in their exploration of all manner of issues surrounding the subject of teen intimacy. Obsession. Promiscuity. Homosexuality. Power plays. Loss of innocence. You name it, they've written it. And they have consistently used tremendous deftness, warmth, and genuine affection in their portrayals of teen relationships. But, clearly, when it comes to sex, love, and TV, Sunnydale couldn't be further in overall attitude from swinging, flirtatious Manhattan.

In this Californian suburb, when a love affair goes bad, it grows fangs. The question is, why?

FATAL ATTRACTIONS

"I'm 17; looking at linoleum makes me want to have sex."—Xander

Part of the answer may be found in taking a look at one of the basic overall premises of the show. Series creator Joss Whedon has stated in several interviews that part of his original concept for *Buffy* involved utilizing basic elements of horror to portray the teen experience through ongoing, rather twisted and dark, metaphors:

> I pitched [the show] as the ultimate high school horror show, very basically taking the pain, humiliation, alienation, and all the problems of high school and ballooning them into horrific proportions. The show only works if it resonates. That's the most important thing.

In other words, the demons Buffy and her friends confront are nearly always more than cardboard creatures for our heroes to defeat. They have emotions, needs, passion, ambition, even humor. They represent something. Just rip away the ugly masks, and you find all of the temptations, dangers, and evils that modern teens find themselves facing every day. We have all watched as the naive characters of the beginning of the series took on and defeated various archetypes of Evil and, in so doing, grew up little by little.

Monsters are more than monsters. Sex isn't just the sex depicted on most TV series. It can destroy. It can transform. The danger can be physical or emotional, or both. But it is never to be taken lightly.

On a purely physical level, several episodes have dealt with the danger that lurks when the body overrides the mind in that teenage, hormonal sort of way. For example, take Xander's close encounters of the wrong kind with the She-Mantis and Mummy Girl in the first and second seasons. In both cases, the attraction is clearly no more than pheromonal and Xander spends a large amount of time walking through the corridors of Sunnydale High in a lust-induced haze. And, in both cases, the danger to Xander is strictly limited to his physical body. Once the siren has been chopped up or turned back into dust, our hero returns to his normal, quick-witted self.

While the relationship of Willow and Oz isn't a fatal attraction in a bunny-boiling sense, it is another example of the dangers of the heat of passion. Literally. Despite Willow's attempts to save it, their romance can't survive once Oz finds another of his kind and his werewolf-strength testosterone kicks in. He is completely reduced to a single, primal urge and either he or "the other woman" are quite capable of ripping Willow to shreds if she gets in the way of their baser instincts. By trying to snap him out of his animal nature, Willow endangers both herself and the werewolf she loves.

But by far the most disturbing of these lustful relationships is the one that has developed between Buffy and Spike over recent seasons. There is absolutely nothing healthy in this relationship other than their mutual libidos. Physical and sexual abuse. Obsession. Jealousy. Psychological torment. The strange allure and addiction of dancing with danger. All of the darkest power struggles of sexual intimacy have been yanked into the spotlight through the mutually destructive acts of these two characters.

The difference here seems to be that, in addition to the physical act of sex having some correlation to endangerment of one's physical body, there is the added complication of a very real danger to the emotional well-being of the participants. While it is safe to say that actual love is not a factor in their relationship, the longer that Buffy and Spike continue their lust affair, the more psychologically damaged by it they become. The complexity of their relationship is more than hunter and hunted, domination and seduction. Spike is continually tortured by his obsession and is particularly dangerous because he is (along with Drew and Angel), according to Whedon, ". . . really a part of Buffy's life, not just external. Something emotional that she couldn't just physically fight." For Buffy, the danger of consorting with such darkness translates into a virtually mortal blow to her spirit. To dance with the dead can kill a vital part of who you are.

It's been hell to watch. But, just as these two have discovered, it's been next to impossible to turn the twisted thing off.

In Sunnydale, there is no such thing as safe sex. But, like, is it okay if you love him?

STAR-CROSSED LOVES

BUFFY: "I love you."
ANGEL: "I love you, too . . . I'll call you."

If simply having sex can get you bitten, maimed, or mutilated in Buffy's world, than what's a teenager in love supposed to do? The prognosis for any sort of long-term relationship looks grim indeed. Grim. But not hopeless. Although Whedon and company seem to be saying that teen intimacy can have serious, even horrific, consequences and should not be taken lightly, they do not appear to come down on the side of total abstinence, either.

Take, for example, the tremendously comic romance of Xander and Cordelia who are, as Whedon puts it, "so very wrong for each other that, of course, they must have each other and they must have each other now." It doesn't work. It can't. But, through that intimacy, both characters reveal aspects of themselves we haven't seen before. Cordelia can be vulnerable. Xander can be tender. Neither is the same person they were before their relationship began. Both have edged just a bit closer to maturity.

In a more dramatic sense, the relationship that develops between Willow and Tara changes forever the shy, little science nerd we once knew and loved. It is more than a gentle discovery of sexual orientation. For Willow, it is a personal revelation that is directly linked to her own empowerment. For the first time in the series, she is not the one in constant need of protection, but is gradually transformed by her bond with her lover into a protective, and even destructive, force that is to be taken deadly seriously.

Buffy's broken heart is revived through her romance with Riley. Anya is humanized (and dehumanized again) by her love for Xander.

But to really get to the pulsing heart of the matter, you have to look at the relationship of Buffy and Angel as the ultimate example in the series of the life-altering consequences of sexuality and love. Says Whedon:

> 'Surprise' and 'Innocence' represent the mission statement of the show more than any other shows we've done because they operate on both a mythic level and a very personal level. On a mythic level, it's the hero's journey. She loses this very important person to her . . . Angel goes bad and now she has to fight him . . . But on a personal level, this is the show about, 'I slept with someone and now he doesn't call me anymore.'

From the beginning, we know they couldn't be more wrong for each other. A vampire. A Slayer. It's worse than Montagues and Capulets. Their doom is inevitable and absolutely riveting. But even as Buffy and Angel's relationship careens out of control, the motives of the creators of the show become a little more clear. Almost nothing could be worse in terms of finding the horror of the high school experience than turning the guy you gave your virginity to into, literally, a soulless monster. The pivotal moment in Angel's bedroom the following day as the two recent lovers face the consequences of their sexual act has got to rank as one of the most devastating of such scenes to ever air on prime-time television.

Both characters are utterly transformed by the intimacy they shared the previous night.

Angel's metamorphosis from tortured soul into monster strikes a terrifying chord with anyone who has felt the vulnerability of love and sexual intimacy. To allow another individual such closeness, physically and emotionally, requires a level of trust that grants the lover a tremendous amount of personal power. Power to hurt. Or betray. In the case of Angel and Buffy, the abuse of that power translates into the emotional rape of an innocent who is learning to love for the first time.

The one point of light here seems to lie in the very gypsy curse that sets the whole thing in motion. Try to forget that the whole thing is irrational. To give a vampire his soul and then, once he achieves a moment of happiness, yank it back away from him again is a ridiculous plan. The fact is, that at least for a moment, Angel truly loves Buffy and he finds ultimate happiness as a result of that love.

The curse does not take effect because Buffy and Angel have sex. Angel's soul is stolen from him because he is in love. Whedon and company seem to be saying metaphorically here that, while sex and love are not one and the same, making love with someone you deeply care about is a somehow sublime, or even profound, experience.

And what of our hero?

Buffy's sexual initiation is the catalyst of an epic journey that has been building for the first two seasons of the show; namely, the crossover from adolescence to young adulthood. According to Whedon:

One of the distinguishing features of the blond girl in the alley who always got killed was that she actually had sex . . . Buffy was created partially to be a stereotype buster on that level . . . the issue of sex was one we were going to have to deal with eventually. . . 'Innocence' represents the effort to do that.

Despite the potential dangers to herself physically and emotionally, Buffy chooses to sleep with Angel and, like most teens, finds herself in way over her head. The results are nothing short of nightmarish.

"I said I didn't want to kill the girl who has sex," says Whedon, "and yet, I punish the hell out of her . . . I believe that Buffy and Angel were in love and that what they did wasn't bad . . . But, inevitably in a horror show, you end up punishing people for everything they do just so you can find the horror, the real emotional horror, of everything they go through."

What makes Buffy such a heroic character is her reaction to that punishment. Yes, there are tears. But there are also rocket launchers.

After Angel summarily rejects her, she is spiritually wounded, but she doesn't crumple up in a corner or retreat to whatever the modern equivalent of a nunnery might be. She tracks the creep down and they fight it out hand to hand. Their battle in the blasted mall is simultaneously an epic fight of Good vs. Evil and, as Angel taunts her in sadistic, sexually explicit fashion, the intensely personal battle of a young woman confronting the man who has wronged her. Says Whedon, "This show was designed to be a feminist show. For her to be so abused by him and for her response to be, as Spike might say, 'kick him in the ghoulies,' it's very primal. It's very important. It's kind of empowering. And I kind of love it."

Buffy is changed forever by her loss of innocence. She is punished. But she is also empowered by her experience as she crosses the line that separates child- from adulthood. She can no longer be the naive young lover she once was; she is warier, worldlier, and a whole lot stronger because of what she has endured. She has passed through the, "baptism of adolescent fire, the romance gone wrong," and emerges as a heroic young woman on the other side.

CONCLUSIONS

"Do you want me to wag my finger at you and tell you that you acted rashly? You did. And I can. But I know that you loved him."—Giles

One of the real pleasures of viewing the *Buffy* series over the years has been to watch as, amid all the prosthetics and gore, the characters have gradually grown up. And a big part of that process for each of them has been to learn how to deal with the issues that arise out of sexual and/or emotional intimacy.

Sex in Sunnydale can be dangerous. Even deadly. But it is not bad in itself. There is often pleasure and even true love. The point is, that like everything else in Buffy's world, there are consequences for every action. Affairs of the body and/or soul should never be entered into lightly.

For these teens, sexual and emotional intimacy is a doorway to adulthood. A means of gaining personal power. And, ultimately, an act of transformation.

Perhaps that is why the final scene of "Innocence" (2-14) has such poignancy. We know how much Buffy has gone through, how much she has suffered because of her choices, and how very much she has changed and matured through that process. Yet, her mother hugs her and says, "You look the same to me."

Despite all the hurt, the loss of innocence, she still retains her Self. Unlike Angel's, her soul is bruised, but still intact. The tremendous courage and integrity she has always possessed have endured the trials of initiation and she has emerged on the other side even stronger than she was before. That is what makes her a hero in the truest sense. And that is what makes love worth taking the risk.

Carla Montgomery began as a reluctant voyeur, but is doing her best to make up for that naughty behavior now. Her essays and short stories have appeared in several anthologies and her commentaries aired on the local NPR station. For really weird story ideas, she highly recommends working as a late-night cop reporter. She currently lives with her family in Utah . . . but that's another story.

Christie Golden

WHERE'S THE RELIGION IN WILLOW'S WICCA?

Yes, Virginia, Wicca is a real religion and there are real witches. And no, Willow is not one of them.

ONE OF THE MANY GREAT things about *Buffy the Vampire Slayer* is it gives hope to the geek in all of us. I'm not talking about the *Über*-geeks Warren, Andrew and Jonathan, but our geek heroes Xander and Willow. Especially Willow, who gives computer nerds a warm and cozy feeling, like we're wrapped in warm blankets. Except, of course, when she's Dark Rosenberg, when she makes everyone want to dive *under* the blankets.

Willow's evolution from computer nerd to powerful sorceress (I chose this word with care, more on that later) has been a fascinating journey over these last seven years. All of the characters on *Buffy* have grown, but Willow's arc has perhaps been the most profound. A very large part of that growth has to do with her becoming, in the words of Anya, "A very powerful Wicca (sic)."

This phrase bugs me for myriad reasons, and I'm going to tell you why. In a nutshell, I'm going to say that while the creators of *Buffy* are presenting Willow as a witch/Wicca(n), they are, alas, wrong. Remember I said that I deliberately chose the word "sorceress" earlier? It's a much more appropriate word, largely because it's a fantasy term that has no real practitioners in the Real World. A "sorceress" can be whatever the writers want her to be. But a witch, or a Wiccan, is something very real, and the creators of *Buffy* don't get it right.

I could go on for a whole book (and many have) exploring the differences between the Hollywood Witch, the Real Witch, the Wiccan, the Neopagan, the Santarian, the Asatruar, etc. but I've only got this one essay. So, for convenience's sake, I'll be working with the following definitions:

HOLLYWOOD WITCH: The version of "witch" we see in the movies.

REAL WITCH or just WITCH: Real live person who may practice spell craft, but who does not necessarily believe in a god or goddess.

WICCAN: A follower of a religion that believes in a god and goddess, works with natural energies, and incorporates spell casting into ritual. Wiccans are usually Witches, but not all Witches are Wiccans.

Is this all clear as mud? It's no wonder the *Buffy* folks have trouble with it.

(*Very important note:* Witches of all kinds [except for Hollywood Witches, occasionally, depending on the script] do not worship or even believe in Satan. Satan is a Christian concept and witches have nothing to do with him. For most people, whose whole definition of "witch" comes from the Salem witch trials, in which innocent folks were accused of consorting with the Devil, this is quite a shocker. But it's also very true.)

Having said all this, I will readily admit that Willow is a "Hollywood Witch," which is now becoming trendy again. The Hollywood Witch is a lot of fun for the writers, the actresses, and the viewers. She usually comes in two flavors, with slight variations.

First, there's the Scary Hollywood Witch, personified by the Wicked Witch of the West and other haggy beings. This is the gal we're all used to seeing around Halloween. Usually she's got green skin, but at the very least, she dresses in black, she rides a broom, and there's a wart.

Then there's the Sexy Hollywood Witch, sometimes overlaid with a bit o' sweetness to make the brew easier to drink. Such witches are Samantha from *Bewitched*, the heroine of *Bell, Book and Candle*, or Sabrina from the *Archie* comics. She's been joined in recent years by the sisters from *Charmed* and *Practical Magic*. It's cool to be a Sexy Hollywood Witch these days.

A Hollywood Witch, be she Scary or Sexy, can be easily spotted by the special effects guy who is always at her side. She chants in a funky language, her eyes go black, lightning shoots from her fingers, winds come out of nowhere (prettily tousling her long hair), things levitate, fly around the room, lose their skins, etc. It's pretty cool.

REAL WITCHES CAN'T DO THIS. And yes, there is definitely such a thing as a real witch.

The greatest problem in the depiction of Willow and her witchiness is that the creators of *Buffy* were not content with making her a sorceress, or even a Sexy Hollywood Witch. They decided to go one step further and fold the current hot religion of Wicca into the mix.

And there, my fellow Willow fans, is where things start falling apart.

The problem lies in the fact that Wicca is a real, genuine, bona-fide religion recognized and protected under the United States Constitution. Despite challenges from such noted conservatives as Jesse Helms, cases such as *Dettmer vs. Landon* (1986) stand to establish its authenticity as a viable religion. Even the *United States Military Chaplains Manual* recognizes Wicca as a religion. Yup, that's right—a Wiccan is every bit as real a follower of her or his faith (Xander's hilarious comment about "manwitches" notwithstanding, there are male Witches and Wiccans and they aren't called "warlocks") as a Methodist or a Jew. ("A Wiccan, a Methodist, and a Jew walk into a bar . . .")

And unfortunately, if one goes by what we've seen on the show and in the various official books such as *The Watcher's Guide*, nobody connected with the show has done a lot of research into what being a Wiccan means.

Heck, they haven't even gotten their grammar right. Willow is repeatedly and very clearly referred to as a "Wicca," which is comparable to saying a "Christia." One who follows the faith of Christianity is a Christian, one who follows the faith of Wicca is a Wiccan.

What's worse is what you'll find in *The Watcher's Guide*. On p. 146 is an essay on "Witches and Sorcerers." Giving credit where it's due, there's a lot of good info on the history of witchcraft, and in general it's a positive piece. And then the words "devotees of the goddess Wicca" appear.

Um. Well. First of all, there *is* no "goddess Wicca." There are many speculations as to the origins of the word "wicca," but it's never been the name of a goddess. The most likely origin is from the Indo-European word *Wikke* or *Weik*, which pertains to magic or sorcery.

Now, admittedly, as I have indicated, it's not as if it would have been easy for the creators of *Buffy* to come up with a nice, simple definition of Wicca that all practitioners would agree on. However, at the risk of not satisfying everyone, let me give it a whirl and we'll see if Willow really can accurately be called a Wiccan or if she's just another Sexy Hollywood Witch.

1. FIRST AND FOREMOST, WICCA IS A RELIGION. Divinity is represented in a pair of opposites: a god and a goddess. The goddess is regarded as the primary divinity and the god is her consort. Some believe that each god and goddess who has appeared in mythology is separate and real; others think that there is a main divinity with different aspects, much the same way an actor can play many roles.

Wiccans often honor the god and goddess through the Celtic Wheel of the Year, with eight holy days known as Sabbats:

February 2: Imbolc (Candlemas, or St. Brigid's Day). This holiday belongs to the goddess. Her light in the world is fire and candlelight, not the sun; we begin to believe that spring really is on the way. (If you view these holidays as spokes on a wheel, its opposite is Lughnasad, which is traditionally a day to honor the god.) In the U.S., this is also Groundhog Day, which is a contemporary "ritual" involving a groundhog testing to see if winter is really over (a sort of divination spell), or if it will last six more weeks—coincidentally, when the next Sabbat is celebrated. Most Wiccans love a good laugh and get a chuckle out of this.

March 21–23: Ostara, the Vernal Equinox. The Christian holiday of Easter is derived from "Ostara" or "Eostre," an Anglo-Saxon goddess of spring. Rabbits and eggs represent fertility and the awakening world. Day and night are of equal length. It lies opposite the Autumnal Equinox, of course.

May 1: Beltane, or May Day. Some traditions, such as the Maypole dance, still survive—and well, let's just say that the rather phallic image of the "maypole" isn't an accident. This holiday marks the union of the god and goddess. The reason there are traditionally so many weddings in June is that it was bad luck to be wed in the same months as the Divinities, but the month after was believed to be blessed. On the Wheel, it is opposite Samhain. Both are major holidays.

June 21–23: Summer Solstice, or Litha, often associated with the Fairy Folk. A very magical time.

August 1: Lammas, or Lughnasad. This was often the first harvest of the autumn, and marks the moment when the god (often believed to live in the crops) willingly sacrifices himself so that humans may survive the winter.

September 21–23: Mabon, or the Autumnal Equinox.

October 31: Halloween, or Samhain (pronounced "sow-ahn"). This is considered the Witches' New Year and is the highest of the holy days. The time between Samhain and Yule, the birthday of the god, is often considered to be time out of time, for reflection and settling into the still, quiet darkness. It's a good time for magic, as the "veil between the worlds" is believed to be quite thin.

December 22: Yule, the Winter Solstice. This marks the time when the days grow longer, the return of the light, the birthday of the sun god.

Wiccans also celebrate what are called Esbats, which are the new moon and the full moon. Witches and Wiccans work with the energy of the seasons and the waxing and waning energies of the moon.

Many things we've learned about Willow seem to contradict or ignore much of the above. Admittedly, there are indeed references to various gods and goddesses. Hecate, the Greek crone goddess who is often linked with Persephone and Demeter to form the Maiden, Mother, and Crone trio of the moon's cycles, is known as "the witches' goddess" and is frequently invoked on the show. And when Willow decided to raise Buffy from the dead, she asked for the aid of Osiris, the Egyptian god of the dead. Perhaps the most "Wiccan" ritual we've seen came at the very last, during the series finale. From what I saw, it appeared to me as though Willow was performing what is known as a "drawing down," when the supplicant draws Divinity directly into herself (or himself— one can "draw down" the god as well). Essentially, it's channeling. For a few moments, Willow actually became a goddess—or The Goddess— and had all Her powers. Kennedy said, "You're a goddess," and she was correct, right down to the hair color change. (Which, by the way, doesn't happen to real Wiccans when they perform this rite.)

But there are goofs that no self-respecting Wiccan would make. Invoking "Diana" as a "goddess of love" is certain to piss off that famous virgin, whose best-known involvement with a suitor ended badly for the gentleman in question when she turned him into a deer and set his own hounds on him. Not exactly the most romantic of encounters.

Oz's comment to Willow in which he said she stopped keeping track of the full moon after he left is also peculiar, since witches make it a point to know when the moon is full, and are aware that its energy is different from the new moon.

Judging by what we've seen on the show, it's safe to conclude that Willow does not look at her magic as a part of a religious, spiritual path, nor does she truly worship and honor the gods she calls on for assistance in her spells.

It would have been nice to see more attention paid to this—I can picture Willow and Tara wearing flowers in their hair and holding hands on Beltane, or doing serious magic on Samhain, or singing "Happy Birthday" to the sun god on Yule.

2. A GUIDING PRINCIPLE OF WICCA IS CALLED "THE THREEFOLD LAW." This is essentially karma—the belief that what you do comes back to you threefold. It's not to be taken literally. It doesn't mean that if you nicely stop to help someone change a flat, that people will stop three times to help you change one. It does mean that if you do something good and helpful, when you are in need of help, you'll have it in abundance.

The converse is equally true. If you do something vindictive and cruel, be prepared for it to come back to you like a boomerang, three times as bad. It's important to understand the Threefold Law if you are someone who shapes and bends things to your will. It's kind of a "Slow Down, Proceed with Caution" sort of thing.

3. ANOTHER PRINCIPLE OF WICCA IS THE PHRASE "AN YE HARM NONE, DO AS THOU WILT." This means, as long as you don't hurt anyone, do what you want. Key phrase: "An ye harm none." This doesn't just mean you can't go out and beat people up and take what you want. This means harm none, including yourself.

To the best of my knowledge, neither of these important philosophies has ever been mentioned on Buffy. One might think such phrases might have given Willow pause long before she became "addicted" or tried to thwart the natural order by raising Buffy.

4. WICCANS USUALLY INCORPORATE RITUAL INTO SPELL WORKING. While the Hollywood Witch only needs her FX guy and some fun-sounding words, real witches require ingredients for spells. They're more like the sage, rose quartz, and green candle ingredients than the eye of newt and fawn blood that we've seen on *Buffy*. (Remember that "harm none"? Killing a fawn is certainly harming it. Wiccans love animals and would never, ever hurt them.)

Wiccans also often use physical components, but don't need them. Their "spells" are prayers, supplemented with a little practical working. The Wiccan god and goddess really do "help those who help themselves." Contrary to the ways in which many other religions view fate and destiny, witches and Wiccans have always known that they need to take an active part in bending and shaping their own lives.

Some quickie examples regarding prosperity: The Hollywood Witch turns lead into gold. A Christian may pray to God for wealth, then sit back and wait for it to appear. A real witch may do a money spell. A Wiccan may pray, but as part of the prayer ritual he'll also do a money spell AND get out the classified ads and look for a part-time job.

Here's a more detailed "for instance." This a possible description of how a Wiccan and a Hollywood Witch might go about casting the same spell.

Say it's a love spell. Our Hollywood Witch manages to obtain a lock of hair of the desired person, or makes a voodoo-type doll, or snaps a picture. Browsing through the mysterious shop on the corner, she finds an ancient tome with crackly, dusty pages. At home, surrounded by about a million candles, she recites a very complicated spell. Bright pink light shoots up from the book. Several blocks away, the desired person's eyes glaze over. He rushes to our Hollywood Witch, her love slave.

The Wiccan might think that her coworker is cute, but she knows she can't "make" him love her. Remember the Threefold Law and "an ye harm none?" If she casts a spell to make someone else fall in love with her when he normally wouldn't, that's violating the other's free will—definitely harming him. Also, she could find herself the victim of others who try to bend her to their will.

So while she might long for this cute coworker, she takes the bigger view. She purchases essential oils, perhaps rose and ylang-ylang, known as romantic scents. She takes a long bath by candlelight using red and pink candles. They're the color of love, and the bath purifies her body and spirit. She might choose to wear something romantic or sexy, in anticipation of the love that will arrive soon. She sits in front of her altar, which is filled with flowers, red candles, and a beautiful seashell. She has perhaps written out a spell, or maybe she makes one up on the spot. Either way, she knows that her own words carry much more weight than some stranger's spells.

She calls upon Aphrodite, the Greek goddess of love, and asks her to send love the Wiccan's way, using the seashell as a focalizing point. She asks for the wisdom to know love when it comes and promises to thank Aphrodite for it when it arrives. And she says, *if it's meant to be,* it wouldn't bother her if that cute coworker happened to notice her tomorrow.

Over the next several days, our Wiccan lady dresses more romantically, uses perfume, and accepts invitations to go out where she'll have a chance to meet men she wouldn't otherwise meet.

They're rather dramatically different takes on the same thing, aren't they? Both are magic, both involve spells, but one is much more real than the other.

One thing I have to address before I close is the infamous "Wicca Group" at which Willow and Tara meet. They're hilarious, and rightfully deserve Willow's contempt. You'll find people like these in Wicca, and they're usually referred to as "fluffy-bunny Wiccans." But I find it very interesting that in the original script there was a mention of "healing energy" that the members used. That line got cut, and when Willow mentioned "spells," they all jumped down her throat for using negative stereotypes. According to *The Watcher's Guide, Vol. 2*, the line was cut for length. While that may be true, I also think it would just get too complicated for the show if there were "fluffy bunnies" out there working magic too, so the writers chose to make the Wicca group "wimmin" completely without power, full only of hot air. Willow comments that she was talking about "real" spells; the irony is, of course, that the healing energy that the Wicca group wimmin performed is much more real and closer to what Wiccans actually do than Willow's FX-created black eyes and levitating tricks.

Now, if we're being honest, watching someone sit around and pray isn't all that interesting, and writers of TV shows know this. The pink lightning and stuff is much more fun to watch. So that's what we get—the Hollywood Witch. There's nothing wrong with her—but she's not a Wiccan.

So, in sum . . . is Willow a sorceress?

Absolutely.

Is she a witch?

Only the Hollywood kind.

Is she a Wiccan?

Sadly, no.

Is she a wonderfully written and acted character on what was one of the best TV shows to ever hit the airwaves?

Oh, heck yeah.

Award-winning author Christie Golden has written twenty-two novels and several short stories in the fields of science fiction, fantasy and horror. Though best known for tie-in work, Golden is also the author of two original fantasy novels from Ace Books, King's Man & Thief *and* Instrument of Fate, *which made the 1996 Nebula Preliminary Ballot. Under the pen name of Jadrien Bell, she wrote a historical fantasy thriller titled* A.D. 999, *which won the Colorado Author's League Top Hand Award for Best Genre Novel of 1999. She wrote "The White Doe" for the* Buffy The Vampire Slayer *anthology* Tales Of The Slayer Vol. I *and "The Sun Child" for the* Angel *anthology* The Longest Night. *Her latest "treks" include* Voyager *novels* Homecoming *and* The Farthest Shore. *The two-part storyline takes place immediately after the* Voyager *finale, in which she takes familiar friends in new directions. Golden lives in Denver, Colorado, with her artist husband Michael Georges and their two cats. Her website is www.christiegolden.com.*

Jean Lorrah

LOVE SAVES
THE WORLD

Buffy's love life may go up and down, but the love within Buffy's self-created family is permanent. The love shared by Buffy, Xander, Willow, and Giles is real and lasting, and constitutes a family more stable and loving than most blood families. As Joss says, "I really want to get this message out, that it's not about blood." When things look bleak in the Buffyverse, sometimes the love between Buffy and Giles, or Willow and Xander, is all that keeps us going. And at the end of season six, this love saves the world. Jean Lorrah tells the story.

THERE IS ONLY ONE THING on Earth more powerful than evil, and that's us," Buffy Summers says at the end of "Bring on the Night" (7-10), verbalizing the theme that has held *Buffy the Vampire Slayer* together from its inception. Who are "us"? By the end of the series, Buffy, Willow, Xander, Giles, Anya, Dawn, and Spike, with the extended family of the surviving Slayers, Faith, Principal Wood, and even Andrew. The first four have been part of "us" from the beginning, while the others have replaced some of the original members of this odd little self-made family.

In his commentary on "Welcome to the Hellmouth," (1-1), on the first season DVD release, producer Joss Whedon says: "The idea of this band of . . . outcasts being the heart of the show and . . . creating their own little family is . . . the mission statement of the show." The theme of a chosen rather than blood-related family develops throughout the first six seasons of the series, until it risks destruction in the final episode of the sixth season, "Grave" (6-22). Yet family is what saves the world at the end of season six and, perhaps more than ever before, the redemptive power of that family is shown in the seventh-season events that follow. The final episode even has the title "Chosen" (7-22), as Buffy's chosen family defeat the final assault of evil in Sunnydale.

At the end of the sixth season, Willow, in a paroxysm of grief over Tara's senseless death, decides to destroy the world. For the first time, the traditional destructive force comes not from without, but from within the group. Jacqueline Lichtenberg, in her essay "The Power of Becoming," has addressed the question of why Willow, who may have misused her powers before but was never a deliberate threat to innocent people, reacts in such an unexpected way. What I want to address is why the world is saved this time not by Buffy, not by the team destroying some outside evil, but by the power of love, in this instance represented in Xander. Only Xander, often considered the weakest of Buffy's cohorts, can reach and persuade Willow, because he and Willow share a lifelong bond that is closer than that of traditional brother and sister.

Xander often articulates the ongoing theme of understanding and forgiveness of anyone who is accepted into this circle of friends. In the fifth-season episode "Into the Woods" (5-10), when Riley is leaving, Xander tells Buffy: "You've been treating Riley like the rebound guy" [he means rebound from Angel, of course], "when he's the one that comes along once in a lifetime. If he's not the guy, if what he needs from you just isn't there, let him go. Break his heart, and make it a clean break. But if you really think you can love this guy . . . I'm talking scary, messy, no-emotions-barred need . . . then think about what you're about to lose."

Buffy is too late to stop Riley from leaving her life, and when she next meets him in "As You Were" (6-15), he has begun his own family by marrying someone else. That episode only makes sense in light of Riley's failure to become a part of the nontraditional family at the heart of *Buffy*. The fact that he consorted with vampires is no reason that he could not be forgiven and restored to grace—look at Angel, at Anya, and, in the seventh season, Willow and Spike.

There is a pattern repeated time and again in *Buffy the Vampire Slayer*: if someone is a member of Buffy's family, then it doesn't matter how far into the dark side that person treads—it is always possible to be forgiven and restored to the family. Only people outside the family do not have that option. Cordelia, hardly the personification of Evil to begin with, was the first to be so redeemed—and look what she has gone on to in the spinoff, *Angel*. Angel was next, paying with his soul for seducing the underage Buffy—disguised in the text as the curse that would not allow him to be happy, which somehow got that celebration of Buffy's seventeenth, not eighteenth, birthday past the censors. Note the parallel in Buffy's relationship with Spike: Angel's rape of Buffy was statutory; Spike's attempt, although unsuccessful, was literal. In both cases, what followed was repentance, absolution, penance, redemption, and restoration to the family. Angel then goes off to create his own family, where we see the same pattern of "membership = forgiveness" that we see in Buffy, while in "Chosen" (7-22) Spike becomes a Champion, the conduit for the power that destroys the Sunnydale Hellmouth, a willing sacrifice that we recognize as a transcendence. If Willow becomes a goddess in the series finale, Spike becomes a saint.

Let's examine this changing but all-important chosen family. When the series opened, Buffy was the daughter of a newly divorced single mother—hardly an unusual situation in the 1990s. However, she has consistently demonstrated her inability to form a traditional romantic relationship with an appropriate partner, being primarily attracted to the very vampires it is her destiny to slay. Her lasting relationships are not romantic ones—it is doubtful that Buffy will ever marry.

Yet Buffy heads a family—one no more dysfunctional than the ones we meet every day. The Scoobies at first consisted of a Slayer, her Watcher, a computer geek, a nerd, and a valley girl. All were human. Soon, though, Angel, the vampire with a soul, became the first nonhuman addition to Buffy's created family. Then came Spike, the vampire who never could be as evil as he wanted to be (consider from first appearance his gentleness with Drusilla). Spike was thrown onto the mercy of the Scoobies and became one of them when the chip was put in his head. He was joined by Anya, a vengeance demon turned human, and finally Dawn, the innocent creation who had no knowledge that she was not really Buffy's little sister but a "key" made to gain what each season's primary villain wants: world power. In the seventh season, extended family are added—sort of aunts, uncles, and cousins—as Principal Wood, Faith, and Andrew join along with the Potential Slayers to form a united front for the final battle.

Dawn is the only member of the family who did not begin as a human—all the vampires once were, and Anya was at one time a woman who wished for the ability to take revenge on men. But Dawn begins as no more a person than the Buffybot: a creature made for a single purpose. By the time the Scoobies work out what Dawn is, the power of their love and acceptance has made Dawn so real that Buffy cannot allow her to be destroyed. And, of course, Buffy's sacrifice of herself to save Dawn parallels the sacrifice of Christ and other redeemer figures: if Dawn was not "real" before that sacrifice, she certainly becomes so then. Although it has never been articulated this way, I think we can assume that Buffy's sacrifice provided Dawn with a soul.

It is Dawn who brings Spike into Buffy's family circle: Dawn trusts him, Spike loves Dawn like a daughter, and Buffy needs him to protect Dawn from both Sunnydale's usual dangers and the truth about her origins. The death of Buffy's mother ends the last traditional family blood tie (for Dawn, as explained above, is not really Buffy's sister, but, like Pinocchio, has been turned into a real person by love). Now everyone in Buffy's family is there by choice. And while all this is happening, Willow slowly turns from computer wizard into a real wizard—that is, into a dangerously powerful witch, at the same time falling in love with Tara and bringing her into the family in the closest thing the series has seen to a successful marriage.

In the sixth season one theme that has been slowly working its way through the series reaches its culmination: with the departure of Giles, all the former adult authority figures are gone and Buffy is left with the responsibility of caring for Dawn and continuing to save the world while coping with earning a living by flipping burgers, paying taxes, keeping a roof over her own head and her sister's, and falling into an uneasy relationship with Spike.

The sixth season explores this nontraditional family not only through Buffy's struggles to be a mother figure, but through the comparison of three relationships: Buffy and Spike, Xander and Anya, and Willow and Tara. Clearly the healthiest relationship is that of Willow and Tara: Buffy's attraction for Spike culminates in his attempting to rape her when she tries to end it; Xander is only too easily tricked into leaving Anya at the altar (after which Anya only too easily first has rebound sex with Spike and then returns to being a vengeance demon); but when Willow and Tara get back together in "Entropy," neither has done anything irredeemable and everyone rejoices.

Nevertheless, the family is disintegrating. Angel is gone permanently, Cordelia with him. Oz and Riley never do succeed in becoming family members. Anya and Spike betray the others, and Tara's death releases

Willow's power in an act of despair. The world threatens to end, just as it does at the end of every season, but this time not only is there no unified family of Scoobies to combat it, but the threat comes from one of their own. Xander's weakness prevents the marriage that might have become a strong center, leaving Anya so demoralized that she has rebound sex with Spike, who is rebounding from Buffy. Spike's despair when their discovery prompts Buffy to reject him with no apparent chance of redemption leads him to attempt to rape her—all in a direct line not caused by but made possible by Xander's leaving Anya at the altar.

But if Xander's weakness is the efficient if not the material cause of the disintegration of the central Buffy family, his strength begins the restoration through his bond with Willow. While he may not be ready to be a husband, he certainly knows how to be the brother Willow needs to bring her back to humanity. As if to highlight the fact that the central family story of the sixth season is different from anything seen on Buffy before, the season's villains, a trio of inept nerds, mock the repetitive action structure of the series. Every season there is some new Evil force out to destroy the universe. In the sixth season, it is the comic relief previously responsible for such inventions as the Buffybot and the invisibility ray who attempt to become a major force for Evil. They can't—they may have high IQ's, but they have neither common sense nor savoir faire. It is by accident that they unloose the Evil in Willow—Evil from the midst of Buffy's family.

Buffy is no match for Willow—she can only try, unsuccessfully, to prevent her longtime friend from performing acts that are, in truth, unforgivable—such as torturing Warren and then executing him by skinning him alive. After that, Buffy is preoccupied with trying to save Warren's two cohorts. Giles acquires special powers with which to attack Willow, but he can only make her emotionally vulnerable to Xander. It is then up to Xander to reach Willow; if he can't, the world ends.

At the end of "Grave" (6-22), Xander says to Willow, "The first day of kindergarten, you cried because you broke the yellow crayon. And you were too afraid to tell anyone. You've come pretty far. Ending the world, not a terrific notion. But the thing is, yeah. I love you. I love crayon-breaking-Willow and I love scary-veiny-Willow. So if I'm going out, it's here. If you want to kill the world, then start with me. I've earned that." And despite her protests, he keeps repeating, "I love you," until Willow collapses in tears and returns to herself.

It really shouldn't surprise us that Xander can reach Willow. It was established early in the series that they are closest of friends, and articulated in the third season, in "Amends" (3-10), when Willow was concerned about her relationship with Xander when she was dating Oz. Buffy told her, "Xander has a piece of you that Oz just can't touch." The love between Xander and Willow long predates Buffy's arrival in Sunnydale. It is agape, true friendship, and this love, not any ass-kicking by Buffy, saves the world.

The seventh season's villain is a return visit of The First Evil from season three. Why the repetition? Have the writers run out of ideas? I don't think so; I think they are highlighting themes that have been backgrounded in the past, and showing that what is happening as the characters grow older is also that they *grow*. The repetition shows us not a circle, but an ascending spiral.

Buffy and her friends have changed drastically over the past few years. Buffy is finally successful and comfortable in her role of mother figure, although she is disconcerted when actually taken for Dawn's mother. She has been given the job of guidance counselor at Sunnydale High—an adult job. The new principal, instead of considering her either a juvenile delinquent or an enemy, respects her as an equal. The high school is open, although parts of it are still being rebuilt—and Xander, after a long series of dead-end jobs, is now in a position of adult responsibility as the head of the construction crew. Willow returns, but has to earn her place in this family again. Anya does penance for briefly becoming a vengeance demon again. Spike returns half mad with having his soul restored—something The First takes advantage of—but he is restored to sanity and far more by the end of the season. Like Willow, Spike becomes transcendent in the final episode: each transformed in a different way through Buffy's acceptance, they once again save the world.

The Buffy family reinvents itself, just as at the beginning of the first season Buffy's own family had been broken, and she had to create a new one. Halfway through the seventh season, Spike redeems himself in Buffy's eyes—in "Never Leave Me" (7-9) she tells him, "I saw you change. I saw your penance." He accepts it and then lives up to it—in "Bring on the Night" (7-10), he refuses to return to evil. The First in the form of Drusilla (who does not fool Spike for a moment), asks him what makes him think he can "be any good at all in this world," and he replies, "She does. Because she believes in me."

The redemptive power of love is articulated in traditional fashion: Spike's soul is restored, which makes him once again capable of sin (as opposed to simple evil). He falls prey to The First because he is in a sense innocent, newly reborn, while at the same time he is an experienced adult subject to adult temptation. He kills. His need for human blood is portrayed as an addiction, which he can overcome through withdrawal, unlike Willow's magic, which is an essential part of her and must be controlled, not left unused. Spike's redemption is actually easier than Willow's, but in the end Spike can only be a martyr, while Willow becomes a goddess.

Spike confesses to Buffy. She forgives him. She calls it penance, but actually she grants him absolution—his penance is the withdrawal agony followed by torture by The First. At the end of "Showtime" (7-11), Spike is indeed restored and Buffy takes him home.

Willow is useful, but is not completely restored to the family until the series finale—both she and others are afraid that her powers could run rampant again. Anya says she, Willow, and the rest of the Buffy family are responsible for the breach in the fabric of the universe caused by their resurrection of Buffy at the beginning of the sixth season—but it was Willow who led them in that venture.

Giles, once a father figure to Buffy's family, returns with several young Slayers-in-training—but it is Buffy who has to demonstrate that if they work together they can win: "If we all do our part, believe it, we'll be the ones left standing." As for Giles, his role has changed drastically. He now treats Buffy as an equal, and until the great betrayal scene in "Empty Places," he lets her lead the fight against The First while he attempts to find and prepare the young potential slayers.

Buffy, Xander, and Willow remain to the end at the core of the family, with Anya still a trusted member and Dawn increasing in strength and confidence. Spike is restored, and when Angel returns to offer himself as Champion, Buffy reminds him that he has his own front to maintain against evil if hers fails, and sends him back to the family he has created in Los Angeles. All of Buffy's immediate family take a parental role with the apprentice Slayers. The central characters have moved from being high school kids with parents or parent-figures in the first season, to all taking the role of parent-figures themselves in season seven—just as happens in traditional families, the children evolve into adults, and in return take responsibility for new children.

Xander's relationship with Willow saved the day at the end of the sixth season, but the series ends with a group effort, the central family of kids who had to grow up too fast in the first two or three seasons dealing with the Potential Slayers who have to grow up even faster.

In the last few episodes Buffy's chosen family is tested nearly to destruction. The young potential slayers squabble and rebel against authority like any group of teenagers. Faith returns, redeemed in her own way, and is accepted into Buffy's family only to betray it by undermining Buffy's authority in "Empty Places." However, Faith quickly recognizes her inadequacy as a parent figure.

Buffy is compared to King Arthur in the final episodes, from her sending Angel away because it is her fight, not his, right down to pulling the weapon with which to defeat The First out of a stone. However, that weapon on the one hand is not a sword but a scythe, the weapon of the Grim Reaper, and on the other hand is not wielded alone: when Buffy is wounded in battle and thinks she cannot continue, she tosses it to Faith. And there is the crux of the difference between Buffy and Arthur (or any other hero of the monomyth): Buffy defies the tradition that has the hero of the monomyth dying in the final battle by fighting alone or with only a single faithful companion at his side. Like a mother providing for her children, Buffy shares her power and survives.

Arthur's round table was his family, and Camelot ended when Mordred succeeded in dividing the ranks of that family. Dawn would be the obvious Mordred analogue, but instead Faith is brought back, Buffy's evil twin, as it were. Faith's betrayal, though, this time lasts only one night; the very next day she cedes authority back to Buffy, sisterhood is restored, and Buffy resolves the problem in a way that would never have occurred to Arthur: she gives her power to all the potential slayers, thereby changing the very laws of her universe.

The only person with the power to confer such powers is Willow, who has not conjured such power since she almost destroyed the world at the end of season six. A year later she redeems herself and becomes a goddess, transforming all the Potentials into slayers, and making it possible for them to hold back The First until the surviving members of Buffy's family can escape.

However, the Hellmouth has been irrevocably opened. In the monomyth, the hero dies saving his society. There is no saving Sunnydale, most of whose citizens have left anyway. Only Buffy's family can be saved, and not without sacrifice. More than half the Potentials die in the fight, as does Anya. But Spike achieves transcendency. If there is any question in the mind of the audience that Spike had redeemed himself (there is plenty in the mind of every character except Buffy), it is dispelled when he becomes the conduit for the energy that destroys the Sunnydale Hellmouth once and for all.

Buffy's surviving family escape, ironically, in a Sunnydale High schoolbus, and pause to take stock. Buffy has come full circle in one sense, but spiraled higher in another. She is once more part of a broken family, one that has lost many of its members not to divorce but to the finality of death. The members of that yet again broken family must move on—some of them possibly to Cleveland—and build new families as Buffy built hers in Sunnydale and Angel his in Los Angeles.

But Willow is now a force for Good as powerful as any Evil they have fought in the past seven years, while Buffy, who may not have the sheer power that Willow wields, is the inspirational force whose idea has permanently changed the universe she lives in. Buffy, Willow, Giles, and Xander, the only survivors of the original Buffy family at the beginning of the seventh season, have all survived to fight again. Xander, despite losing an eye, is still the one who sees clearly, and the one who keeps up everyone's hopes.

Redemption and survival seem to be the final themes of *Buffy the Vampire Slayer*, made possible through the creation first of the tightly-knit central family, and then the extended family that can even admit and protect a weak link like Andrew.

A highly untraditional family, perhaps, but a successful one because of its bonds of love.

New York Times *best-selling author Jean Lorrah is the author of the award-winning vampire romance* Blood Will Tell, *the award-winning children's book* Nessie and the Living Stone, *and the acclaimed Savage Empire series. She is co-author of* First Channel, Channel's Destiny *and* Zelerod's Doom, *part of the cult classic Sime~Gen series.*

Margaret L. Carter

A WORLD WITHOUT SHRIMP

Joss loves to play mind games with us. Like in the opening credits to "Superstar,"
in which Jonathan is featured as the star of the show. Or in "Normal Again,"
where Joss leaves us with the prospect of the entire series being the delusional
imaginings of a psychotic Buffy. Or in "Buffy vs. Dracula," in which Buffy
suddenly and inexplicably has a sister. It gets a bit confusing. Do the monks
change history in creating Dawn or do they just change everyone's memories
(and create physical changes like photos, etc.)? Does Anya create an alternate
universe or does she just tap into an existing one? (And if there is an infinite
number of alternate universes, can we collect an army of Buffys to fight the next
Big Bad? . . . I guess this will have to wait for the movie.) Margaret Carter
sorts this out for us.

ALTERNATE REALITIES ARE NEAT," declares Anya in the *Buffy the Vampire Slayer* episode "Superstar" (4-17). Apparently the creators of the series agree, for the malleable nature of "reality" proves to be one of the *Buffy*verse's central themes. Anya reminds us of the infinite variety of possible worlds and the great differences that seemingly minor changes can produce: "You could, uh, have a world without shrimp. Or with, you know, nothing but shrimp" ("Superstar," 4-17). Or Buffy could inhabit a world with or without a younger sister. The advent of Dawn at the end of the first episode of season five sharply draws the viewer's attention to the fluidity of this fictional

176

universe. The transformation of the *Buffy*verse by the sudden appearance of Dawn ("sudden" to the audience, not to the characters, who "know" Buffy has always had a sister) highlights the importance of the "alternate reality" theme in this series. Most television programs imitate the presumed stability of the primary world, the "real" world we live in. At most, the average series may feature an occasional fantasy sequence or *It's a Wonderful Life* pastiche. *Buffy the Vampire Slayer*, in contrast, presents several alternate reality episodes that produce major dislocations of the world as the characters know it. This recurring motif infects the *Buffy*verse with a fundamental instability. The introduction of a younger sister retroactively transforms Buffy's entire family history. Cordelia wishes into existence (or possibly just reveals) a timeline in which Buffy never moved to Sunnydale. Jonathan works a spell to create a timeline in which he stars as a superhero. And the episode "Normal Again" (6-17) reveals a timeline in which Buffy is, rather than the powerful Slayer, a helpless mental patient. Unlike most secondary (i.e., invented) worlds, the reality of *Buffy* undergoes frequent, unsettling alterations.

All these episodes produce deviations from the "original" reality of *Buffy*, the world we viewers recognize as being altered when Dawn appears, which I refer to as the dominant reality, or dominant timeline. The magical transformations in the various episodes create alternate realities, worlds that resemble our own but deviate at some point in their history to generate timelines that can vary widely from the dominant one as a result of a single critical change. I use "alternate reality" and "alternate universe" interchangeably. Note, however, that the various transformed realities in the series are not all of the same type, but belong to at least two different categories. If the alternate reality exists in complete independence from the dominant timeline, I classify it as a separate dimensional plane. Alternate realities that replace the dominant one and run in the "real time" of the characters' lives can be labeled alternate histories. I consider "The Wish" (3-9), for example, to belong to the first category and "Superstar" (4-17) to the second. As for the "demon" or "hell" dimensions often mentioned in the series, they exist on other dimensional planes but do not qualify as alternate realities in the sense being considered, because they do not conform to the model of a universe that parallels ours except for the ramifications of one critical change.

For instance, Dawn's insertion into the story reshapes the dominant reality of the *Buffy*verse, thereby situating every episode after that one in a parallel universe. Dawn's arrival retroactively alters the *Buffy*verse's past as well as its present, so that the changed past becomes the "real" past. The fact that the audience remembers a different history does not invalidate the reality of the "new" past within the universe of the series. By all criteria the characters can apply, including confirmation from other people in the external world (with a few exceptions to be discussed below), their memories reflect objective fact. Moreover, the parallel worlds briefly experienced by the characters possess objective reality. I maintain that they do not exist solely in the characters' minds. They exist alongside the dominant reality, with no necessarily compelling reason to privilege that timeline over the alternate ones. By their existence, they foreground the malleability of the universe inhabited by the *Buffy* characters.

As mentioned, each of the *Buffy*verse alternate realities creates a parallel world through some relatively minor "alteration" in the dominant reality as the characters know it. Events in postseason five episodes and events in "Superstar" (4-17) feature one change and its consequences integrated into an otherwise unchanged timeline. After the nullification of Jonathan's spell in "Superstar" (4-17), the characters remember the events (at least dimly), and actions taken during the period of altered reality have consequences in the restored dominant timeline. "The Wish" (3-9) also begins with a single change and explores its consequences, but Cordelia's visit to that reality occupies no time in the dominant reality. With the reversal of her wish, she returns to the instant when she made it, and neither she nor Anyanka remember the alternate world. "Doppelgangland" (3-16) later suggests that the world spawned by Cordelia's wish has an independent existence on a separate dimensional plane. As for Buffy's alternate life in "Normal Again" (6-17), it occupies a space-time completely distinct from the dominant timeline and thus can claim the status of a true parallel universe.

It may be objected that "Superstar" (4-17) and the entire sequence of events after the first episode in season five do not occupy alternate universes, but the original universe with altered memories. This objection, however, makes an unwarranted distinction between perception and reality. The audience, standing outside the *Buffy*verse, is aware of both realities, old and new. To the characters, though, the old reality does not exist and never has existed. In the context of the respective episodes, Buffy has always had a sister named Dawn, and Jonathan has always been a superhero. As far as any practical effects are concerned, the world as they perceive it in the present and remember it in the past is the only reality. On an emotional level, they idolize Jonathan and love and protect Dawn even after they become intellectually convinced of the magical alterations that have produced these situations. That perception and reality are, in practical terms, indistinguishable, is particularly highlighted by "Normal Again" (6-17), as discussed below.

Thus we find no valid distinction between the world as perceived by the characters and as it "really is." Particularly when applied to the past, this dichotomy becomes meaningless. If a character's own memory and the consensus of his or her companions' memories recall the past in a certain way, and if all external sources that can be checked confirm this recollection, in what sense can this remembered past be considered "not real"? Although as viewers we assume the dominant *Buffy*verse timeline in "Normal Again" (6-17) to be real and the asylum experiences delusional, within the world of the episode neither realm can be privileged over the other. Similarly, the characters' current memories of a Sunnydale and a Summers household that include Dawn are neither less nor more "real" than the previous, and now erased, memories of a Dawnless world were during the period before Dawn's advent. The various magics that create the parallel worlds retroactively rewrite reality. The term "rewrite" is deliberate, since the fluidity of the Buffyverse's reality draws attention to its fictional nature. After all, the dominant reality of the *Buffy*verse is, in what we call the "real world," only the invented setting for a television series, and "rewriting" is precisely what the writers of the series did at the beginning of season five.

Each of the three alternate worlds considered here—found in "The Wish" (3-9)/ "Doppelgangland" (3-16), "Superstar" (4-17), and "Normal Again" (6-17)—comes into existence (or, possibly, the characters simply become aware of its existence) through the force of desire. In each case, one character's will finds expression in an altered reality. And, in each case, a relatively small shift in the dominant reality causes an alternate world to branch off at the point of the change. In the world of "The Wish" (3-9), Buffy is still the Slayer, but she operates in Cleveland instead of Sunnydale. "Superstar" (4-17) alters the personality and biography of Jonathan, while leaving all other aspects of reality unchanged except insofar as Jonathan's transformation affects them. "Normal Again" (6-17) introduces Buffy to the timeline that would have unfolded if she had remained in the institution where she spent a brief period as a patient right after learning of her destiny. We may note that the outside world, not just Sunnydale alone, reflects the repercussions of these changes. In Cordelia's "bizarro" realm, Giles telephones Buffy's Watcher in Cleveland, and Buffy travels to Sunnydale from there. In "Superstar" (4-17), Jonathan has coached the U.S. Women's Soccer Team, starred in *The Matrix*, and invented the Internet, actions that must certainly affect the world as a whole. The reshaping of the past along with the present does not change Sunnydale alone. As for "Normal Again" (6-17), we see none of the alternate reality outside the mental ward; however, a world in which either (1) demons and monsters do not exist, or (2) Buffy has not embraced her destiny of fighting the monsters, would be a radically different place from the dominant reality of the *Buffy*verse.

The role of desire/will in evoking the alternate reality is most obvious in "The Wish" (3-9), when Cordelia wishes Buffy had never come to Sunnydale, and in "Superstar" (4-17), when Jonathan works an augmentation spell to transform himself into "a sort of paragon, the best of everything." The transformed reality of "Normal Again" (6-17), however, also expresses desire, but in a less direct way—Buffy's yearning to be "normal," an ordinary girl, a wish demonstrated on many occasions, such as her tryout for the cheerleading squad and her campaign for Homecoming Queen. As Dawn accuses, "It's your ideal reality, and I'm not a part of it" ("Normal Again," 6-17). Willow later recognizes the same unacknowledged desire: "You're trying to sell me on the world. The one where you lie to your friends when you're not trying to kill them? . . . And insane asylums are a comfy alternative?" ("Two to Go," 6-21). The alternate timeline Buffy imagines (or possibly accesses) as a result of the demon's venom gives her back her parents as well as a stunted version of a normal life. In that place/time, she does not have to fight monsters, her parents are alive and together, and, as an only child with a serious illness, she has their full attention.

Buffy's "shadow" (in the Jungian sense, a repressed or neglected aspect of the self) appears in at least two guises in this episode. In the mental ward, we see Buffy as the ordinary girl she has, on one level, always longed to be. Ironically, in this "normal" world where demons do not exist and the Summers family unit remains unbroken, Buffy herself is normal only in the sense of having no superhuman powers. Her shadow self, a helpless, terrified schizophrenic, is far from the conventional definition of "normal." Within the dominant reality of Sunnydale as we know it, Buffy's shadow expresses itself in the outbreak of violence against her friends. It seems likely that she harbors repressed resentment against them for bringing her back from Heaven. In the context of the alternate reality of the mental ward, the asylum itself fills the role of Heaven. The doctor reminds Buffy: "Last summer, when you had a momentary awakening, it was them [her friends] that pulled you back in" ("Normal Again," 6-17). As Willow later taunts her, "The only time you were ever at peace in your whole life is when you were dead" ("Two to Go," 6-21). In the *Buffy*verse dominant reality, Buffy was in Heaven during that period of "peace"; in the alternate reality, she was in the asylum, momentarily "awakened" and, presumably, happy in the awareness of her parents' presence and love. Her covert hostility against the Scoobies for dragging her out of this "peace" finds an outlet in her attempt to kill them.

Another incarnation of Buffy's shadow appears in "The Wish" (3-9), Buffy as she would have become without the guidance of Giles and the friendship of the Scoobies. This alternate-world Slayer, hardened and cynical, unable to "play well with others" ("The Wish," 3-9), foreshadows Faith, even in her clothing style, although without (as far as we can tell) Faith's blatant sensuality. Survival and destruction consume all other facets of this Buffy's personality. The bizarro realm also displays the shadow selves of Willow and Xander (whose personalities and mannerisms, interestingly, parallel those of Drusilla and Spike, who apparently never visited Sunnydale in this timeline, where the Master still rules). The bizarro-world Willow appears deliberately constructed to embody the extreme opposite of the gentle, shy girl familiar to viewers. Vamp Willow's foreshadowing (in "Doppelgangland," 3-16) of dominant-world Willow's later coming out as a lesbian is, of course, obvious and often noted. As the dark side of Willow, however, her vampire incarnation also foreshadows her embrace of evil at the end of season six. The incarnation of a character's shadow is displayed most explicitly in "Superstar." When Jonathan transforms himself into a "paragon," Giles explains, "In order to balance the new force of good, the spell has to create the opposing force of evil, the worst of everything" ("Superstar," 4-17). As in *The Strange Case of Dr. Jekyll and Mr. Hyde*, an attempt to suppress the negative aspects of humanity only makes them break out more powerfully. Jonathan's augmentation spell unleashes a force of evil that literally shadows him. The weakness suffered by Jonathan when Buffy attacks the monster confirms that the creature is the rejected part of himself. Therefore its destruction causes the world to revert to its dominant-reality status.

In each of these alternate universes, at least one person realizes that reality has been manipulated, that something is "wrong." In "The Wish" (3-9) Cordelia, as maker of the wish, and Anyanka, as granter of it, know the world has changed. Adam, the Initiative's demonic cyborg, recognizes in Jonathan's reshaped universe: "None of this is real. The world has been changed. It's intriguing, but it's wrong" ("Superstar," 4-17). Why does Adam alone remain unaffected by Jonathan's spell? His explanation—"I'm aware. I know every molecule of myself and every-thing around me"—is unconvincing. Perhaps some aspect of his unique status as a demon-machine hybrid renders him immune to magic, at least of this kind. This possibility, however, only provides a rationale for the commentator role he fills as the audience's representative within the story, aware (like the viewers) of both realities, original and transformed. In my opinion, the audience does not need a character to perform this function, since, just as with the arrival of Dawn, we can hardly avoid noticing the transformation of reality.

As for the overarching shift in the dominant reality, the rewriting of *Buffyverse* history catalyzed by the advent of Dawn, certain people recognize her as "not real." This recognition comes from the brain-damaged and the mentally ill, including Joyce Summers when her brain tumor grows out of control. An impaired mental state, apparently, con-fers resistance to the magic used by the monks who transformed the Key into Buffy's sister and altered everyone's perception accordingly. Unlike Adam's immunity to Jonathan's spell, which remains unex-plained and leads nowhere, this recurring theme of mental derange-ment illuminates the issue of perception versus reality. The few people who know the "truth" in each of these alternate realities represent a minority view. Those who deny Dawn's reality are literally insane. Anyone who, in "Superstar" (4-17), spoke up to insist that Jonathan did not star in *The Matrix* or invent the Internet would be dismissed as delusional. In "Normal Again" (6-17), Buffy's belief in demons and her own Slayer destiny marks her as mentally ill in the alternate real-ity, but in the dominant reality of the *Buffyverse* we know, her growing belief that Sunnydale and her friends do not exist manifests itself as a mental breakdown. If "reality" can be defined in postmodern style as "consensus reality," those who contradict the consensus by denying the Master's control of Sunnydale, Jonathan's heroic achievements, or Dawn's relationship to Buffy must be victims of delusion.

What evidence do we have for and against the objective existence of each of these parallel worlds? If every possible change in the course of events can cause a separate timeline to branch off and develop according to the logic of its own history, an infinite number of alternate worlds can come into existence, each objectively "real" in its own dimension. This concept appears, of course, in many science fiction novels, such as Robert Heinlein's *Number of the Beast*, in which even imaginary universes—every one ever conceived—have concrete existence on their own dimensional planes. It first appears that the bizarro realm of "The Wish" (3-9) is only an altered Sunnydale warped by Anyanka's magical response to Cordelia's desire. As Larry succinctly evaluates the situation, "The entire world sucks because some dead ditz made a wish?" The premise seems to be that the bizarro world simply replaces the dominant reality. Anyanka's assertion to Giles, "This is the real world now" echoes bizarro-world Buffy's flat declaration, "World is what it is. We fight. We die." "Doppelgangland" (3-16), however, complicates this assumption. Anya appeals to her demonic patron to "fold the fabric of time." Yet, when Willow joins Anya in the abortive spell and glimpses the bizarro realm, she says, "That wasn't just some temporal fold, that was some weird Hell place." This remark gives the first hint that the alternate reality has an objective existence in a parallel dimension alongside the dominant reality as we know it. Vamp Willow's physical arrival in dominant-world Sunnydale, in my opinion, confirms this hint. The tangible existence in the "real world" of a character from another timeline suggests that both worlds exist simultaneously.

Dialogue from the episode seems to confirm this interpretation. For example, Anya says to Vamp Willow, "You know this isn't your world, right?" Vamp Willow replies, "No, this is a dumb world. In my world, there are people in chains, and we can ride them like ponies." Later she tells dominant-world Willow, "Your little schoolfriend Anya said that you're the one that brought me here. She said that you could get me back to my world" ("Doppelgangland," 3-16). Whether Cordelia's wish created the bizarro realm or simply accessed a dimension that already existed, it seems clear that this realm now has an independent existence, as a locale from which Vamp Willow can be summoned and to which she can be returned. While the "real" Willow's spell must have reached into the bizarro world's past in order to extract Vamp Willow before her death, this point need not prove fatal to the objective reality of the other realm. Time may flow differently in the two worlds, as in many fantasies of cross-dimensional travel (such as C. S. Lewis's *Narnia* series) and in the third-season *Buffy* episode "Anne"

(3-1). Note the implications of Vamp Willow's mission statement to her vampire lackeys: "This world's no fun anymore. We're going to make it the way it was" ("Doppelgangland," 3-16). To her, the bizarro dimension is the "real" world, while what we think of as the dominant reality is an alternate (and inferior) timeline. Reality in the *Buffy*verse depends on one's point of view. Whether Cordelia's wish created a new universe, as Jonathan in a sense did in "Superstar" (4-17), or only allowed access to a previously existing realm, that dimensional plane now has objective existence.

When Jonathan uses an augmentation spell to make himself into a "paragon" in "Superstar" (4-17), reality reshapes itself to fit his transformed status, rewriting past history. For example, now everyone remembers that Buffy gave Jonathan the "Class Protector" award, rather than vice versa. As discussed above, what consensus reality accepts as the truth about the past *is* essentially the truth. Subject to the magical alteration of past and present, however, the established story line continues with respect to the hunt for Adam and the tension between Riley and Buffy. The changes effected by the spell have been seamlessly integrated into the preexisting reality, just as, in the dominant timeline, reality has changed only as far as necessary to integrate Dawn's past into the remembered past. To Anya, the world created by Jonathan's spell is real, and any alternative seems wildly implausible: "You could even make a freaky world where Jonathan's some kind of not-perfect mouth breather." When the Scoobies begin to suspect the truth, Riley ventures the question, "So if this is the world he created, what's the real world like?" Willow, who expresses fear of the changes that will result from reversing Jonathan's spell, says after the dominant reality has been restored, "I can't believe we believed it." "It seemed so real," Riley confirms, to which Buffy responds, "Well, in that world, it was real." Buffy's comment reinforces the point that "reality" can be subjective.

Unlike "The Wish" (3-19), "Superstar" (4-17) involves some overlap between the two versions of reality. After the spell is broken, the inhabitants of Sunnydale do not instantly forget Jonathan's world. "I think some people are kind of angry," he notes. He mentions that "the twins moved out," implying that the two young women are still living with him when the reversal occurs. (Since his luxurious home obviously ceases to exist when the dominant reality is restored, do the twins suddenly find themselves in Jonathan's "normal" residence, perhaps the basement seen in season six?) We notice that some events that occurred in Jonathan's world have become part of the dominant reality's past. For instance, when Buffy tells Jonathan that he "can't keep trying to make everything work out all at once, with some huge gesture," he reminds her that he gave her similar advice about her relationship with Riley, advice she then puts into practice ("Superstar"). We may conclude that the alternate world of "Superstar," unlike the world of "The Wish," does not exist independently alongside the dominant reality, but while Jonathan's spell remained in force, that world was as "real" for its duration as the dominant timeline is in the series' present.

What about the alternate world of "Normal Again" (6-17)? On the surface, Buffy's experiences in the mental ward appear to be delusions evoked by the demon's venom. Do we see any evidence that these experiences are actually glimpses into a parallel timeline that split off from the dominant reality at the point of Buffy's brief commitment to a mental hospital years earlier? Perhaps we are seeing, as Spike puts it, "Alternative realities. Where we're all little figments of Buffy's funny-farm delusion." Buffy wonders, "What if I never left that clinic?" and her "delusions" show her probable fate if she had remained a mental patient. The final scene of the episode suggests that she has seen an actual alternate reality rather than the phantoms of her own mind. Note that in the closing scene, set in the institution, we see Buffy in a catatonic state. Since she has no awareness of her surroundings, that scene cannot be presented from her point of view. Without Buffy as viewpoint character, we must assume the action is being shown from an omniscient perspective, as objectively real. The placement of this scene at the close of the episode reinforces this assumption. The institutional psychiatrist in the alternate timeline has, so to speak, the last word. This alternate world, unlike that of "Superstar" (4-17), occupies a completely separate and independent dimension from the dominant reality. Whatever the "intent" of the writers, we can evaluate only the events we see in the episode as filmed, and what we see in the final scene of "Normal Again" (6-17) is a separate, self-consistent world.

In this episode several lines of dialogue draw deliberate attention to the fictionality of the dominant-world *Buffy*verse. For instance, Xander protests, "What? You think this world isn't real just because of all the vampires and demons and ex-vengeance demons and the sister that used to be a big ball of universe-destroying energy?" ("Normal Again," 6-17). The doctor in the mental ward reminds us of the retroactive alteration of the dominant reality by the introduction of Dawn: "Buffy inserted Dawn into her delusion, actually rewriting the history of it to accommodate a need for a familial bond." "Rewriting," of course, precisely defines what the program's creators did when they "inserted Dawn." When Buffy comes around to the belief that her life as a mental patient is a fact and the dominant timeline a delusion, she echoes Xander's comment: "'Cause what's more real? A sick girl in an institution . . . Or some kind of supergirl—chosen to fight demons and—save the world?" From our vantage point as television viewers inhabiting our own primary reality, of course, the former seems more credible. In terms of plausibility, the *Buffy*verse is to the mundane "real" world of the television audience as Jonathan's world is to the *Buffy*verse dominant timeline. To add "The Wish" (3-9) to the analogy, in the hierarchy of plausibility the bizarro dimension stands somewhere between the dominant timeline and Jonathan's world. The metafictional references in "Normal Again" draw attention to the malleability of the "real" throughout the series. To propose an extreme instance, what if Willow had carried out her threat against Dawn in "Two to Go" (6-21)? If Willow's power caused Dawn to revert to pure energy, would the monks' spell reverse itself and restore the dominant timeline to the condition it would have reached at that point if Dawn had never existed?

The advent of Dawn at the beginning of season five and the glimpse of Buffy's own alternate life in "Normal Again" (6-17)—as it would have unfolded in a mundane world like our own, in which demons, vampires, and Slayers are purely imaginary—reveal how malleable, fluid, even fragile, this dominant reality is. The parallel worlds in "The Wish" (3-9) and "Superstar" (4-17) also draw attention to this fluidity. So do less durable windows into alternate timelines, such as Xander's view of his supposed future in "Hell's Bells" (6-16). Although this precognitive glimpse turns out to be a deception perpetrated by a malicious entity, it is certainly a possible future, one path Xander's life with Anya might follow. Another temporary alteration of the timeline occurs in the *Angel* crossover episode "I Will Remember You" (1-8), in which the Oracles agree to erase the previous twenty-four hours, allowing only Angel to retain the memory of that brief fragment of alternate history. The bits of metafictional dialogue in "Normal Again," by foregrounding the fictional status of the *Buffy*verse as a whole, further emphasize the fluidity and fragility of the "real." In short, the theme of alternate realities lurks at the central core of *Buffy the Vampire Slayer*. The general of the Knights of Byzantium predicts that if the Key is activated, "The walls separating realities will crumble" ("Spiral" 5-20). To a greater or lesser extent, however, the erosion of this wall has already occurred many times.

Marked for life by reading Dracula *at the age of twelve, Margaret L. Carter specializes in the literature of fantasy and the supernatural, particularly vampires. She received degrees in English from the College of William and Mary, the University of Hawaii, and the University of California. Her nonfiction works include* Dracula: The Vampire and the Critics, The Vampire In Literature: A Critical Bibliography, *and* Different Blood: The Vampire as Alien. *She is also the author of a werewolf novel,* Shadow of the Beast, *and three vampire novels,* Dark Changeling *(2000 Eppie Award winner in horror),* Sealed In Blood, *and* Crimson Dreams. *With her husband, retired Navy captain Leslie Roy Carter, she coauthored a fantasy novel* Wild Sorceress. *She has recently ventured into erotic romance with three vampire novellas, "Night Flight," "Tall, Dark, and Deadly," and "Virgin Blood" from Ellora's Cave (www.ellorascave.com). Visit her website, www.margaretlcarter.com.*

Lawrence Watt-Evans

MATCHMAKING ON THE HELLMOUTH

Pop quiz: Who is the ideal mate for Buffy?

a) *Angel*

b) *Riley*

c) *Spike*

d) *Clem*

e) *None of the above*

Actually, it's someone you would never guess, as proven by this essay by Hugo Award–winner Lawrence Watt-Evans.

A s THE CHOSEN ONE, the Slayer, Buffy Summers is doomed to spend her life battling monsters. Is she doomed to loneliness, as well? Must she go through life unpartnered? Sure, she has her friends, but let's face it, so far her love life has been a disaster—every relationship has failed spectacularly. Only three ever really even got off the ground, and all of them crashed and burned. Angel's curse pretty much destroyed any chance for long-term happiness there, she and Riley never managed a solid emotional connection, and Spike—well, that was messy, wasn't it?

So who's out there who might be a fit lifemate for the Slayer, the Chosen One?

First off, I think we can immediately eliminate any ordinary, untrained human being. Those around Buffy are inevitably going to encounter the creatures of the night—demons, vampires, evil gods, the entire panoply. We got a look at this all the way back in the first season, with Owen in "Never Kill a Boy on the First Date" (1-5), and again with Scott in the third season, and even Parker in the fourth. Anyone in Buffy's life is going to get involved in her Slaying, and a normal man's life expectancy in such a situation, Xander notwithstanding, is not likely to be very great. Bringing a new arrival up to speed, teaching him to cope with the menaces Buffy faces, would be risky and time-consuming, to say the least. Furthermore, an ordinary mortal boyfriend's presence is likely to endanger Buffy, as well, as she finds herself worrying about defending her man at times when she really doesn't need any distractions.

But wait, you may say—what about Xander himself? He's somehow managed to survive seven years facing the darkness; he clearly has *something* going for him.

True enough, Xander has proved himself in the field of battle, but let's face it, often he survived only because Buffy deliberately shut him out of whatever was going on. That sort of exclusion is one thing for a friend; it's something else entirely for a lover.

Besides, there's all that history. There was a time when Xander and Buffy might have happened, but that time is long past. They've lived too close to each other for too long. They know far too much about each other's exes—can you honestly think that Xander would not mention Spike in some unfortunate fashion during the inevitable lovers' spats that crop up in any relationship? That wouldn't exactly go over well with a touchy Buffy, would it?

And it seems pretty clear that Buffy likes a little darkness, a little violence, in her men. Every relationship that's gone anywhere at all has been with someone holding back a dark power or secret of some kind—Angel suppressing Angelus, Riley, the drug-enhanced secret government agent, Spike, with only the chip preventing him from being a monster. Some might argue that this string was merely bad luck, but her behavior makes this unlikely; Spike, probably the series character with the greatest insight into people's motives, has certainly told her that she's drawn to the dark, and her denials, never very convincing, eventually ran out entirely. Her relationship with Riley, let us note, seems to have begun to collapse almost as soon as he was free from Professor Walsh's drugs and persuasion, while learning that Angel was a vampire only increased her lust for him. Her affair with Spike only took off when she discovered that he could fight her again.

Perhaps it's because of her own internal darkness, the fact that by her very nature as a Slayer she is as much a destroyer as a protector, or maybe it's just an extreme form of the common female interest in bad boys, but whatever the reason, she is indeed attracted by men with dark secrets and hidden power. Much as she may hate to admit it, she's drawn to that danger, that possibility of the loss of control, and Xander doesn't have it. Oh, he has a temper, he can hold a grudge, but that's not the same thing. Buffy wants someone who tests the boundaries, who risks unleashing his own darkness and Xander doesn't fit that profile—and given his abject terror of becoming his father, he wouldn't *want* it, even if Buffy was part of the package.

So ordinary men, including Xander, are out. Extraordinary men we'll get to in a moment, but first let's consider some other categories.

I think we can immediately eliminate virtually all vampires. Vampires are, as Buffy told Spike repeatedly during season six, not men, but dead, soulless *things*. These may work as sex toys, but not as partners and lovers.

There are vampires with souls—two of them, anyway—who get around the "soulless thing" problem, and who can defend themselves, but neither of them is really going to work.

Angel has the gypsy curse on him, of course, whereby a single moment of true happiness will turn him back into the soulless, sadistic monster called Angelus. We've already seen that a night with Buffy is enough to provide that moment—and even if it actually isn't anymore, even if Willow's version of the curse doesn't have that problem, even if worrying about the possibility would mar Angel's happiness enough to prevent the transformation, Angel and Buffy are not going to take that chance.

And that's just one reason they won't reunite. As Angel told Buffy in "The Prom" (3-20), he thinks she deserves a more normal life than he can ever provide, someone who can give her children. Whether he's right or not, merely the fact that he believes it will doom any relationship they might have.

In a way, they have each idealized their image of the other until they can't possibly stay together successfully—Angel sees Buffy as a creature of light who he cannot be worthy of, who he can never give what she deserves, rather than as a flawed and human girl, while Buffy sees Angel as an ancient, dark, and powerful figure, recognizing nothing of the Irish ne'er-do-well Liam was, nor of what a doofus Angel can still sometimes be.

That takes Angel out of contention, even though Buffy may still think of him as the great love of her life.

Ignoring for the moment his apparent destruction, that leaves one other ensouled vampire, one who loves her, one who got his soul restored entirely in hopes she could learn to love him—but Buffy has pretty definitely established that she doesn't love Spike and doesn't want to, soul or no soul. Respect him, yes; love him, no.

A third vampire acquiring a soul is extremely unlikely; acquiring a soul and remaining sane *and* being someone suited to Buffy is just not going to happen.

Not a vampire, then. Another variety of demon, perhaps?

Who? Most of them are pretty thoroughly evil, many are of subhuman intelligence, and I can't see Buffy settling for either evil or stupid. There are a few who are neither, such as the estimable Clem, but we haven't seen any who really look like relationship fodder, nor have we seen any human-demon hybrids and other monsters who show much promise. Also, let's face it, most of them are ugly, and Buffy does like a handsome face and well-built body.

What does that leave?

It leaves men who are *not* ordinary mortals, men who can take care of themselves when faced with supernatural menaces of all sorts. Men like Riley Finn.

Let us look, then, at what made Riley special—and what went wrong with the Riley-Buffy pairing.

Riley was extensively trained and fed performance-enhancing drugs; he was big and strong and smart, knew how to fight, and had an idea what he was up against. That made him *almost* as effective at monster-fighting as a Slayer. Physically, he could hold his own.

Emotionally, though, he and Buffy never quite meshed. Much as he admired her strength and power, it also did intimidate him a little. He wanted to be worthy of her; he wanted her to admire him as he admired her.

Buffy didn't cooperate. She's never been very impressed by mere physical prowess; she's spent too much time beating on creatures twice her size.

Also, she never really opened up to him emotionally. Angel and Spike, perhaps by virtue of their centuries of experience, have always been able to read Buffy in a way that poor innocent Riley could not. He needed her to *tell* him what she was feeling, what she wanted, and she never did.

That's inherent in their personalities. Riley is very much a team player, while Buffy, much as she appreciates and relies on her friends, is basically a loner, and has always been aware that she is the Chosen One, emphasis on the "One."

And there's that whole darkness issue. Riley saw that Buffy was drawn to the dark, that however much she might like him, she found him unexciting in his wholesomeness. The thrill of the forbidden was not there. He tried to find the darkness within himself, and only managed the sordid in his visits to the vampire hookers. Buffy found that repulsive rather than exciting.

Might it have worked out anyway? Need every relationship be thrilling to succeed? Buffy got over her revulsion, and was willing to carry on—but Riley wasn't looking for simple companionship. He was passionately in love with Buffy, and wanted passion in return. Buffy wasn't ready to provide it.

I think we really need to consider that relationship a near-miss.

Could another highly trained human do better? Maybe. But we'd need to find a man who doesn't mind being outclassed by his girlfriend, who fights for the good guys but has a little darkness in him . . .

It's not an easy combination. In particular, if we're talking about *physical* training, a man like that is going to be unlikely. You don't build serious muscle without a little pride and a lot of testosterone; combine that with a streak of wildness, and you're probably not looking at someone who wants to live with a girlfriend who can punch him out.

Is there some other sort of training that might serve?

Well, of course there is: mental training, which in the *Buffy*verse is going to include magic.

We've certainly seen *that*. Buffy has always had other people around as her support structure, doing her research and providing the occasional spell—people like Willow and Giles.

Imagine if Willow were a straight male. She has power enough to defend herself; she has dallied with the darkness. She and Buffy are friends, able to live in the same house without fraying too many nerves.

She is, however, female, and Buffy, unlike Willow, is pretty definitely heterosexual. Not gonna work. We know from "Him" that Willow could probably change either her own sex or Buffy's orientation, but I can't see that happening. Willow knows better (now) than to mess with such things.

So Willow the witch is eliminated, but entirely on the basis of her sex. Is there anyone like her who doesn't have that particular drawback? What magic-using males have we seen?

Well, Giles is the obvious one, and he certainly has toyed with the darkness, both as Ripper in his youth and, when pressed, more recently—as Ethan Rayne or Ben/Glory could testify.

But he's too old for Buffy, and has played the surrogate father so long that quite aside from the age difference it would undoubtedly feel incestuous for them both. I don't think that's the sort of darkness Buffy's after—it's not so much dark as just icky.

What about Ethan Rayne, then, since we've mentioned him?

No. Far too untrustworthy. Buffy wants a man who can watch her back, as Angel did, or Riley, or Spike. Ethan would be much more likely to decide he'd rather run and protect his own hide.

But if we've eliminated Giles, Buffy's own Watcher, are there any other Watchers who might serve? Watchers younger than Giles, but with something of his style and experience? Not just any Watcher will do; we've seen too many who were stiff-necked fools with no real-world experience. Are there any more Watchers who are not hidebound morons?

With the Watchers' Council largely destroyed, the odds of finding a suitable survivor don't look promising.

Who does that leave, then? Must we resort to creating a new character—a male witch, or a sympathetic Watcher?

I think not. There is one more possibility. I have in mind a man a few years older than Buffy, but not old enough to make a relationship awkward; a man who has been fighting the forces of darkness for years, both alone and as part of a team; a man who knows and respects Buffy; a man experienced in the use of magic, greatly learned in the history of the arcane, and able to hold his own in a fight. This man was trained as a Watcher, but is no longer beholden to the Council. He has walked on the dark side, flirted with evil—and more than flirted, on occasion. While capable of passion, he does not demand the sort of commitment Riley hoped for; he knows how to give a woman her space.

And there's pretty good evidence that he's not bad in bed.

I refer, of course, to Wesley Wyndham-Price.

Before you reject the idea, think it over carefully. Oh, it's true that when they last worked together he was an utter twit, and Buffy despised him; it may take some time for Buffy to get over that, but as we have all seen, he has grown far beyond that now. Buffy, too, would quickly see as much, should they meet again. Wesley is not the inexperienced coward she knew; he has faced his fears and found courage, and survived everything from slime demons to a slit throat.

Yes, his interests lie elsewhere at the moment, and Buffy is not currently resident in Los Angeles, but these are trivial obstacles, easily dealt with. Let Wesley finally give up all hope of gaining Fred's affection, send Buffy to the city to face some menace there, and there you are.

Imagine it—the rogue demon hunter fighting back to back with the Slayer . . .

It would be perfect.

Which, of course, is why it will never happen. Joss Whedon doesn't believe in happy endings.

But if he did . . .

———————

Lawrence Watt-Evans is the author of some three dozen novels and over a hundred short stories, mostly in the fields of fantasy, science fiction, and horror. He won the Hugo Award for Short Story in 1988 for "Why I Left Harry's All-Night Hamburgers," served as president of the Horror Writers Association from 1994 to 1996, and lives in Maryland with his wife, two teenaged kids, a pet snake named Billy-Bob, and the obligatory writer's cat.

Nancy Holder

SLAYERS OF THE LAST ARC

With the airing of "Chosen," the "Buffy era" (as the late 90's to early 00's will come to be known) is finally over. We will all mourn its ending in our own ways. Some will bitterly conclude that the series had run past its prime in any event (see Larbastier's essay in this volume). Others will, in desperation, turn to Angel, which, for all its recent brilliance, can never replace the hole in our psyches left by Buffy's departure. Yet others will pine for possible sequels featuring Dawn or Faith or Giles, or for the major motion picture that surely will come soon. Nancy Holder chooses to celebrate the ending with an examination of Buffy's final story arc. She describes how well it fits an ancient and profound mythological structure, which perhaps goes a little way towards explaining the uncanny way the final sequence—and, even more, the entire series—got under our skins and touched us in ways no show ever had before.

W ITH THE ANNOUNCEMENT that *Buffy the Vampire Slayer* was ending its seven-year run, viewers went on high alert and speculation mounted about how Joss Whedon and his staff would conclude Buffy's story. There had been discussions about the fate of the show before, by savvy fans who knew that Sarah Michelle Gellar's contract was due to run out at the end of season seven (as were the contracts of most of the regular cast.) They were aware that Gellar could decide to renew her contract, but the prevailing feeling was that she would not. Surely for a show titled *Buffy the Vampire Slayer*, the character of Buffy Summers was pivotal—or was she? If Gellar left but the show went on, would it be revamped (sorry) and titled *Slayer*, as it had originally almost been called? Would Buffy die? Would Faith survive and take over the job? Would Buffy "jump" into Faith's body? Would the Buffybot provide a model for a new Slayer? Would Dawn take on the mantel? What about a new unknown becoming the Chosen One?

During the course of season seven, most of the possibilities fans discussed among themselves were brought into play. The opening shot of "Lessons," the last season's first episode, shows the assassination of a Potential (though not revealed to be so at first.) Potentials were murdered; Willow had visions; The First drove the newly ensouled Spike even crazier, and haunted the living with their dead. Potential Slayers by the dozens hurried to Buffy for safety, and Giles returned to mentor and guide them. In "Potential" (7-12) it appeared that yes, Dawn was in line to become the next Slayer. Then in "Dirty Girls" (7-18), Faith herself showed up. And the race to figure out how Buffy would end was on.

The official announcement drew casual *Buffy* viewers into the guessing game, and the puzzle mainstreamed to the point that the media began running articles about the end of "The best show that you (probably) didn't watch" (*San Diego Union*, May 18, 2003.) Pieces appeared in publications such as *The New York Times*, *Entertainment Weekly*, and *Buffy the Vampire Slayer Magazine* itself, all posing the Big Question: What's going to happen?

Joyce Millman of the *New York Times* wrote:

> Frankly, as long as Whedon doesn't try to tell us that the whole series was a figment of Buffy's imagination, I'll be happy. I'll be even happier if the finale grandly articulates, one last time, the show's main themes: woman power, friendship, growing up and sacrifice.
>
> (appearing in the *Kansas City Star* April 21, 2003)

Entertainment Weekly asked Whedon which of "our favorite characters" were scheduled to be "slaughtered." And although he wouldn't say, he did promise "one hell of an ending."

It's my position that he delivered, and that the ending he provided took off in a fabulously clever miniature arc consisting of the last five episodes, which delivered on three levels: as a mini-quest of its own; as the satisfying conclusion of season seven; and as the well-structured and premeditated closure to the entire *Buffy the Vampire Slayer* series.

Although the fate of the series was unknown at the beginning of season seven, there was a definite consciousness on the part of Joss Whedon and the writing staff that they needed to guide the show toward possible closure. As Co-executive Producer Marti Noxon noted, in an interview in *Buffy the Vampire Slayer Magazine* in the June/July 2003 issue, "The way that Joss designed the final episodes left things very flexible. Even though it's a complete end to the series and you'll feel very satisfied, it also leaves open a lot of possibilities."

Those possibilities have now been revealed, and as of this writing (June of 2003), the fan boards have lit up with arguments and debates about the show's finale. Some fans feel cheated, arguing that if the original concept was that there can be only one Slayer, there should only ever be one Slayer. Others are exuberant that the new, improved, open-ended nature of Slayerdom—that there are now many Slayers—may indicate that spin-offs of many forms will be the offing.

Taking all that into account—and having read all twenty-two scripts of season seven back-to-back—I'd like to offer that what Whedon and Company did to end the series "works" in every sense of the notion of mythic storytelling. And nowhere is this more evident than in the last arc of the show. That this is an arc was suggested by Marti Noxon herself when she stated *in Buffy the Vampire Slayer Magazine,* "Faith's arrival in episode eighteen obviously sets off some fireworks that will propel us into our season's end."

First, on *Buffy* and arcs: In its first season and a half, *Buffy the Vampire Slayer* started out as an anthology show, with primarily standalone episodes featuring "monsters of the week"—the "phlibotenum," in the *Buffy*speak of the show's writers' room. Although the evil Master dwelled in his underground prison, the individual episodes were not linked week-by-week to his presence. Instead, monsters drawn to the evil energy of the Hellmouth provided the forces of darkness that Buffy and her friends had to battle, as in *The X-Files* or the first season of the more current *Smallville.* These were episodes such as "Teacher's Pet" (1-4) and "Go Fish" (2-20).

However, once the show established Buffy's world and the operating definition of her heroic nature, the storylines expanded into arcs that lasted a few episodes—the arrival and demise of Kendra in the *Becoming* arc, for example—to the notion that a Big Bad would dominate each season: Mayor Wilkins for season three, Glory for season five; and arcs that extended past seasons: the duo of Spike and Dru, introduced in "School Hard" (2-19) in season two and, one might argue, extending until the end of the show. But as the story of *Buffy* herself unfolded, all seven seasons become a linear, organic whole, and as I posit, the last arc not only underscores this, but provides a perfect conclusion to the 144-episode-long Hero's Journey that Buffy undertook.

The notion of a universal Hero's Journey in the mythos of humanity was first popularized by folklorist Joseph Campbell in his book, *Hero with a Thousand Faces*. Campbell held that there are universal storytelling elements to be found in myths and legends worldwide, and he described these elements in Jungian terms of archetypes and stages. The subject of many books, TV series, and documentaries, his work probably entered the cultural mainstream when George Lucas cited his influence on the development of *Star Wars* ("It's possible that if I had not run across Joseph Campbell, I would still be writing *Star Wars* today," he has been quoted as saying.)

Then Christopher Vogler, now a story consultant at Fox, took Campbell's work and applied it to his own observations about story and structure as he evaluated over 10,000 screenplays. His book, *The Writer's Journey: Mythic Structure for Writers*, provides a template for describing this last arc of *Buffy the Vampire Slayer*. And using his template, I'd like to bolster my argument that Joss Whedon's last arc for *Buffy* "works" beautifully.

Vogler's modifications of Campbell's journey lists twelve major steps, or Stages, in the journey of a Hero:

1. Establishment of the Ordinary World
2. The Call to Adventure
3. Refusal of the Call
4. Meeting with the Mentor
5. Crossing the First Threshold
6. Tests, Allies, and Enemies
7. Approaches to the Inmost Cave
8. Ordeal
9. Reward (Seizing the Sword)
10. The Road Back
11. Resurrection
12. Return with the Elixir

Each season of *Buffy* follows this model on its own, including the shorter first season (as *Buffy* was purchased for a twelve-episode run as a mid-season replacement.) But in the last five episodes, this model expanded to create a mini-epic, or Journey, of its own: First, the Ordinary World is established: a young Potential is running for her life from the Bringers, who have already been established as minions of the bad in previous episodes. We are on the outskirts of Sunnydale, home of the Slayer, and to whom the Potential is running for safety. To Revello Drive, to be precise.

This is the Slayer's Ordinary World, and recognition of the ordinary world is crucial if one is to leave it in order to embark on a path to a more extraordinary world.

The Potential—named Shannon, in the script—leaps into Caleb's truck, and at first assumes that she is safe for the moment. Then Caleb quickly reveals himself to be the leader of the Bringers, brands her, and asks her to deliver a message to the Slayer. She agrees, he guts her, and pushes her out of the truck . . . knowing full well that agents of the Slayer are traveling close behind him.

Sure enough, Willow's car screeches to a halt and Willow and her companion get out of the car. Willow rushes to the aid of the Potential, who will deliver the Call to Adventure to Buffy . . . and Faith stares out at the landscape and reminds the viewer that the call has been delivered within the boundaries of Buffy's ordinary world:

FAITH: "Yep. Guess I'm back in Sunnydale."

("Dirty Girls," 7-18)

Buffy hears Caleb's message from Shannon—which the viewer will later learn is "I have something of yours"—and Buffy decides to answer the Call to Adventure (Stage 3) by attacking Caleb immediately, before he expects it. The Call to Adventure is the second stage of the Hero's Journey: The call is initially refused—not by Buffy herself, but by her followers—the Potentials and the core Scoobies—who suggest that she's impulsively leading them into a trap.

Buffy's mentor, Giles, who arrived in "Bring On the Night" (7-10), also advises against the foray, but Buffy ignores him. One might also argue that Giles's position in this case is as another Campbell archetype, the Threshold Guardian—those who attempt to dissuade the Hero from her path.

Buffy leads the girls on the assault on the vineyard, thus crossing the First Threshold (Stage 5)—with disastrous results. Her gambit fails; she has grossly underestimated the strength of her enemies, and some of her warriors are killed. Xander is terribly maimed.

Now comes the Stage 6 of Buffy's journey, that of undergoing Tests and gathering Allies and Enemies. With her failure at the vineyard fresh in the mind of her followers, alliances shift. Kennedy and the other Potentials question her fitness to lead. Faith inadvertently corners their allegiance by providing them with some much-needed R&R; it is when Faith is threatened by the cops that the girls finally become the army Buffy needs to destroy The First—and who then turn against her. Wood fires her from her job because it's distracting her from her true mission. And Giles sends Spike out of town, highlighting Buffy's mistrust of him since "Lies My Parents Told Me" (7-17), in which Giles conspired with Robin Wood to kill Spike.

> BUFFY: "You sent away the guy who's been watching my back. Again. I think—"
> GILES: "We are *all* watching your back."
> BUFFY: "Yeah. Funny how I don't really feel that lately."
> ("Empty Places," 7-19)

Making matters worse, Caleb approaches her on her home turf—her office at school—and knocks her unconscious.

Failing all her tests of leadership, her order to return to the vineyard is refused and her followers mutiny. At her nadir, she is stripped of her leadership and sent into exile.

> BUFFY: "I don't understand. Seven years I've kept us safe by doing this, exactly this, making the hard decisions. Suddenly you're all acting like you don't trust me."
> GILES: "But didn't you just tell me today that you don't feel like you can trust us?
> ("Empty Places," 7-19)

Even Dawn turns against Buffy. Her only ally is Spike, who seeks her out and stands by her. He provides her with crucial information for the battle to come, and rallies her.

SPIKE: "You were their leader and still are. This isn't something
   that you gave up; it's something that they took."
BUFFY: "And the difference is?"
SPIKE: "We can take it back."

("Touched," 7-20)

This period of Tests, Allies, and Enemies culminates in Stage 7, which
is the Approach to the Inmost Cave. Buffy returns to the scene of her
most crushing defeat, the vineyard, specifically to retrieve what belongs to her, circling back to the original Call to Adventure issued by
Caleb and finally answering it. Caleb attacks her again; this is the third
time she has faced him in battle, and this time she wins. She retrieves
the scythe, which is the symbol of her right to lead.

Meanwhile, her rival, Faith, has led her followers into disaster. Buffy
saves both Faith and the surviving Potentials, and they return to base
camp—the Summers home. Her followers accept her return, and she
resumes her position as commander-in-chief, the scythe firmly in her
possession.

FAITH: "It's old. Strong. And it feels like . . . like it's mine. So I
   guess that means it's yours."
BUFFY: "It belongs to the Slayer."
FAITH: "Slayer in Charge, which I'm guessing is you."

("End of Days," 7-21)

Buffy's not so sure of that; and she continues on the Hero's Journey
to the Inmost Cave, launching on a quest to discover the origins of the
scythe. Guided by Giles' and Willow's research, she meets another
Mentor—the ancient Guardian named "She," who explains that the
scythe was imbued with power to benefit the Slayer.

SHE: "Use it wisely. . . and perhaps you can beat back the rising
   dark. One way or the other, it can only mean an end is truly near."

("End of Days," 7-21)

And this is where the mini-arc takes off to provide the closure for
the entire series as a whole, and not just one single season: *through the
revelations provided by She, Buffy changes the Ordinary World.* She comes
to understand that the Shadow Men forced the First Slayer to swallow
the demonic essence that created the line. Becoming the Watchers,

they laid down the rules that there would be only one Chosen One at a time—reinforcing that notion time and again with tests like the Cruciamentum "Helpless," (3-12); and conferring anxiously among themselves when first Kendra and then Faith were called, seemingly out of order, because Buffy had died and been revived—a total of twice ("Prophesy Girl," 1-12 and "The Gift," 5-22). Buffy had already broken their rule without realizing the import.

It is her enemy, speaking through the slain Caleb, who provides her with the answer to breaking free of the legacy imposed by the Shadow Men/Watchers upon Slayers since the beginning of time:

> BUFFY/FIRST: "Into every generation, a Slayer is born. One girl in all the world. She alone will have the strength and skill to fight the . . . well, there's that word again. What you are. How you'll die. Alone."
>
> ("Chosen," 7-22)

These have been the opening words of every episode of *Buffy the Vampire Slayer* since the show's premiere. They are the ground rules of Buffy's universe, her Ordinary World. Throughout the run of the show, the fact that Buffy died and then was revived (in "Prophecy Girl," 1-12) has been factored into the existing notion that there can be only one Slayer at a time. The presence of additional Slayers was considered an anomaly—and not the establishment of a new set of rules.

> BUFFY: "In every generation one Slayer is born because a bunch of guys that died thousands of years made up that rule . . . So I say we change the rules. I say my power will be *our* power. Tomorrow Willow will use the essence of this scythe, that contains the energy of so many Slayers, to change our destiny."
>
> ("Chosen," 7-22)

As she concludes her speech, she asks each Potential present to make a choice: to accept the power of a Slayer now, rather than to passively wait for it to be given to her, due to a random death of another girl she might never know.

It is for the Hero herself to understand that, through Willow, she has the power to change the world forever—literally. And she chooses to do so. Thus is Buffy's entire journey distilled into the five-episode arc that concludes the show.

The decision made, this final episode then masterfully resumes the path of the season seven's original quest: to destroy The First; but also refocuses the Journey on the establishment of a brand new Ordinary World (Stage 1), in which a new Hero's Journey can begin.

Back in the Egyptian temple monument, when Buffy spoke with She, she also received an amulet from Angel, another of her allies. He told her she would need a champion to wear the necklace in order to prevail. Though his Mentor (Lilah, of Wolfram and Hart) is unreliable, both he and Buffy at least accept the amulet as part of the requisite items needed for her to win the day. Thus she has amassed her weaponry and her army, and now stands firmly at the door of her Ordeal. This is underscored by scenes showing the warriors on the eve of the big battle, a traditional trope of the Hero's Journey: a few of the troops playing a game (in this case, a dungeons & dragons game); talking quietly; making love; and connecting, possibly for the last time.

The day of reckoning dawns. It's Ordeal time (Stage 8). Buffy deliberately opens the Seal of Danzalthar by combining her own blood with that of her followers. Willow is preparing the spell that will imbue all the Potentials with Slayer power. Other warriors are taking up their positions: Xander and Dawn, Anya and Andrew, Giles and Robin Wood. Old and new strategies shift into play: brute Slayer strength, magick, and, unknown to the legions of evil, a Hero leading an army of Heroes, all prepared to launch their own Journeys.

> BUFFY: "From now on, every girl in the world who might be a Slayer, *will* be a Slayer. Every girl who could have the power, will have the power. Who can stand up, will stand up. Every one of you, and girls we've never known, and generations to come . . ."
>
> ("Chosen," 7-22)

With these rousing words in their minds, all the Potentials are Slayers, and any one of then could carry the day. The great battle ensues, filled with the elements Vogler describes as vital to the crisis: tasting death (seeing some of the Slayers die); the elasticity of emotion (mixing humor and pathos, for example, Andrew's speech where he wants to thank his friends and family before he dies); seeing the Hero appear to die (Buffy's seemingly mortal wound); and the Hero witnessing and possibly causing death (wearing the amulet Buffy gave him, its power sears Spike's soul and causes the huge explosion of light into the cavern). Buffy suffers a crisis of the heart, in which she says, finally, to Spike, "I love you," then must leave him to die.

The Slayers prevail (Stage 9), and now begins Stage 10 of the Hero's Journey: the Road Back—getting out of the cavern and out of danger. All the survivors save Buffy make it out and scramble onto the bus, but Buffy is left behind because she said goodbye to Spike. It is left to her to have one last star turn as she leaps from crumbling building to crumbling building as the hellmouth collapses, chasing the bus, which symbolizes safety.

Once she reaches the bus, it is time for Stage 11: Buffy's final Resurrection. For the Slayer who has been brought back twice from deaths she has willingly chosen in the line of duty, this third death is startlingly different: she becomes a normal human being with the opportunity to live a natural life. Buffy is no longer the Chosen, no longer unique.

> FAITH: "Yeah, you're not the one and only chosen anymore. Just gotta live like a person. How's that feel?"
>
> ("Chosen," 7-22)

This is Buffy's Return with the Elixir, which she presents at journey's end. She is changed, and she has changed the destinies of untold numbers of girls—and of viewers, who can now foresee many different paths for the Slayer "franchise," as Noxon terms it in an interview. And it is for that reason that I suggest this ending is structurally the soundest and most emotionally satisfying piece of storytelling Whedon could have devised for Buffy.

In her essay for the *New York Times*, Joyce Millman projects her hopes for the finale:

> I want Buffy to die and become an immortal goddess . . . I can see the series' last moments now: Buffy's ascension unleashes a surge of positive energy that empowers the forces of good.

I posit that the finale Joss Whedon provided does unleash a surge of positive energy that empowers the forces of good, at the same time concluding the final arc of the show, thus providing a sense of closure to that dynamic thread; and additionally circling backward—or perhaps, spiraling upward—to promises of the journey laid out in the premiere, seven seasons previous, exploiting the mythic structure of the Hero's Journey to create an extremely satisfying, balanced end.

————————

Nancy Holder is a four-time Bram Stoker Award-winning author, and was nominated a fifth time for one of her Buffy *novels. She also received a special award from amazon.com for* Angel Chronicles Volume 1. *She has written or co-written over three dozen projects in the BTVS and Angel universes. The* Watcher's Guide, Volume 1, *coauthored with Christopher Golden, appeared on the* USA Today *Bestseller List and was described in* Entertainment Weekly *and the* Wall Street Journal *as "superb." She lives in San Diego with her seven-year-old daughter, Belle, who recently cast her friend Kate Liang as the Dancing Taco in an independent after-school production.*

Visit:

www.joss-whedon.com

Take a tour
through Joss Whedon's brain

Test yourself at the Joss Whedon
quiz

Win a *Buffy the Vampire Slayer*
Season 4 DVD

Joss Whedon:
The Genius Behind Buffy

"Possibly the finest book of the century; it's exactly like *A Tale of Two Cities*, but with 30% more me."

—Joss Whedon

"Candace Havens nails the guy who nailed the zeitgeist. This dishy dissection of a true TV genius is smart, surprising and vastly entertaining—just like *Buffy* itself. Even Sunnydale know-it-alls will adore this book."

—Michael Logan, *TV Guide*

Joss Whedon explores the life and work of the brilliant Joss Whedon, the creator of *Buffy the Vampire Slayer*, *Angel*, *Fray* and *Firefly* and the Academy Award nominated screenwriter behind *Toy Story*, *Speed*, and *Alien Resurrection*.

When Joss Whedon set out to create *Buffy*, he wasn't just looking to create a successful show. Whedon deliberately set out to create a cult phenomenon. "I wanted *Buffy* to be a cultural phenomenon, period . . . that was always the plan," Whedon confesses. *Joss Whedon* describes the reasons behind Whedon's intense creative drive and shows how he, very deliberately, crafted a cult sensation.

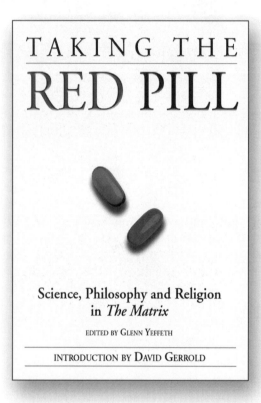

Now Available from BenBella Books:

—WINNER—

LORD RUTHVEN AWARD
for Best Vampire Novel Winner,

LORIE AWARD
for Best Paranormal Romance

"Lorrah's vampire lore and the twists and turns her revelation of it entail make her novel—an interesting combination of mystery, romance, and horror—worth reading."

—Booklist